The Horse at Gettysburg

Published by Gettysburg Publishing, LLC
www.gettysburgpublishing.com

Front Cover Images:

    Horse is "Maverick", owned and photographed by the author.

    "Retreat by Recoil" painting by Don Troiani

Back Cover Images:

    Horse is a Friesian named "Abe" from Rock N Oak Farm in Gettysburg, Pennsylvania, owned by Dr. Carla Huitt. Photographed by Caroline Stover.

    Photo of "Dead horses of Bigelows (9th Massachusetts) Battery" courtesy of the Library of Congress

Cover Design by Caroline Stover

Maps by Hal Jespersen, www.cwmaps.com

Library of Congress Control Number: 2021931483
ISBN 9780999304969

Printed and bound in the United States of America

First Edition

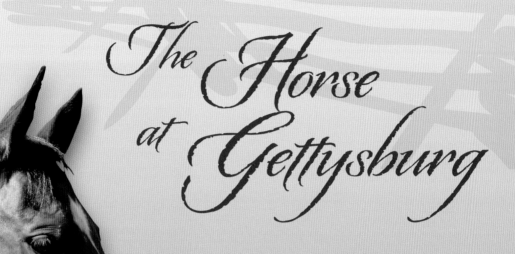

The Horse at Gettysburg

PREPARED for the DAY of BATTLE

CHRIS BAGLEY

GETTYSBURG
PUBLISHING

Dedicated to the Horse.
May you know a life without war, neglect, or abuse.

ACKNOWLEDGMENTS

In 2016, John and Terry Latschar allowed a newly licensed Battlefield Guide to conduct horseback tours of this hallowed ground. Their patience and guidance gave me a newfound appreciation for these animals. Then, two years ago, the idea for this book came to light. From the beginning, my wife, Becky, who always supports me, gave her sometimes brutally honest critiques and patiently put up with countless re-reads. The Gettysburg National Riding Stables Horse Rescue staff and wranglers (Meg, Shawn, Amanda, Chris, Alicia, Jessica, Samantha, Kylie, Shea, Landry, Maya, Allie, Mike, Pam, Becky, Jackie, and Asher) always found time to teach, answer questions, and patiently endure my many equestrian shortcomings, despite the time-consuming hard labor required to care for and manage these equines.

Many thanks to John Heiser, a Historian at Gettysburg National Military Park, Timothy Smith and the Adams County Historical Society, and the U.S. Army Heritage and Education Center in Carlisle, PA for providing invaluable assistance in finding documentation and resource materials for this book. I also want to thank the Association of Licensed Battlefield Guides Library and Files and to extend a notable mention to Licensed Battlefield Guides Rob Abbott, Britt Isenberg, Michael Phipps, James Hessler, and John Krepps, who kindly took the time to offer their feedback regarding this manuscript.

Many others have helped contribute to this project, whether they be a reader or contributor of maps, photos or paintings: Mr. Ken Rich, Hal Jespersen, Don Troiani, Colonel Craig Huddleston USMC Retired, Hanna Lipsey, Dr. John Pinkowski, Shannon Cessna, Molly Gerber, Allison Stover, Mike Bagley, Jamie Moore, Friends of Point Reyes Morgan Horse Ranch, Pam and the staff at Hickory Hollow Farm, Samantha Riggs, Laura Stamler, Alaina Stamler, Janelle Abrams and Maya Swiderski. To my dad, Wil Bagley, my son Ryan, and daughter-in-law Angie, thanks for everything. If I have neglected to render thanks to anyone who assisted me along the way, please accept my sincerest apologies.

This venture would not have been possible if it were not for the efforts of Mr. Kevin Drake and the team at Gettysburg Publishing. Their time, patience, and guidance made this book a reality.

Finally, I would like to thank Maverick, who adopted me as his human. The hours spent with you gave me a newfound respect for the horse. Thank you for your patience, for suffering through my many mistakes, and for simply being a friend and companion.

Any errata contained within these pages lies solely with the author.

ABBREVIATIONS

ACHS: Adam's County Historical Society

ALBG: Association of Licensed Battlefield Guides

GNMP: Gettysburg National Military Park

LOC: Library of Congress

OR: Official Records of the War of the Rebellion

SHSP: Southern Historical Society Papers

USAHEC: United States Army Heritage and Education Center

"The greatness of a nation and its moral progress can be judged by the way its animals are treated."

FOREWORD

There have been hundreds of books written about the Battle of Gettysburg, which was both the largest land-based conflict in the history of the New World as well as a turning point of the American Civil War. Likewise, there have been hundreds of books written about horses, ranging from their breeding and care to their singular impact upon mankind and civilization. But this book offers a unique perspective, combining a brief overview of the Battle of Gettysburg with a layman's introduction to horses in warfare.

The Horse at Gettysburg is intended to demonstrate that if it weren't for the labor of horses, the Battle of Gettysburg would never have been possible. Horses brought the cavalry and artillery to the battlefield, horse-mounted couriers were a principle means of communication between units, horses hauled away the wounded, and horses and mules moved everything necessary to feed, arm, and supply the opposing armies. Just one example of the critical role horses play in the Civil War era is General Lee's warning to President Jefferson Davis shortly after the Battle of Gettysburg. General Lee reports that due to a lack of horses, "I have been obliged to diminish the number of guns in the artillery and fear I shall have more to lose."

Most aficionados of the Battle of Gettysburg can recite the basic statistics: An estimated 165,000 Union and Confederate soldiers present and 51,000 casualties. But how many can recite the equine statistics? An estimated 80,000 horses and mules accompanied the armies to Gettysburg, and an estimated 5,000 died in the battle. If those horses were provided with "full rations" during battle as recommended by the army manuals, it would have required 96,000 pounds of grain per day, 1.12 million pounds of forage (hay or grass) per day, and a daily average of between 400,000 and 600,000 gallons of water.

Beyond those basic numbers, a thorough understanding of the Battle of Gettysburg requires an understanding of the unique relationship between soldier and horse, which was played out during the battle. Each of those 80,000 horses and mules had to be specially trained for their battlefield role, whether that be as an officer or cavalry mount, part of an artillery team, or part of a wagon team hauling everything needed to supply and support 165,000 soldiers. In most cases, and this was particularly true for personal mounts, the training created a special relationship between the horse and rider. Neither the horse nor the rider went into battle alone. On the battlefield, man and beast were dedicated partners.

The value of *The Horse at Gettysburg* lies in the combined overview of the battle itself and the critical role of horses in the battle. Topics covered in this book range from the types of horses commonly bred in the Civil War era and the specialized training that is required to prepare them for the day of battle to tactical concerns, such as the (surprising) difficulties that horses had navigating the irregular terrain at Gettysburg and the limitations of a horse's field of vision.

The strength of the book lies in the examination of the relationship between the soldiers and their horses during the stress of combat. Sometime those relationships are humorous, such as the real reason General Meade's horse ran away with him, and sometimes they are poignant, such as a courier's understanding that he must ride his horse to death due to the pressures of delivering extremely time-sensitive messages.

Considering that both the Army of the Potomac and the Army of Northern Virginia could move only by foot power and horsepower, it is somewhat surprising that there are few studies which examine the relationship and interdependence of soldier and steed. This brief study helps fill that void.

Terry L. Latschar
Licensed Battlefield Guide, Gettysburg National Military Park
Former Park Ranger, Gettysburg National Military Park

TABLE OF CONTENTS

Chapter 7   135

Chapter 8   167

Chapter 9   173

PREFACE

Northern and Southern armies that met at Gettysburg relied upon horses. The skill and bravery of both man and beast have been retold over the years through publications, lectures, tours, and programs. The geographic field of Gettysburg offers some of the most challenging terrains to traverse on horseback. The area has diverse topography, from rolling ridges and open fields to steep hills, large rocks, and immense boulders. Severe heat and humidity, coupled with heavy rains, compounded the misery endured by both sides. The three days of bloody combat resulted in massive casualties and taxed the town of every vital resource needed to cope with its aftermath. Where does the horses' status, their history, the aftermath of the battle, and future of horses belong in this national tragedy? To answer these questions, let us embark on a journey and of the events from a unique perspective.

"Look back at our struggle for freedom, trace our present day's strength to its source; And you'll find that man's pathway to glory is strewn with the bones of the horse."

— AUTHOR UNKNOWN

INTRODUCTION

People who pass through the town of Gettysburg will experience scenes from a bygone era—People mounted on horses, touring the battlefield. Whether riding trail horses and carriages from Gettysburg's local tour businesses or riding on privately owned horses, tourists are in a unique position to view the hallowed ground by the same method that moved men and armies well over one hundred fifty-seven years ago.

Today, people driving through the countryside can scarcely pass a field and see these animals grazing without pointing out the window and mentioning the obvious, "Horses!" These noble beasts strike a note within people. Children are thrilled riding on the mechanical "quarter" horses at a local store or the pony rides at the county fair. In moments like this, children and adults are transported back to a time not long ago where these animals played a significant role in everyday life. Mounted cavalry, cowboys in the Wild West, and the American Indian fill the imagination. The foundation of North America was predicated on the very existence of these animals. They served as beasts of burden pulling plows, carriages, and wagons. As viable means of transport, these animals, when trained and saddled, carried both the lowliest and loftiest of persons.

As this country grew, so did the vision of the United States' destiny. The Civil War was known by many names—The American Civil War, The War Between the States, and the War of Northern Aggression— They are all synonymous to describe the period of 1861-1865. By the end of this war, 624,000 Americans gave, as Lincoln noted, their "last full measure of devotion." Half of them died of disease. Soldiers were not the only ones who perished. The loss of horses and mules nearly tripled that of their masters—1.5 million, half of them also dying of disease.

A question you may ask is, "Why Gettysburg?" Occurring halfway through the Civil War, Gettysburg was a significant turning point of the war, as it was the first major victory for the North, and notably it was the subject of the most famous and recognized speeches ever given, the Gettysburg Address. It became one of the most massive clashes with an estimated 165,000 combined troops locked in three days of bloody combat over the course of days, resulting in 51,000 men killed, wounded, missing, and captured. Approximately 80,000 horses and mules aided these armies in their arrival at this peaceful town of 2,400 citizens: The cost in horseflesh was roughly 5,000. Today, the field is among the most extensive and best-kept gardens of stone and bronze in the world. The impressive monuments that feature the battle's horses can be easily admired by those who come to learn about the battle and experience the history of these hallowed grounds.

We can imagine how impressive these animals were on the battlefield, and we recognize their more famous masters, like Lee, Meade, Longstreet, and Reynolds, but what do we know about the great horses who played such a huge part in the war, such as Traveller, Baldy, Hero, and Fancy?

To use the vernacular of the period, horses that received training and were ridable were called, "broke." Once broke, the horses were desensitized to the external stimuli (e.g. the firing of weapons, fluttering of flags, sounding of bugles, and rattling of equipment) that soldiers experienced during battle. Through this process, a bond formed between man and horse, and their mutual respect, trust, acts of care, and companionship fueled this relationship. The soldiers know their lives may be forfeit at any moment— The animal that is taught to trust and obey commands does not have that awareness. Perhaps therein, a source of pity for these creatures finds its way into the hearts of many during this time of chaos and destruction.

Kings of men, political ideologies, politicians, and governments from the earliest days of history drove (and still drive) kingdoms and countries into war after war. The horse, on the other hand, if given a choice, would be content to be a horse, living in herds, grazing as their days pass. Man could not leave them to live in this peaceful way, though. Instead, man altered their lives at will, and the horses were turned into expendable implements of war, impressed, trained, and prepared for battle. Their story deserves telling from a time not so far removed.

"The horse is prepared for the day of battle, but deliverance is of the LORD."

— PROVERBS 21:3

CHAPTER 1

"The horse is God's gift to mankind."

— ARABIAN PROVERB

The horse's story begins hundreds of years before the summer months of 1863. Christopher Columbus arrived in the Caribbean in 1492, and soon after, he started his exploration of the New World. With him, he brought horses. Only the hardiest of animals survived the long and dangerous journey. Once established, it was not long before breeding farms fostered the first native-born equines—their numbers grew, and the animals flourished.

Not long after, in the year 1519, Hernando Cortez and Spanish Conquistadors began the exploration of the New World in the area of modern-day Mexico. To accomplish this mission, he and his fellow explorers also brought horses. The Mayan people had never seen horses prior to this expedition, as the North American continent had been void of these animals since the last ice age, which they did not survive. The natives thought the horses to be "gods" and had a shrine built to honor Cortez's horse "El Mozilla."[1]

If one removed all of our present-day sources of modern transportation, imagine the ensuing problems, how do you survive? As the colonies (and later the fledgling United States) prospered and grew, so did the reliance upon the equine population. As horses with pedigrees from mainly Europe and the East soon bred, this led to new horse breeds that remain with us to this very day, such as Thoroughbreds, Quarter Horses, Morgans, Saddlebred, Standardbred, Draft, and countless others. Like people, equines come in all shapes, sizes, and colors: Bays, palominos, roans, buckskin, black, grey, sorrel, chestnut, paints, appaloosas, pinto, and just about every combination the imagination can muster came into being. A thorough discourse of horse and mule breeds, colors, and equine terms are discussed in this chapter below.

---

1   Tamsin Pickernal, *The Majesty of the Horse an Illustrated History*,: Quintessence Edition (London: B.E.S Publishing, 2011) 18-21.

Numerous breeds and color schemes were present on the battlefield at Gettysburg. Some are described in detail, such as the bay, Thoroughbred, or sorrel. For those only casually acquainted with these terms, they require an explanation. To the lay person, horse breeds and colors may appear indistinguishable. The specific breed of the horse is more than just a term; it determines that horse's abilities and temperament. These days, people often pick a horse that suits their personality, but back in the era of the Civil War, the horse's breed was especially important because the animal's capabilities needed to match its purpose. This was certainly true when choosing a horse that would be well-suited on the battlefield. Let us explore some "horse lingo" that a horse handler uses when talking about horses, as well as the different breeds and colors. Here is a brief list of definitions, followed by the anatomy of equines, to aid readers unfamiliar with these terms:

Broke or Broke In: A trained horse deemed rideable.

Bridle: A complete headset that includes headstall, bit, chinstrap, and reins.

Colt: An uncastrated male horse under the age of four.

Draft/Draught: A larger, heavy horse.

Equestrian: A person who is skilled at riding a horse.

Farrier: An individual skilled in blacksmithing and shoeing horses. Also, a specialist in hoof care.

Filly: Female horse under the age of four.

Foal: A baby horse, aged up to one year.

Gelding: A male horse that is castrated.

Green Horse: An untrained horse. Persons unfamiliar with horses or how to properly ride can also be referred to as "green."

Groom: A person/soldier who will look after the horse's hygienic needs such as brushing and hoof care.

Halter: Headgear used to lead a horse.

Hands: A unit of measurement utilized to determine the height of a horse. One hand equals four inches.

Lameness or Lame: Anything either disease or trauma-related that affects the horse's ability to move or stand.

Mare: A female horse over the age of four.

Nearside: The left side of a horse.

Offside: The right side of a horse.

Pace: A two beat gait where the front and rear legs on the same side move forward together.

Gait: The speed and tempo in which a horse moves its legs and feet. Walk, trot, canter/lope, and gallop are examples.

Saddle: A seat placed on the horses back for the rider to sit. Saddles usually have a saddle pad or blanket placed underneath to help protect the animal from developing sores.

Horseshoe and Shod: Horseshoes help protect the horse's hooves. Shod simply means an animal that has had shoes applied by a farrier.

Sire: Father of a horse.

Snaffle bit: A metal bit with rings on each side that works off of direct pressure. It provides no leverage. A curb bit applies leverage to the animal's head and chin. A curb bit is distinguished by shanks/cheekpieces on the outside. Each had a set of reins.

Sound: A horse in good health.

Stallion: A male horse over four years that is not castrated.

Stud: A stallion kept for breeding.

Unsound: A horse that is unhealthy or lame, or otherwise unusable.

DIAGRAM OF ANATOMY

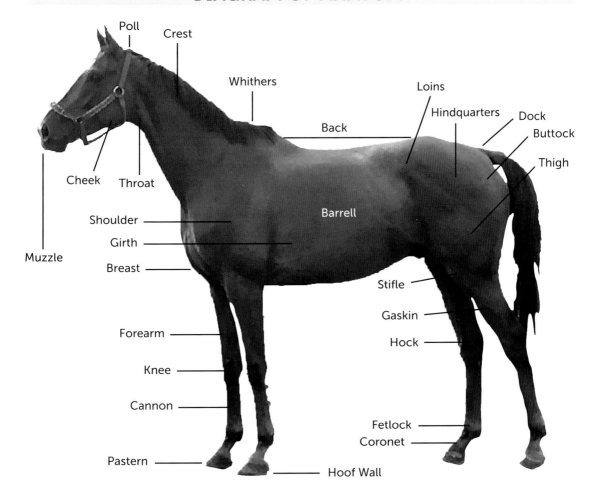

"Wandering Mind/Willie," a Thoroughbred. Photograph courtesy of Alaina Stamler.

The height of a horse is measured in hands. From the highest point of the whithers, past the shoulders to the ground. One hand is 4 inches. A horse that is 16 hands would be about 5 feet 4 inches from its whithers to the ground, or 64 inches.

"Wandering Mind/Willie," a Thoroughbred. Photograph courtesy of Alaina Stamler.

BREEDS

THE MORGAN HORSE

The year was 1793 in the state of Vermont when a man by the name of Justin Morgan purchased a bay colt of Thoroughbred and Arabian descent. As this animal reached adulthood, he stood 14 hands and weighed about 1,000 pounds. Morgan named this animal "Figure." Figure was used as a stud, and no matter the lineage of the mare, Figure's offspring were always the same: They looked just like their sire. Thus, the Morgan horse was born, so named after his master. Justin Morgan found Figure to be of even temperament, and the horse was as fast as he was healthy, winning quarter mile races and log-hauling events against horses more massive than he.

Morgans usually stand 14-15 hands and weigh 1,000-1,200 pounds. They are characterized by a small to medium-sized head, wide ears, flared nostrils, an arched neck, a short back, and well-muscled hindquarters. The manes and tails of these animals are noted for their flair and style. Morgans come in a variety of colors, including bay, brown, black, and chestnut.[2] This breed eventually became the official mount of the U.S. Cavalry, and the National Park Service uses them to this day in mounted patrols.

"Maverick," a Morgan. Photograph courtesy of Philip Straub, Manager of the Morgan Horse Ranch, Point Reyes National Seashore, CA.

---

2   Susan McBane, *The Illustrated Encyclopedia of Horse Breeds.* (Edison, NJ: Wellfleet Press, 1997) 194-197.

THE THOROUGHBRED

The Thoroughbred is possibly one of the most recognized names in horse breeds, we may easily recall names such as Man-O-War, Secretariat, American Pharaoh, Nyquist, Always Dreaming, and Justify, who are all notable winners of the Kentucky Derby. What else do they all have in common? They are all American Thoroughbred horses. Thoroughbreds trace their lineage back to England when Arabian and Eastern horses were bred with other horses of English stock. Built for stamina and endurance, they found use in horseracing, the game of polo, and hunting. As they made their way to the then New World, the breed began to thrive and prosper.

They can be rather 'high-strung' and temperamental. They usually stand 15-16 hands and can weigh 1,000-1,400 pounds on average. Their appearance is characterized by a lean, straight head with full, large eyes and large nostrils, a muscular neck, and strong well-developed hindquarters. These animals can come in a variety of colors, frequently bay, brown, chestnut, roan, black, and gray.[3]

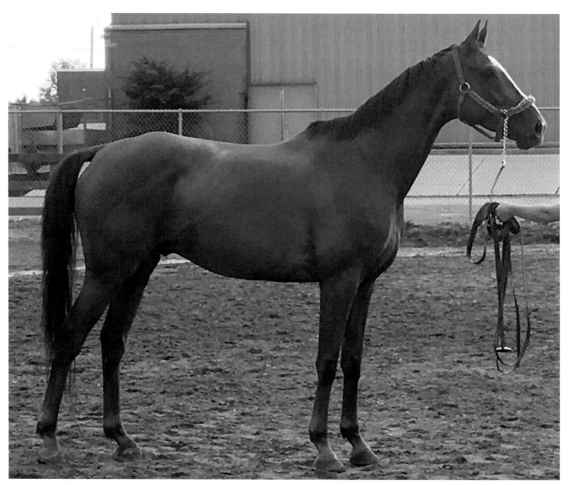

"Wandering Mind/Willie" a Thoroughbred. Photograph courtesy of Alaina Stamler.

---

3   Fran Lynghaug, *The official Horse Breeds Standards Guide,* (Minneapolis, MN: MBI Publishing Company, 2009.) 642-645

THE QUARTER HORSE

The Quarter horse lineage can be traced from Iberian and oriental stock as well as horses brought from England. Early Settlers needed animals that were versatile for everyday duties, such as riding, farm work, and moving cattle. They are also known for their explosive speed over short distances.

The early American colonies relished horse racing as entertainment, and the race-tracks were usually a quarter mile long, thus giving rise to their name, "Quarter horse." These animals are fast and agile with good instincts. Their even temperament makes them ideal for just about any task, and even today they remain a popular breed.

These equines usually stand 15-16 hands and weigh in between 1,000-1,200 pounds. They can be described as thick, musclebound animals. The neck, shoulders, hindquarters, and thighs are dense and full. Their back and barrel are usually shorter. The nostrils are large, and their muzzle (nose and mouth area) are tight. They can present with just about any variety of color patterns.[4]

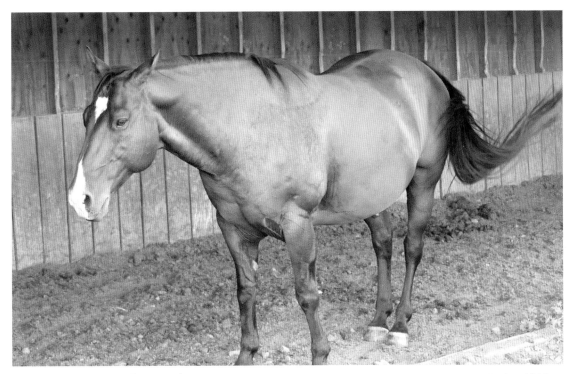

"Jack," a registered Quarter horse. Photograph by the author, courtesy of the Gettysburg National Riding Stables Horse Rescue in Gettysburg, PA.

---

4   Susan McBane, *The Illustrated Encyclopedia of Horse Breeds*. (Edison, NJ: Wellfleet Press, 1997.) 176-179.

THE SADDLEBRED

Anyone familiar with Confederate Commander General Robert E. Lee may recall the name of his horse—possibly the most famous horse of the Civil War—a Saddlebred named Traveller. Saddlebreds descend from Morgan and Thoroughbred stock. They stand approximately 15-16 hands and can weigh in the vicinity of 900-1,200 pounds. They come in a variety of color schemes.

Traveller, like many horses, was renamed several times. He was born in 1857 on the Andrew Johnston Farm in Greenbrier County in what is now West Virginia. Here, he was named Jeff Davis. His sire was Grey Eagle, and his mother was Flora. Ironically, the man to break and train the future Confederate commander's horse was a slave named Frank Winfield Page. Page rode these animals, including Jeff Davis, all day until they were made gentle. Jeff Davis went on to win first place at local fairs from 1858-1860. Following the start of the Civil War, Jeff Davis passed into the possession of an officer named Captain James William Johnston. It was in 1861 that Lee saw this animal and inquired if he might purchase him. To Lee's disappointment, Johnston already promised to sell Jeff Davis to Captain Joseph Broun. As fate had it, Lee later saw Broun and

inquired how his colt was doing. Broun had since changed the horse's name to Greenbrier. Broun offered Greenbrier as a gift, but Lee insisted on paying for him. The cost of the transaction was $225.00 in Confederate currency. Lee changed the animal's name one last time to the one he is now known as: Traveller. Lee had him appraised in 1864 for the sum of $4,600.00 in Confederate currency (the high appraisal price was due to the inflation of Confederate money toward the war's end). This mount became Lee's favorite, and thus Traveller was known to serve his master throughout the war. Lee died in October of 1870 and Traveller soon after in 1871. This great horse is buried near the Lee family crypt. [5]

Lee described his companion, who stood nearly 16 hands and weighed 1,100 pounds, as a "dappled gray with black points," meaning his lower legs, mane, and tail were black in color. In a letter to his cousin Markie, who had asked for a description of Traveller, Lee writes:

"Traveller" and Robert E. Lee. Photograph by A.H. Plecker, Library of Congress. A.H. Plecker

5   Robert Pendelton, *Traveller. General Robert E Lee's Favorite Greenbrier Warhorse* (Victoria, B.C.: Trafford Publishing, 2005), 7-9, 11.

"If I were an artist like you, I would draw a true picture of Traveller, representing his fine proportions, muscular figure, deep chest, short back, strong haunches, flat legs, small head, a broad forehead, delicate ears, a quick eye, small feet, and black mane and tail. Such a picture would inspire a poet, whose genius could then depict his worth and describe his endurance of toil, hunger, thirst, heat and cold; and the dangers and suffering through which he passed. He could dilate upon his sagacity and affection, and his invariable response to every wish of his rider. He might even imagine his thoughts through the long night marches and days of the battles through which he passed. But I am no artist Markie and can therefore only say he is a Confederate gray."[6]

Saddlebreds afford their rider a smooth, comfortable ride, as these horses are known for their "running walk." This gives a relaxed, yet brisk, pace. These animals are very spirited but have a gentle temperament. Their form is characterized by a long neck and slim build with pointed forward-facing ears and a longer back and barrel. Their hindquarters are flattened with long legs and a high-pitched tail. Their beauty makes it easy to see what attracted Robert E. Lee to this breed of horse.

THE STANDARDBRED

If the Thoroughbred is synonymous with the Kentucky Derby, then the Standardbred is synonymous with harness racing. This breed combines the Thoroughbred and Morgan, resulting in a horse that stands 15-16 hands weighing an average of 800-1,000 pounds. Like other horses, they were bred to fill a specific need; in this case, pulling lightweight carriages with a reasonable degree of speed. Their pace is a coordinated movement where the hind leg on one side and the front leg on the opposite side strike the ground at the same time. This results in a speed that is somewhat akin to the Saddlebred—faster than a walk but not quite a trot. It is not uncommon to see these horses pulling buggies along the roadways in Amish communities.

They can appear as a more petite Thoroughbred. Their back is slightly longer, having well-muscled loins with a sloping tail. The neck is somewhat longer as well, joining its well-muscled shoulders. As with many horses, the nostrils are large. Their color can range from brown, black, or chestnut.

Union General George Gordon Meade's favorite mount at Gettysburg was named Baldy. Baldy kept such a peculiar gait and pace that many other mounted soldiers had difficulty keeping up with him, for his norm was neither a walk nor a trot. While Baldy's breed is not known for certain, based on descriptions historians know of him, he could have very well been a Standardbred.

Baldy was purchased by Meade following the First Battle of Bull Run. During that time, he was utilized by General David Hunter. Baldy was wounded and sent to Wash-

---

6   A.L. Long, *Memoirs of Robert E. Lee His Military and Personal History* (New York, Philadelphia and Washington: J.M. Stoddart and Company. 1886), 131.

ington D.C. to recover. Meade bought him from the Army Quartermaster for the sum of $150.00. Meade recollected that he was entirely ignorant when it came to judging "horse flesh," but his purchase that day served him well. To his wife, George Meade wrote, *"As to horses I did the best I could, the truth is the exposure is so great, it is almost impossible to keep a horse in good health."* [7]

Baldy was wounded a total of six times, including one sustained during the Battle of Gettysburg. Meade eventually sent him via an orderly to Philadelphia in the spring of 1864. There, Baldy, now referred to as "Old Baldy," lived out the remainder of the war and survived Meade by ten years. Baldy was approximately eight years old when he was first purchased by Meade, making him nearly thirty years old at the time of his passing. Old Baldy can be viewed to this day, as his head and neck are preserved in Philadelphia at the Grand Army of the Republic Civil War Museum and Library. [8]

"Baldy," the mount of General George Gordon Meade, post-war. LOC.

Below: "Old Baldy." Photograph courtesy of the Grand Army of the Republic Civil War Museum and Library of Philadelphia, Herb Kaufman, Curator.

---

7   Meade to his wife in George Meade, Life and Letters of George Gordon Meade (New York: Charles Scribner's Sons, 1913) vol. 1, 229, 232-233.

8   Ibid., 227.

THE BELGIAN (BRABANT)

The Belgian, one of the larger breeds of horse known for its size and strength, is a draft horse. Of a gentle and docile disposition and standing from 15.3 to 17 hands, these animals can weigh as much as 2,000 plus pounds. The name of this horse is derived from the geographic area in French Ardennes, Belgium. These animals can come in a variety of color patterns. The bodies of these animals are very well-muscled with thick legs and a shorter neck and back. Other styles of draft horses can include the Percheron, as shown below.[9]

Belgians can take a rider, but their sheer size makes them better designed for pulling heavy equipment, cannon and their compliments, as well as substantial carts and wagons.

"Gus," a Belgian Draft. Photograph courtesy of Gettysburg National Riding Stables Horse Rescue in Gettysburg, PA.

At right: "Mystic," a Percheron mix. Photograph by the author, courtesy of Shannon Cessna, Cessna Stables, Lodi, Ohio.

9   Susan McBane, *The Illustrated Encyclopedia of Horse Breeds.* (Edison, NJ: Wellfleet Press, 1997.) 116-119.

THE MULE

We have all heard the simile, "stubborn as a mule." People automatically picture these animals as lazy and unwilling to do just about any task. During battles like Gettysburg, mules generally were purposely kept away from the action. They are quickly excited and nervous, making them ill-suited for use during maneuvers involving artillery or cavalry, or even as a personal mount. Perhaps these animals are just a bit smarter than their equine relatives. Mules will not allow themselves to be overworked—hence their stubborn reputation. When the firing and the chaos of battle drew closer, their "fight or flight" instinct told them to wrestle free of any constraints and flee as far away as possible. Mules, therefore, were relegated to pulling wagons. Their contribution was to keep the literal "wheels of war" turning. Wagons carrying food, forage, supplies, ammunition, and other necessities become the job of this animal.[10]

Mules are a cross between a male donkey (called a "Jack") and a female horse (mare). All mules are sterile and therefore cannot reproduce. They exhibit traits of both parents. From a distance, they may look like a horse, but upon closer inspection, the distinguishing longer ears and muzzle are noted. Their coat, which can come in a variety of colors, is coarser than that of the horse. They stand about 15-16 hands. Even though a male mule is sterile, they were gelded or castrated to soften their temperament. [11]

The one person whom the mules dared not cross was the "Mule Driver." This individual was exceptionally skilled with the "black snake," which was the whip carried by the driver. The Achilles heel of a mule is its ears. One or two well-placed "cracks" of the whip near the mule's ear was all it took for the immediate obedience to orders. They are also known kickers. John Billings, a soldier in the Union Army, related an amusing anecdote:

> *"a driver walking unpresumptuously by a mule when the animal kicked him, knocking the man to the ground. The assaulted, as if this were a common occurrence, proceeded to the wagon, retrieved a stake, and delivered a blow which sent the mule to the ground. The man returned the stake to the wagon and continued on his way. The mule recovered shook his head, and a new-found truce was declared; each was understanding the other."[12]*

The old saying, "A horse will accept your leadership, but a mule will ask for your resume" possibly led Billings to muse, *to "break a mule...start with his head."[13]*

Mules do have a distinct advantage over horses; they are hardy animals adapted to severe working conditions and unforgiving terrain. They can endure longer times

---

10   John Billings, Hardtack *and Coffee. The Unwritten Story of Army Life* (Boston: George M. Smith and Company, 1887) 284, 286-287.

11   Fran Lynghaug, *The official Horse Breeds Standards Guide,* (Minneapolis, MN: MBI Publishing Company, 2009.) 395-399.

12   Ibid., 287.

13   Ibid., 288.

of either poor or no feed with the ability to eat just about anything, even brush or tree branches. It is said that in one case, a driver left his blue wool overcoat unattended. It was found by his mule, who promptly turned it into a tasty snack. [14]

"Nellie Mule." Photograph by the author, courtesy of Gettysburg National Riding Stable Horse Rescue in Gettysburg, PA.

14   Ibid., 282.

HORSE COLORATION

Horses come in a variety of colors and color patterns. As these animals age—or even with the changing of seasons—their coats can appear lighter or darker. Melanin determines human skin color as well as the pigment of the horse's skin and horsehair/coat color. At the time of the Civil War and the subsequent Battle of Gettysburg, one might see a variety of coat colors and facial markings.

THE BAY

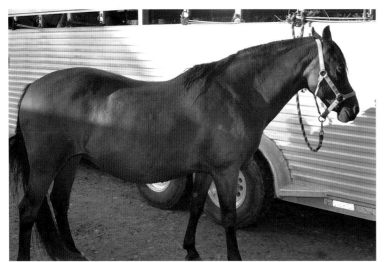

A horse that is considered a bay will usually have a light to very dark brown coat with black points, meaning a black mane, tail, and lower legs.

"Spirit," a bay Morgan. Photograph by the author, courtesy of Hickory Hollow Farm in Gettysburg, PA.

THE SORREL

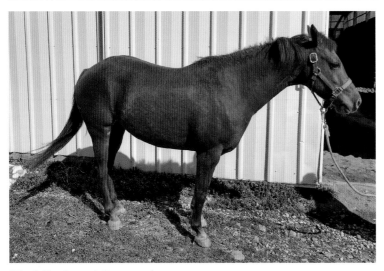

A sorrel is a horse that is reddish to reddish-brown, and even a deep darker brownish coloration known as chestnut and seal. The mane and tail is usually of the same color. A horse of this color, and other colorations may have white markings on its face (called a star or a stripe) and its lower legs (referred to as socks).

"Tesla" a Sorrel Quarter horse. Photo by the author. Courtesy of Becca Lengacher.

Nellie displaying her seal/dark chestnut color. Photograph by the author, courtesy of Gettysburg National Riding Stables Horse Rescue in Gettysburg, PA.

THE ROAN

Roans are a solid color horse with interspersed white hairs that give its coat a greying effect. A black horse with white hair is known as a blue roan. A bay horse with white hair is known as a red roan. Sorrels with white hairs are called strawberry roans.

"Strawberry," a strawberry roan. Photograph by the author, courtesy of Gettysburg National Riding Stables Horse Rescue in Gettysburg, PA.

"Skye," a blue roan. Photograph by the author, courtesy of Hickory Hollow Farm in Gettysburg, PA.

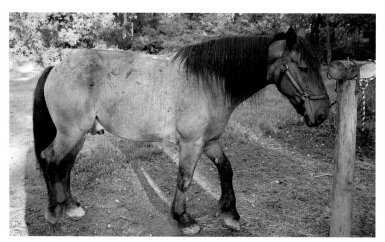

"Taz," a red roan Brabant. Photograph by the author, courtesy of Hickory Hollow Farm in Gettysburg, PA.

THE BLACK HORSE

A black horse is precisely that. These animals may have white markings on their face or lower legs.

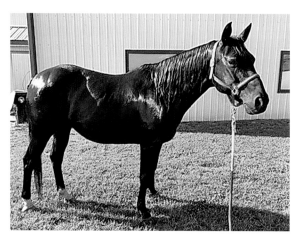

"Jett" a black Quarter horse. Photograph by and courtesy of Maya Swiderski.

THE PALOMINO

These beautiful animals can be cream-colored or blonde with a white mane and tail. White leg markings are not uncommon.

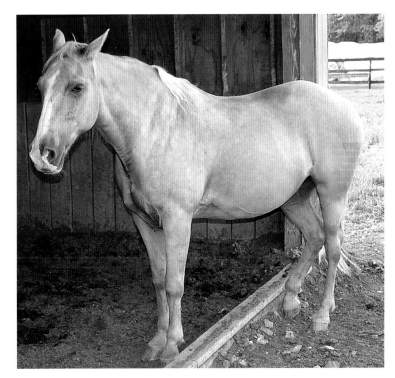

"Sebastian," a palomino. Sebastian also has a white facial stripe. Photograph by the author, courtesy of Gettysburg National Riding Stables Horse Rescue, Gettysburg, PA.

"Nugget," a golden palomino. Palominos can also be a darker golden color. Photograph by the author, courtesy Gettysburg National Riding Stables Horse Rescue in Gettysburg, PA.

THE BUCKSKIN

With a black coloring to the mane, tail, and lower legs, these animals have golden to tan-colored coats.

"Mark," a buckskin with black points. Also visible along the barrel and hindquarters are examples of dappling.
Photograph by and courtesy of Molly Gerber.

THE GRAY

Grays come in a variety of shades ranging from almost white to a darker iron color. These animals may appear "flea-bitten," which describes a gray coat with interspersed black hairs that give this appearance. Traveller, the famed horse of General Robert E. Lee, was a dappled gray. This dappling primarily consists of darker rings or circular patterns of hairs with lighter centers, spanning the horse's coat. Many gray horses may have black points with black in the mane, tail, and lower legs. While many gray horses appear as though they are white, they are not. Pure white horses are rare. Their skin carries no pigment, and these animals will have no change in color throughout their lives.

"Gabe," a Thoroughbred who is a flea-bitten gray. Photograph by and courtesy of Allison Stover.

THE PINTO AND THE PAINT HORSE

A pinto is a black and white or brown and white horse with either a black or white mane and tail, or a mixture of both. These are also called skewbald or piebald horses. Skewbald, specifically, refers to a horse of any color other than black and white. Piebald refers to a horse that is black *and* white. A paint horse can be confused with all these color types, but a paint horse doesn't refer to a color; rather, it refers to a horse with a known pedigree of Thoroughbred or Quarter horse lineage.

"Pretzel," a grullo paint. Photograph by the author, courtesy of Gettysburg National Riding Stables Horse Rescue in Gettysburg, PA.

"Caesar," a paint Quarter Horse. Photo by the Author. Courtesy of Gettysburg Riding Stables Horse Rescue in Gettysburg, PA.

Despite the wide variety of coat colors, the military frequently chose darker-colored horses. Horses with lighter colors tended to stand out in combat, thus putting both animal and soldier at risk. The Union procured darker-colored horses to blend into surroundings. On the other hand, Confederate cavalrymen, as well as officers of both armies, procured their own mounts, which resulted in horses of varied colors.

CHAPTER 2

"For want of a Nail, the Shoe was lost; for want of a Shoe the Horse was lost, and for want of a Horse the Rider was lost; being overtaken and slain by the Enemy, all for want of Care about a Horse-shoe Nail."

— BENJAMIN FRANKLIN, POOR RICHARD'S ALMANACK, JUNE 1758

ACQUISITION, CARE, AND MAINTENANCE

Ben Franklin summed up perfectly what many horse owners to this very day realize. Horses, being expensive and time-consuming, are an investment. They require a great deal of care, and if not adequately maintained, they will become a lost investment. During the Civil War, men of both armies depended upon these animals. Ensuring their proper care (even though they were expendable) kept the gears of each turning. Horses were purchased by the U.S. Government, and the Quartermaster issued receipts that redeemed for their cost. Usually, the price of the animal was approximately $140.00-$195.00, with the average being about $150.00.

Horse cost varied by their function. The cost of a cavalry horse ranged from $144.00-$185.00, artillery horses $161.00-185.00, and the mule about $175.00. The Confederate Government purchased horses as their Union counterparts did, and at the onset of the War, the costs were comparable. However, by the war's end, depreciation of Confederate currency and inflation drove the prices much higher. During the conflict, both sides captured/appropriated horses while on the campaign. They were distributed as needed or sent back to their respective countries. [15]

Many readers may have already determined which breed of horse suits their personality and which colors they may find aesthetically pleasing. Unfortunately, if you were a Union enlistee, you didn't have a choice— You were issued a horse. Horses were provided by the U.S. Government and issued feed and forage, as well as the other necessities required to care for them. Officers, on the other hand, procured their own mounts and thus had the advantage of choosing the animal that matched their needs. They received a monthly feed and forage ration from the government for their

---

15   Gene C. Armistead, Horses and Mules in the Civil War (Jefferson, NC: McFarland Publishers, 2013) 26-28.

animals based upon their rank. This in essence determined the number of horses an officer owned:

Major Generals: up to seven horses.
Brigadier Generals: up to five horses.
Colonels of cavalry: up to five horses. Other branches of service allowed up to four.
Lieutenant Colonels/Majors of cavalry: up to four horses. Other branches of service allowed three.
Captains of cavalry: up to three horses.
Captains and Lieutenants of other branches: up to two horses.

A typical officer's allowance per day was fourteen pounds of hay and twelve pounds of oats, corn, or barley (oats were preferred). One hundred pounds of straw per animal per month were also provided for bedding purposes. [16]

Confederate animals also required quality feed and forage, but as the war progressed, the South's ability to produce essential crops declined. This caused the daily rations for these animals to dwindle, and consequentially, many died from disease and malnutrition. Southern officers, like their Union counterparts, drew their animal's rations based on rank. The ration per animal per day was fourteen pounds of hay and twelve pounds of oats, corn, or barley.[17] The Confederate Quartermaster provided feed and forage as follows:

Brigadier Generals: up to four animals.
Colonels of engineers, artillery and cavalry: up to three each.
Lieutenant Colonels, Majors and Captains of the general staff, engineers, light artillery and cavalry: up to three each.
Lieutenants in the engineers, Lieutenants of light artillery, and cavalry: up to two each.

Regardless of the armies for which they served, these horses, like people, required that their daily caloric needs be met in order to maintain their overall strength and health. And also, like people, the more active the horse, the more calories were needed to sustain activity. When animals were taxed by covering vast distances, carrying men, pulling wagons and cannon, and thrown into battle, naturally their caloric needs increased.

The horses of the Civil War also required adequate water intake. Not surprisingly, equines that are deprived of water intake become easily dehydrated. One result of dehydration is colic (also known as a bowel obstruction), which for equines, can prove fatal. A minimum of five to ten gallons of water per day per animal is necessary, and with the extreme summer heat and excessive sweating, the amount of water needed to keep a horse in good health increases even more.

16   The United States Department of War. Revised Regulations of the Army of the United States. 1861. Dover Publications. Mineola, NY. 2013. Article XLII. 1122. Page 166.
17   Regulations for the Army of The Confederate States, War Department Richmond, January 28th, 1863. James A. Seddon Secretary of War. Article XLI. 1008. Page 103.

When planning military maneuvers, the armies, planned and allowed for the acquisition of water from running streams or wells. Gettysburg hosted nearly 165,000 soldiers combined, and the number of horses and mules from both armies possibly exceeded 80,000. Hence, it was no surprise to find local wells completely dry. The contamination of wells and streams due to blood, excrement, and decomposing bodies following the battle only added to this logistical nightmare.

PERSONAL MOUNTS

Like their Union adversaries, Confederate officers purchased their mounts while the artillery were issued horses. However, one of the most significant differences was that of the cavalry. Confederate cavalrymen, unlike their northern counterparts, had to provide their mounts. Upon enlistment or muster, the trooper's horse, which was likely a companion and friend from their own home, was appraised and assigned a monetary value (usually a standard amount). The government provided food, forage, and shoes, plus forty cents per day toward the care of the horse. If the animal was killed in battle or died of wounds sustained from actual combat, the trooper was promised reimbursement by the government based on the assigned value of that horse.

Confederate horseman, however, were lucky to receive a full payment if anything at all. Then, after the loss of his horse, the trooper had the responsibility, at that point, to attain another horse. Replacing an animal is possible, but the loss of a friend and perhaps a reminder of home and time without war had no real monetary value. Some procured a replacement (remount) that had been captured and considered contraband, or they were furloughed home to acquire another mount. During the Gettysburg campaign, Confederates chose from the many horses taken from the untouched Pennsylvania countryside. Either way, a cavalryman without a horse is an infantryman. If the trooper's mount died from any other cause, whether disease, deprivation, exposure, or capture, the loss belonged to the soldier, and he received no reimbursement.[18]

In Confederate service, there were considerable variations in the age, size, color, gender, and breed of horses present for duty, especially for officers and cavalry units. The Union army, on the other hand, had regulations for the procurement purchase and requirements of their equine recruits. Cavalry mounts were to be between five and nine years of age and between 15-16 hands tall.[19] Before the Battle of Gettysburg, the selection of horses and mules was not standardized. It was essential to purchase animals in great numbers, and consequently, the quality was found, in many instances, lacking.

To the layperson, walking into a corral full of horses and picking usable and sound animals proved a daunting task. By 1863, complaints arrived about the dubious quality of horseflesh. At this time, recommendations were already underway to remedy the situation. Colonel Daniel Rucker proposed to have experienced cavalry officers inspect

---

18   See Harriet B. Mesic, *Cobb's Legion of Cavalry* (Jefferson, NC: McFarland & Co. Publishers, 2009) 4. Also, Edward G. Longacre, *Lee's Cavalrymen* (Mechanicsburg, PA: Stackpole Books, 2002) 42-45.
19   Blake Manger, *Traveller and Co. The Horses of Gettysburg* (Farnsworth House Military Impressions, 1995) 48.

potential animals for service at a depot. Civilian contractors arrived, and their animals examined. If they passed a rigorous inspection, they were purchased at standard prices. This procedure became official just a few short weeks following Gettysburg. The Cavalry Bureau came into existence on July 28, 1863, and a series of cavalry depots were established. The largest of these, and the one that served the armies of the eastern theater of the war, was located at Giesboro, Maryland just outside of Washington D.C. Camp Stoneman, named in honor of Major General George Stoneman, the first chief of the Cavalry Bureau, the depot sat due east across the Potomac River (the modern-day location of Joint Base Anacostia-Bolling).[20]

In years past (and even today), prospective recruits entering military service had to pass a physical examination to ensure an individual was fit for military service. If an individual was declared unfit for military service, they were classified as "4-F." It is reasonable to assume that horses endured similar testing and exams.

CAVALRY REQUIREMENTS AND PROCEDURES

The process of obtaining mounts for U.S. Cavalry service was not as simple as purchasing what "appeared" to be a sound quality animal. Horses that were prospective cavalry mounts arrived at an inspection depot. The inspectors of these animals were the "experts" of their era and charged with weeding out equines that did not meet army regulations. The process continued as follows:

1. "A register kept at each depot on which contractors registered their names, the number of horses they have contracted to deliver, the beginning and end of each contract, and the number presented for inspection each day.

    Inspections are made according to this register. Any contractor not present when his turn comes was required to wait until the horses of those who shall then be waiting shall be inspected. The 'senior inspector' caused the horses furnished under each contract to be placed in the inspection yard at least twenty-four hours before examining them; at which time he required every person except his assistants to leave the yard, and permit no other person to enter it, or handle the horses, until the inspection and branding is completed.

2. The check was conducted with a view of obtaining sound and serviceable horses, and in such a way as to make it to the advantage of the contractor to identify his interest with those of the Government; therefore, all horses presented that is manifestly an attempt at fraud on the Government, because of incurable disease, or any purposely concealed defect whatever, shall be branded on the left shoulder with the letter "R."

---

20   Erna Risch, *Quartermaster Support of the Army: A History of the Corps. 1775-1939* (Washington, DC: Center of Military History U.S. Army, 1989) 377-378.

3. Horses that are rejected for being underage, in poor condition, or temporarily injured by transportation or otherwise, shall be lightly branded on the front part of the forehoof, near the coronet (the rear leg just above the hoof) with the letter "R", not to exceed in length three-fourths of an inch. Should any horse thus marked become fit for service before the expiration of one month, he may be again presented for inspection, provided the contractor, before submitting him, shall notify the inspector or inspectors of the fact, that the animal had previously been rejected. Inspectors will be particularly careful in making these re-inspections, and any horse once rejected, that is presented without the required warning, shall be considered as an attempt at fraud upon the Government and be treated as prescribed in paragraph 2.

4. All horses rejected are removed as soon as they pass from the hands of the inspectors, from the immediate vicinity of the corrals in which those accepted are kept.

5. When horses are doubtful, before branding, they may be kept three or four days, under guard, at the expense of the contractor, be again rigidly examined, and then finally disposed of by the above rules. No mares are accepted.[21]

6. In the inspection of horses, inspectors proceeded as follows: The horses are led one by one as fast as needed, from the receiving yard, by a halter or snaffle bridle, without blinds or saddle; then ascertain his height by actual measurement. He should be between fifteen and sixteen hands high. Examine his mouth and determine his age and that his teeth are sound. When the teeth have been tiled or otherwise tampered with, to conceal his age, he shall be treated as an attempt at fraud. No horse undersize, or less than five years of age, or over nine, are approved, except when he is in every other way suitable for cavalry service. In no case are horses over ten years of age are permitted. Next, the inspector examined the eyes to see that they are sound. Following this, the ears are assessed to ensure that they are clear of disease, particularly on the inside. The head of the animal is then examined to ensure that there are no diseases or material imperfections. The legs are then checked carefully for spavins, splints, sprains, curbs, and other defects.[22]

7. Each foot examined to see that there are no cracked, split, or pumiced hoofs, corns, or evidence of the acute founder.[23] The feet must be sound in all respects. Next, examine the general appearance of the horse; that his coat is sound and good, withers not too high nor too heavy; that the length of the

---

21 Horses that were used by Confederates or as a personal mount in either army could be male or female. The Union Army procurement allowed for male horses only and preferred them to be gelded (castrated). The presence of mixed genders in close proximity to each other, in fact, may result in unintended consequences

22 Spavins, splints, sprains, curbs, and other defects can indicate cysts around or in the joints, especially in the "hock," which may indicate previous injuries or arthritis.

23 Acute founder can be defined as laminitis or an inflammation of the hoof and its connective tissues.

loins is in proportion to the rest of the body; the back sound and free from knots, and old sores temporarily healed; the belly large and not pinched up After having gone through the previous, the horse is led off, first at a walk, then at a trot. Observe how he moves, that his feet do not interfere, and that his motion is free from stiffness. The animal is then turned short round to the right and left to ascertain any injury to the chest or shoulders. The animal is then mounted, and vigorously exercised for several minutes, to see that his breathing and endurance are acceptable; that he has the strength to carry his rider; he does not stumble and has been adequately broken.

8. After the inspection had ended, and no serious defect discovered the horse is returned to the stand of the inspector, and, under his observation, branded on the left fore- shoulder with U. S., in the usual manner. The initials of the name of the inspector, together with that of the contractor, are also be branded on the neck, under the mane, in such manner that each horse can be traced to the inspector and contractor by whom he was brought into service. This brand need not be too large, yet large enough to identify the inspector's name first, and then that of the contractor.

9. All branding irons when not in use are kept under lock and key in charge of the quartermaster receiving the animals. Every precaution must be taken to prevent rejected horses from being put among good ones and branded as passed. Gates of corrals are secured at night by locks, and military guards when practicable, stationed to prevent tampering in any way with the enclosure or the horse.

10. Horses are fed at the expense of contractors until they have been branded and accepted.

11. A complete record of all inspections was kept at the office of receiving quartermaster on duty at that post. Copies of these records are forwarded at the close of each contract and give detailed information concerning the entire range of responsibilities involved in the purchase, care, and inspection of horses for cavalry service at that place.

12. The following certificates are made on the inspection report of the inspector when he is a commissioned officer. The affidavit attached is for civil inspectors and must be qualified in the manner prescribed by the present regulations and orders of the army. It should be for convenience printed upon the voucher."[24]

---

24 This process can be found in United State Serial Congressional Serial Set. Washington: U.S. Govt. Print Off., 1893-1896 Volume 3142 Issue 1. Report 2534. Page 590-594. John Spicer vs The United States. The afore mentioned suit included a Circular from the War Department, Cavalry Bureau. The circular titled "Instructions for the Inspection of Cavalry Horses dated February 5th, 1864 was submitted as evidence. Prior to Gettysburg, the procurement and inspection of horses perhaps followed along these lines; Although primary documentation in this area was not found, it did demonstrate the commitment to produce quality horses within a year of the battle.

ARTILLERY HORSE REQUIREMENTS

Just as cavalry horses had requirements, so did artillery horses. The main task of these animals was to pull cannons, limbers, and caisson. This work, in many cases, required strong draft type animals. The requirements for these horses were:

» Five to seven years old
» 15.3 hands (plus or minus 1 inch)
» Broken to the harness
» Free of vice
» Full chest and shoulders to support the collar
» Broad, deep loins
» Solid hindquarters
» 1,000-1,200 pounds
» Healthy large hooves and a willingness to be shod

Artillery horses were expected to pull approximately 600 pounds each, excluding that of the cannoneers. Each piece required six animals. The piece consisted of the actual cannon, carriage, and the limber. The caisson also needed an additional six animals.[25]

Six horses were required to pull this three-inch ordnance rifle and its limber. Pictured: Battery "A" 4th US Artillery, located on Hancock Ave in Gettysburg National Military Park (GNMP). Photograph by the author.

---

25 William F. Barry, French, William H., Hunt, Henry J. *Instruction for Field Artillery, Prepared by the Board of Artillery.* J.B. Lippincott and Co. 1860) 46-50.

Artillery Caissons. Six horses are required to pull each caisson. Three horses positioned on each side of the pole. Pictured: Battery "A" 4th US Artillery, located on Hancock Ave in Gettysburg National Military Park (GNMP). Photograph by the author.

Horses of younger ages were preferred, but how did they ensure that the purchased horses met this requirement? To a non-expert, it is difficult to tell the age of a horse, especially if the animal's history is unknown. To be sure, an examination of the animal's teeth was necessary to understand its approximate age and state of health. Government agents and soldiers who evaluated the equine candidates were on hand to inspect the teeth, particularly the corner incisor. A horse's set of teeth, unlike that of a human, does not stop growing/erupting during its lifetime, and characteristics in its teeth are telling of the horse's age. At about age 10, the corner incisor will begin to display a groove traveling down the center of the tooth until it reaches the base. This is called Galvayne's Groove. As the horse ages and the teeth continue to grow and erupt, this groove will disappear as gradually as it appeared. The surface shape of the horse's molars, the tooth color, and the slope of the tooth changes over the lifetime of the horse. A close examination of the mouth of the horse proved to be an effective tool in understanding the age and health status of the horse. This method, while not one-hundred percent foolproof, served as a guide when estimating the age of the animal.[26] This, perhaps, gives new meaning to the old saying "never look a gift horse in the mouth!"

26   Susan McBane, *The Illustrated Encyclopedia of Horse Breeds* (Edison, NJ: Wellfleet Press, 1997) 23.

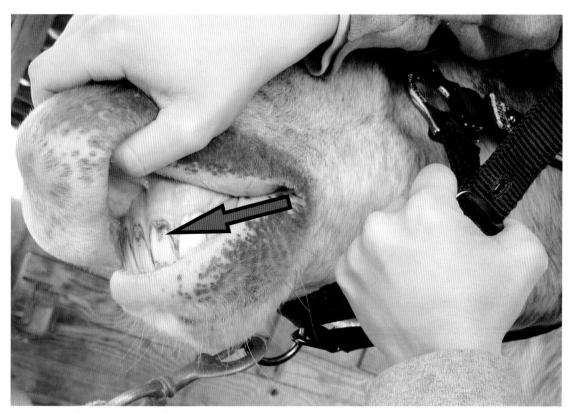

A Galvayne's Groove is indicated by the red arrow in the photo. "Murphy" is approximately thirteen to fourteen years old. Photograph by the author, courtesy of Samantha Riggs.

FARRIERS AND VETERINARY CARE

The horse's overall appearance communicates a great deal about its health. Height, weight, the assessment of its eyesight, and overall temperament and disposition are also observed. The hooves of these animals are also revealing. Observing the animal's posture and assessing for any abscesses or cracks in the hoof can demonstrate if the equine is fit for military service. As far as temperament is concerned, the horse must display a willingness to be shod (a term for the application of horseshoes) by a farrier. It became apparent to men of both armies that the services of farriers were a vital component to the health of their horses. These individuals not only shod horses, but many were skilled at blacksmithing. Shoeing an animal is not only labor intensive, but it can also be dangerous. Attempting to shoe an uncooperative horse can cause the horse to startle and kick, placing those nearby at risk of severe injury and even death. Each hoof can vary in shape and size. The farrier determines the size of the shoe needed and must customize it to the animal. This requires heating the metals to make them malleable, then using a hammer and anvil to shape the shoe. The farrier not only removes the old shoe but also trims, files, and cleans the hoof before the application of the new shoe. Animals today, depending on the frequency of their use, may need to be shod every six weeks.

A U.S. Government horseshoeing facility circa April 1865. LOC.

Farriers use similar implements, tools, and techniques today that were utilized during the American Civil War. Photograph by the author.

A farrier prepares a hoof for shoeing. Today this remains a highly technical job, requiring sound horse handling skills as well as blacksmithing ability. Photograph by the author.

A horse's hoof is inspected by a farrier after shoeing. Photograph by the author.

Artillery Forge by Edwin Forbes. LOC.

It's easy to lose sight of the amount of metal and labor necessary for the hoof health of the Civil War horses. An estimate of the number of horses and mules used during the Civil War approached three million. At four shoes per animal, that equates to twelve million shoes. If these animals were shod just once a month for the four years of the war, this required more than 576 million shoes. To aid this undertaking, the military's farriers utilized traveling forges complete with necessary tools and supplies.

CARE OF HORSES

Veterinary services were also needed to ensure these animals received proper medical care if they became sick or wounded. Veterinary science at the time of the war, like the medical care of soldiers, was lacking. Infection, pathology and the medical knowledge to prevent infection had yet to be discovered, and antibiotics were not developed until the early twentieth century. The adage of a "horse doctor" is not too far from the truth, considering in lieu of any formal training, some soldiers received a copy of the book, *Every Man His Own Horse Doctor*. This publication went over ailments and potential equine cures and treatments. Needless to say, that in the hands of the untrained soldier, who may not have had access to the proper types of medicine, treated the animals often with deadly results. Confederates who owned their animals were expected to care for them with little or no formal veterinary training. When provisions were finally made to have an official 'doctor' for these animals, the position was taken by men who were not necessarily medically trained, but rather just had a familiarity with horse care.[27]

Major General George McClellan observed the need for specific formal training for both farriers and veterinarians and responded by preparing instruction and textbooks. Cavalry schools and depots soon introduced both.[28] McClellan recommended that only the brightest and best recruits receive instruction and argued that their monthly pay was consummate with those talents. The first requirement was simply to have an interest in horse care and the willingness to serve in that capacity. 'Veterinarians' selected had often served as army surgeons in the cavalry. These individuals had sound horse handling skills as well as good judgement in the horses well-being, and their future assistants also required some form of medical training. McClellan recommended that each company of cavalry, at full strength, had one farrier and one veterinarian with the rank of sergeant. Farriers, too, required a background in blacksmithing, in addition to the ability to shoe and care for the animals. In addition, each regiment of cavalry was to have one chief veterinarian, who held the position of Sergeant Major or a commissioned officer. [29] Eventually, the regimental veterinary surgeon received a monthly payment of $75.00.[30]

These animals were certainly expensive investments, and the enormous need for horses grew at such a rapid rate that on February 11, 1863, the U.S. Government appropriated $23,189,000.00 for the purchase of cavalry and artillery horses and a further $19,125,000.00 for forges, blacksmithing supplies, tools, and medicine for horses and mules.[31] Government spending of over $42,000,000.00 for these animals, at the time, was an astounding sum. While it was true that, like their masters, many of these animals died from wounds sustained in battles such as Gettysburg, keeping the horses healthy between campaigns and battles proved to be just as difficult. Malnutrition, especially for the Confederacy in the later stages of the war, claimed the lives of many animals. For both armies, exposure to the elements, poor roads, constant saddling and harnessing, and brutal working conditions took its toll. If these conditions were not bad enough, disease made it even more difficult.

Diseases of the hoof, such as founders/laminitis (inflammation of the connective tissues that join to the bone in the hoof), were not uncommon. The causes varied from poor nutrition, sepsis (blood infection), and trauma or injury to the hoof. Hoof diseases affected the horse's ability to stand and walk correctly due to severe pain. The result: a lame horse or mule. An ounce of prevention is worth a pound of cure, in this instance. Farriers ensured the animal's shoes were changed and the hoof adequately

27 Amelia Grabowski and Katie Reichard, Every Man His Own Horse Doctor. National Museum of Civil War Medicine. August 30th, 2017.

28 George B. McClellan, Regulations and Instructions for the Field Service of the United States Cavalry in Time of War (Philadelphia: J.B Lippincott &Co., 1861) 13.

29 Ibid., 14-15.

30 General Orders of the War Department 1861-1863. Volume 2, General Order 73, March 24th, 1863 (New York: Derby and Miller Publishers) 78. The monthly pay of a Private in the Union army was $13.00 per month. Comparatively, the Confederate army paid the same rank $11.00 per month. The Regimental Veterinary Surgeon's pay was substantially more.

31 Ibid., General Order 40. Number 19. February 11, 1863, page 22.

cleaned and trimmed. Adequate rest and nutrition, as well as tending to injuries, helped prevent this disease.[32] Animals who spent too much time trudging in the warm mud, which was the case just before and following Gettysburg due to rain, were predisposed to developing "grease heel." This condition occurs when the skin beneath matted hair around the hoof becomes irritated, swollen and itchy. As the hair falls out, thick greasy discharge issues from the hoof and skin, and the area develops sores. The subsequent bacterial infections only worsened the ailment. Treatment included keeping the area clean and dry.[33]

Horses and mules, like people, are prone to infectious communicable diseases from both bacteria and viruses. Diseases called glanders and farcy are two of the most deadly and contagious diseases that plagued horses and mules during this time period. Also contagious to people, these highly infectious diseases were spread rapidly from one animal to another by communal watering troughs, direct contact, body fluids, and airborne inhalation. Contamination resulted in pustules and sores with active drainage, cough, fever, diarrhea, and labored breathing. Today, glanders and farcy can be treated with strict isolation and the use of multiple antibiotics, but during the Civil War, it was a death sentence to both man and beast.[34]

Many horses were victims of other communicable diseases such as distemper, also commonly known today as "strangles." This infection, caused by a Streptococcus equi bacteria, manifests with symptoms such as labored breathing, fever, cough, and loss of appetite. Today, it is treated with isolation, antibiotics, and antibacterial cleansers for water and feeding troughs. During the American Civil War era, it cost many equine lives.

Men of both armies did their best to care for these animals with the limited knowledge and experience of the times, yet the United States with its vast resources held a distinct advantage in the rehabilitation of wounded and ailing animals. The Federal cavalry depots such as Giesboro were used to treat such animals. It had a staff of 1,500 and 100 blacksmiths, and initially it was designed to hold 12,000 animals. Within a short period of time, it expanded its size to accommodate 15,000 animals and finally six months after its opening, it increased in size to house an astounding 30,000 horses and mules. At its peak, 21,000 horses and mules occupied this facility.[35] Many of these animals were rehabilitated and used again. Those that were unfit were sold, or, if too infirmed or contagious, euthanized.

If an individual owns a horse or manages animals, he or she likely agrees on one fact: The horse or mule comes first, then what time is left in the day, if any, is open to accommodating personal time. It is not uncommon to see owners and wranglers with coffee in hand heading to the stable or corral early in the morning. Animals are fed

---

32 Laurie Bonner, "Twelve Ways to Protect Your Horse from Laminitis," Equus *Magazine,* issue 439: April 2014.

33 Greasy Heel. *Equimed.* July 22, 2014.

34 G. Terry Sharrer, "The Great Glanders Epizootic, 1861-1866: A Civil War Legacy," *Agricultural History,* vol. 69, no. 1 (1995): 79–97.

35 David James Gerleman, "Unchronicled Heroes: A Study of Union Cavalry Horses in the Eastern Theater, Care, Treatment and Use. 1861-1865." (Ann Arbor. UMI Dissertation Services, 1999) 278-279. USAHEC

Giesboro Point Cavalry Depot 1864. LOC.

Giesboro Cavalry Depot. LOC.

and watered, they are carefully brushed and groomed, and their hooves are cared for. Their stalls cleaned, and fresh bedding and hay is placed. By the time the owner and stable hands get to that morning's cup of coffee, it is usually stone cold. Regardless of the season, this scenario repeats day in and out through the scorching summer heat, bitterly cold winter days, and in rain and snow.

Care for these animals during the Civil War was as demanding as it is now— animal duties always came first. The day began with the soldiers being awakened by the sounding of the bugle call "Reveille" at dawn. The soldiers in the cavalry and artillery then proceeded to hear "Stable Call." At "Stable Call," the animals were fed and groomed, and it wasn't until after these tasks were completed that the soldier had their own breakfast call. Individual bugle calls throughout the day indicated the time for watering the horses and mules, and finally at the end of a long day of training or campaigning, they again heard the stable's evening call to feed, water, and care for their animals.

Brigadier General John Gibbon chronicled in great detail the care that the animals should receive. Horses and mules were sponged down, including the eyes, nose, mouth, and "the fundamentals," which referred to the sheath, if caked in dust. If the horses were too sweaty, they were dried with straw. He noted that in muddy conditions, more attention was needed to the lower legs and hoofs, with the shoes inspected and hand-washed and dried daily. He also observed that horses may not eat if extremely hot, due to their overwhelming thirst. Allowing them to "cool off" for an hour after reaching camp and before watering them is the best routine to follow. This time also allows the water to warm, as cold water to a thirsty animal may be injurious. They were instructed that a diet with fresh vegetables such as carrots, beets, and turnips helped maintain a healthy animal. Working a horse immediately after eating was not recommended. These animals, at least the artillery horses, were capped to travel no more than thirty-five to forty miles per day while in harness. Even then, the mileage should not be a daily occurrence if avoidable.[36] For many of these creatures, the close attention they received in no way made up for the endless days and nights of campaigning and battles where rest, forage, and water for both man and beast were limited. Willard Glazier of the 2nd NY Cavalry Regiment recollects many of these deprivations:

> *"The usual Sunday morning inspection was omitted on account of rain. The rain had fallen for many days, almost incessantly. The regiment has been earnestly at work throughout the day in building stables for the horses, which have suffered greatly from being kept standing too long in the mud. Under these circumstances our horses are afflicted with the scratches, many of them so badly as to render them unserviceable, and occasionally they lose their lives.*
>
> *By this cause and through hard work my little black mare, which I drew by lot at Camp Sussex in the autumn of 1861, has at last suc-*

---

36   John Gibbon, *Artillerist's Manual Compiled from Various Sources and Adapted to the Service of the United States* (New York: D. Van Nostrand, 1860) 1st ed. p. 396.

cumbed, and, with a grief akin to that which is felt at the loss of a dear human friend, I have performed the last rite of honor to the dead. The Indian may love his faithful dog, but his attachments cannot surpass the cavalryman's (Sic) for his horse. They have learned to love one another in the most trying vicissitudes of life, and the animal manifests affection and confidence quite as evident as a human being could.

The cavalier, it is true, is often compelled to drive at a most fearful rate, as when bearing hurried dispatches, or making a charge, frequently causing almost immediate blindness to the animal. Or, maybe, he continues on a march for many days and nights in succession, as on a raid, averaging at least sixty-five miles in twenty-four hours, with little water and less forage; unable to remove the saddle, which has to be tightly bound, until the animal is so badly galled that the hair comes off with the blanket at its first removal.

Sufferings like these often cause the death of a large proportion of command, and to a careless looker-on, these things would appear to be mere neglects. But these cruel military necessities only develop more perfectly the rider's sympathy for his suffering beast and bind them in closer and more endearing bonds.

Some men would rather injure themselves then have their horses harmed, and the utmost pains are taken to heal them if they are wounded. Each regiment has its veterinary surgeon, whose skill is taxed to the utmost in his branch of the healing art.

Among the most touching scenes, we have witnessed, are those in which the mortally wounded horse has to be abandoned on the field of carnage. With tearful eyes, the rider and perhaps owner turns to take a last look of the "unchronicled hero," his fellow-sufferer, that now lies weltering in his blood, and yet makes every possible effort to follow the advancing column. The parting is deeply affecting.

Often the cavalryman finds no object to which he may hitch his horse for the night save his hand; and thus, with the halter fast bound to his grasp he lies down with a stone, or perhaps his saddle, for a pillow, his faithful horse standing as a watchful guardian by his side. At times the animal will walk around him, eating the grass as far as he can reach, and frequently arousing him by trying to gain the grass on which he lies; yet it is worthy of note, that an instance can scarcely be found where the horse has been known to step upon or in anywise injure his sleeping lord. Such a scene the poet undoubtedly had in his mind when he sang:

> *The murmuring wind, the moving leaves*
> *Lull'd (Sic) him at length to sleep,*
> *With mingled lullabies of sight and sound.*

Such experiences as these had taught me to love my faithful and true friend. But I found I was not the only man in the command who was bereaved of his first love. Only a few horses of the original number which we drew still remain and several of them are either partially or totally blind, though yet serviceable. The hardships of the camp and the campaign are more destructive of animal than human flesh. Men are often sheltered from the storm when the horses are exposed, and the men are sometimes fed when the horses have to go hungry.

In battle, the horse is a larger mark than the man, and hence is more frequently hit, so that more than twice the number of horses fall in every engagement than men. The cavalryman is more shielded from the deadly missile than the infantryman. The horse's head and shoulders will often receive the bullet which was intended for the rider's body. This is true also of the elevated portions of the saddle, with the rolls of blankets and coats and bag of forage. A difference has also been noticed between the casualties in cavalry and infantry regiments under equal exposure. This difference is wholly explained when we consider the jolting and swift motion of the man as his horse leaps forward in the fray, making him a very uncertain mark for the enemy.[37]

37 Willard Glazier, *Three Years in the Federal Cavalry* (New York: R. H. Ferguson and Company Publishers, 1870) 131-133.

CHAPTER 3

"The horse, the horse! The symbol of surging potency and power of movement, of action."

— D.H. LAWRENCE

PREPARING FOR THE DAY OF BATTLE

Perhaps D.H. Lawrence, in his description above, was not too far from the truth. The first time an inexperienced rider mounts a horse can be very daunting, and rightly so! Each horse is unique in character and personality. Some are docile, and some are quite spirited. Horses are herd animals, and each herd has a hierarchy. 'Alphas' tend to rule the herd, and the social structure will go down the line until the most docile equine is found. Their senses are acute. Heightened eyesight with excellent night vision and a keen sense of hearing and smell aid in their survival. The rationale is straightforward—horses are prey—and their attention to detail around them is necessary for the evasion of predators. There are only two things that spook a horse: Things that move, and things that do not. And, while social and curious, their instinct for survival can, in many cases, cause them to run first and ask questions later. It is an odd thing, then, that animals like these can become, with proper training, implements of war. It is their versatility and adaptability that made them vital to the war effort.

Imagine being a member of the military at the onset of the Civil War and you are assigned a horse. It arrives— now what? Do you place a saddle on its back, mount, and ride off? Perhaps in the movies and western novels this is true, but more likely the animal will be too frightened and skittish. Its flight or fight instincts are on high alert. At this point, it is not a question of *if* you will be injured, but *when*.

The weight of an adult horse varies, but, on average, they weigh 1,000 pounds—their sheer size warrants caution and prudence. As prey animals, a herd of horses may react to a perceived threat *en mass*; if one runs, they will all run and ask questions later. Imagine hundreds of green Union recruits and an equal number of green horses, each uncertain what will happen next. This sets the stage for a comedy of errors with sometimes injurious and deadly consequences. Training one horse can be challenging, but training scores of inexperienced men and animals at the same time presents a dilemma. The training received had to be done as quickly and efficiently as possible and preparing both man and steed for the day of battle taxed each to their limits, as well as the horse masters who instructed them.

Confederates held very distinct advantages in the early stages of the war. When the war erupted in 1861, Confederates, for the most part, were already accomplished horseman both in riding ability and care of their animals. The South was more rural and agricultural, where horses played a vital role in the day-to-day life. Union soldiers, on the other hand, came from a more diverse background. These men had a variety of occupations in urban areas where horses were used for pulling wagons and carts, which resulted in cavalry and artillery recruits who had little or no riding experience. Training a soldier to become a competent horseman took, at the very least, one or two years. For a brief period, Confederate soldiers enjoyed this superiority, but in a short time, that gap closed.

As far as training is concerned, for the horse to respect you and carry out your commands, you must first respect the horse. Equines today, as well as at the advent of the Civil War, respond to gentle training. Gentle (in terms of training a horse) does not mean pampering, but rather firm and fair instruction. The soldier, regardless of rank or branch of service, must become the leader and a source of strength and trust for the horse. Then, and only then, will a bond form between them. To better understand what it took to train a horse for war, we must look at how these animals are trained today to realize that in the not-too-distant past, methods were not entirely different. Perhaps at this point, our newly found steed must do one thing: Take the first step and follow the leader.

MODERN TRAINING METHODS

Today horse training often takes place in a round pen. The pen ensures the animal will not flee the trainer or the training for the duration of the session. The trainer can leave its confines, but the horse cannot. Safety first for both man and beast.

"Maverick" in a round pen.
Photograph by the author.

Trainers utilize tools as aides, such as halters, lead ropes, training sticks equipped with a thick leather or rope-like cord. The horse must come to accept these tools. Initially, a horse-in-training may be startled by the unfamiliar objects, but with time and desensitization, it will become less reactive. An approach and retreat method are used, at first bringing the 'scary' or 'startling' object into view briefly, then withdrawing it. This way, the horse learns it is non-threatening, and as it becomes more accustomed to the training tools, the trainer brings the objects closer and closer until the animal accepts them and eases into a relaxed state. Equines are naturally curious and will often (cautiously) inspect these items. The trainer watches the horse carefully for cues. Natural respirations, licking of the lips, a chewing motion, blinking, and standing with one leg slightly bent are all indications that the animal is at ease.[38]

Horses, by nature, only move when it suits them. One of the first tenants in training a horse is to cause it to do the thing it hates the most—move its feet. The trainer controls the animal's movement and direction with little more than a hand signal or vocal cue. A mounted rider communicates with his or her horse by the application of additional cues such as leg pressure to the lateral aspects of the horse's body and with the use of equipment like reins, riding crops, and spurs. How long does this take? Honestly, it varies from horse to horse. Before a horse is mounted, however, essential training must be completed. This training is called "groundwork." One thing is certain—the animal must be allowed to make mistakes. We, as humans, learn similarly. The trainer will apply pressure to elicit a response. The horse gradually learns that if it responds correctly to that pressure, the pressure is released. In other words, the relief from the pressure is an incentive to learn the correct response. This is the first step in earning the animals respect and trust, and also forms a bond between man and beast.[39]

Groundwork looks similar to this— While in a round pen, you point in the direction you want an unseasoned horse to travel, it will ignore you. Point while giving a verbal cue, like a clicking noise, and still, you may get no response from the horse. Now, introduce the training stick and cord. These instruments serve as an extension of the trainer's arm and are never used to beat the animal. While pointing and clicking, the trainer may direct the training stick toward the hindquarters in a smacking motion, typically striking the ground. The amount of pressure applied to the horse should be the minimal amount of pressure required to elicit the correct response. Once the correct behavior is achieved, the stimuli (whether that be pointing, clicking, or whipping motion) is immediately withdrawn. Eventually, over time, as the training progresses the animal it will be saddled, mounted and ridden using similar principles. Utilizing advance and retreat, application of pressure training, the correct use of training aids, and the desensitization of startling objects and noises can turn even the greenest horse into a respectful friend and trusted riding companion.[40] Training a horse requires dedica-

38   Clinton Anderson. *Lessons Well Learned. Why My Method Works For Any Horse* (North Pomfret, Vermont: Trafalgar Square Books: 2009) 23-27, 166.

39   Ibid., 91-93.

40   Clinton Anderson, *Training on the Trail. Practical Solutions for Riding* (Boulder, CO: Equine Network, 2005) 2. See also Sean Patrick, *The Modern Horseman's Countdown to Broke* (North Pomfret, VT: Trafalgar Square Books, 2009) 14-20.

tion, consistency, and time. The one luxury armies do not have during war is *time*. The animals and the soldiers had to be trained as quickly as possible in order to prepare for battle. Fortunately, there were manuals designed to instruct soldiers to manage and train both their horses and themselves. With the guidance of these manuals, and under the supervision of veteran soldiers, the "Civil War Horse" emerged.

It is ironic that J.E.B. Stuart's Confederate Cavalry rode around General George B. McClellan's Army of the Potomac so effectively, even though it was McClellan who, in 1862, published the book *Regulations and Instruction for the Field Service of the U.S. Cavalry in Time of War*. McClellan was also designed and patented the famed McClellan Saddle and Bridle, which was widely used during the American Civil War.

Photograph of an unidentified Union soldier on horseback, 1861.[41] LOC.

---

41   For more illustrations depicting the McClellan saddle and bridle see: Jean Roemer, *Cavalry, Its History, Management and Uses in War* (New York, NY: D. Van Nostrand, 1863) 499, 511.

TRAINING DURING THE CIVIL WAR ERA AND USE: CAVALRY, ARTILLERY, MEDICAL, AND SUPPLY

In 1855, prior to the American Civil War, Captain George McClellan, received orders from Jefferson Davis, the Secretary of War, to travel to Europe as a military observer during the Crimean War. While there, he gathered the information that aided and advanced the U.S. military's capabilities, training, logistics, and overall strength.[42] Other manuals also existed, such as *Nolan's System for Training Cavalry Horses* by Captain Kenner Garrard of the 5th U.S. Cavalry.[43]

The abuse of equines achieved nothing then, nor does it today. It accomplished nothing more than turning an otherwise willing animal into a frightened, nervous, and potentially hostile brute. The armies recognized this and fortunately took steps to ensure gentle but firm treatment. That is not to say that abuse did not happen, but according to the training manuals, it was greatly discouraged. Striking and beating these animals today is viewed as animal cruelty, and rightly so. During the American Civil War, it was certainly cruel, but it was also counterproductive, as the goal was to establish trust and obedience between man and beast.

Upon arrival at the training area, a new equine recruit (often referred to as a remount), was led by mounted men on trained horses. Here, a remount was only required to follow. From that point, the animal became accustomed to having a saddle placed on its back, its hooves lifted and handled, and its shoes struck, all the while receiving gentle reassurance and allaying any fears. Punishment of these animals was strictly reserved for vicious behavior, not ignorance.[44]

The horse's training furthered. Upon becoming accustomed to the new stimuli, a bridle is placed on the horse's head and a bit is placed in its mouth, somewhat simultaneously. This requires the animal to lower its head and open its mouth. For a trainee, this can be an intimidating task that required the use of the pressure and release approach. The application of downward hand and finger pressure to the poll (or top of the horse's head) causes the horse to move away from that pressure, eventually by lowering its head. After repeated practice, the horse will lower his head at even the slightest amount of downward pressure. An explanation of the bit placement requires some knowledge of the mouth of a horse. The animal has six large front teeth on the top and on the bottom of its jaw called incisor teeth. They are used to clip the grass as it grazes. Just behind the incisors, there is a large gap called an interdental space, followed by more teeth used to chew or masticate. It is this space in which the bit sits.[45]

---

42 Alan Axelrod, *Generals South/Generals North* (Guilford CT: Lyons Press, 2011).

43 Kenner Garrard, Nolan's System for Training Cavalry Horses (New York, NY: D. Van Nostrand. New York, 1862). Nolan, a Captain in the 15th Hussars of England, wrote the Principles of Equitation When this publication was no longer in print, a new manual was written with some additions to preserve the methods of training.

44 George B. McClellan, *Regulations and Instructions for the Field Service of the U.S. Cavalry in Time of War* (Philadelphia: J.B. Lippencott & Co., 1862) 153.

45 Mary Delory, " Dentistry: A Look Inside." *The Horse Your Guide to Equine Health Care,* April 1, 2009.

When a thumb or finger is inserted into the interdental space, the horse can be taught to open its mouth just long enough to guide the bit into position. This task is accomplished by standing on the animal's left (near) side, next to its head and slightly forward of the shoulders. Many a student, soldiers included, learned the hard way by attempting to muscle the poll downward and shove the bit into the horse's mouth. This always concludes with the recruit and horse becoming frustrated. With horse training, one lesson builds upon the next. Lowering a horse's head is one thing but placing a hand into a large animal's mouth can be unnerving, at least at first. With time and practice, it became second nature.[46]

Once correctly placed, the bit exerts pressure in the mouth by use of the reins, which are attached to the bit. The applied pressure to the sides of the mouth guides the horse to the left or to the right, depending on the movement of the reins. Combined with the bridle, the rider controls the backing motion of the horse as well as the upward and downward movement of the animal's head.

Noble D. Preston, a member of the 10th NY Cavalry and a unit historian, wrote that breaking in a green horse, especially with regards to saddling and bridling, was not always a simple task:

> *"The breaking of green horses to the saddle furnished great amusement to the men, and the boasting of some of them as to their superior horsemanship was put to the crucial test. In some cases, the determination to make good their vauntings(sic) resulted in bruised limbs and aching heads, for there were many high-spirited and some vicious steeds among the seven hundred and thirty-two that had been issued to the regiment."[47]*

Private Levi F. Hocker of Co. F, 17th Pennsylvania Cavalry Regiment, in uniform with pistol and sword, on horseback, 1862. This photograph displays a properly placed curb style bit. LOC.

---

46   Sean Patrick, *The Modern Horseman's Countdown to Broke*, (North Pomfret, Vermont: Trafalgar Square Books. 2009) 84-87.

47   Noble D. Preston, *History of the Tenth Regiment of Cavalry New York State Volunteers, August 1861 to August 1865* (New York, NY: Appleton and Company) 33.

Once accustomed to the placement of both saddle and bridle, the animal was led out. Each horse was lined in offset ranks and separated about three paces from the next. With an instructor present, each trooper had to be taught the proper way to mount. The recruit would approach the horse and make his presence known by gently caressing the animal in a reassuring manner. Then, the order "stand to horse" was given, and the trooper would stand adjacent to the horse's head and shoulder on the near side (left) with the reins in the right hand. The next command, "prepare to mount" is given. At this point, the soldier would place the rein over the horse's head, and while keeping the rein in hand and moving to the left stirrup, he placed the left boot into the stirrup. The left hand (still holding the rein) grabs the horse's mane while the right hand gripped the cantle of the saddle (rear of the seat). Finally, the last command, "mount," was issued. The recruit used a springing motion and raised himself, and for a very brief moment, held his position before gently swinging his right leg over the horse, seating himself into the saddle and securing the right boot into the stirrup. Then, the animal was given another reassuring pat on the neck. In modern training today, riders almost always mount on the left (or near side) of the animal, but troopers frequently learned to mount on either side of the horse.[48]

Once in the saddle, the soldier had a new and elevated point of view. If the mount stands fifteen hands, this height measures five feet from the front hoof to the withers, meaning the new recruit now sat about seven to eight feet above the ground. An experienced horseman rarely gives this a second thought, but the neophyte now has a commanding yet precarious view. Finally, the order to "close ranks" required the horse and rider to fall into one line, with only a small distance of separation between the pairs.

A view of Cemetery Ridge astride a horse standing 15 hands. Photograph by the author.

Below: Two horses and personal space. Photograph by the author, courtesy of Gettysburg National Riding Stables.

---

48 George B. McClellan, *Regulations and Instructions for the Field Service of the U.S. Cavalry in Time of War* (Philadelphia, PA: J.B. Lippencott & Co., 1862) 154.

Many a mishap occurred during training. Horses, like us, are interested in having their own personal space. This makes placing horses in formation a difficult task. Equine and rider need to move together, leaving only a small space in between each animal. When the horse's space is encroached upon, an untrained animal may act out by biting or kicking the offender and its rider. If the rider is not in control of his horse, the consequences can result in a melee, proving dangerous to all involved. Gradually more horses would be introduced into the formation, while at the same time, the trooper learned to control the animal with the rein, leg, spur, and boot pressure.

Henry P. Moyer, a bugler for the 17th PA Cavalry, Company F, related a scene not too uncommon for green recruits and their mounts:

> *"Those drills-will they ever be forgotten by those who participated in them? No, as long as memory will serve us, we will remember them. Many of the horses we had received had never been ridden before. There was rearing and kicking, running and jumping, lying down and falling down, men thrown by their horses, kicked and getting hurt in various ways. There was crowding in the ranks, getting out of place and striving to get back into place again, pushing forward and hanging back, some any old way but the right way. All sorts of mishaps occurred, which caused a great deal of discomfort and amusement at times. But by patience, continued effort and practice, these difficulties rapidly disappeared, and both men and horses soon acquired a knowledge of the art military characteristic of professionals."[49]*

Unlike the many Union soldiers, most Confederates, on the other hand, were adept in their riding ability, and furthermore, each trooper was already accustomed his own animal, accouterments, and weaponry. Perhaps their most significant challenge was a lack of organized drill and uniformity. Richard Lee Tuberville Beale, who rose to the rank of Brigadier General in the 9th Virginia Cavalry during the war, noted in his writings the difficulties endured at the onset of the war:

> *"The appearance of the regiment at this time was but a slight improvement upon that ascribed to one of the companies the years previous. Three of the companies had been partially armed with inferior carbines and pistols by the counties in which they were raised; most of them were supplied with such sporting guns as could be collected by the officers from the people of the country. The equipment of the horses was of the most inferior kind and varied with the means of the individual troopers. No regular squad or regimental drill had been regularly ad-*

---

49   Henry P. Moyer, *History of the Seventeenth Regiment Pennsylvania Volunteer Cavalry* (Lebanon, PA: Sowers Printing, 1911.) 27-28.

*opted, and the supply of books of tactics was wholly inadequate to the
wants of the officers."[50]*

One such book was written by a Colonel J. Lucius Davis entitled *Troopers Manual,*
which was based upon Poinsett tactics and used in the U.S. Mounted Arm from 1841 to
1861.[51]

The Confederacy and the Union faced remarkably opposite challenges: The Union
army had excellent means and supplies of every kind (including horses), but its men
were not skilled in their use, and the Confederacy had limited resources, but its troopers had exceptional riding and horse handling skills. As the war progressed, the difference between their respective abilities levelled out, though in the end, the South was
still faced with a lack of resources.

McClellan's manual continued to be of service, not only for mounting, reining,
guidance on spurs and riding crops used to control the horse, but also the manual
provided lessons on the speed at which the animals are made to move. It was (and still
is) necessary to learn the proper incremental gaits of a horse and to control those gaits
appropriately. First, the rider signaled to the horse to move at a "working walk," which is
an *active* walk whereby the horse is not just lazily walking along, but rather the animal
is alert and ready to accept the next command. From here, the rider increased the pace
to a trot, then to a canter, and finally to a gallop through the use of leg pressure, spur,
rein and if so equipped, a riding crop.

This team of man and beast trained to handle very difficult terrain— battlefields did
not always exist on idyllic flat, grassy spaces. They learned to climb and descend the
steepest of inclines and leap over obstacles such as depressions, fences, tree stumps,
and other similar obstacles. This training, too, was done in gradual phases, and simula-
tions of natural objects called "ditches and bars" were presented and used.

When teaching the horse to leap an obstacle, each recruit would walk his animal
by the reins to the obstacle, pause, and then walk around it (not over it). As training
progressed, the soldier would run alongside the horse to the barrier, and then he leapt
over it himself, all the while an instructor trailed closely behind the animal and, if necessary, used a whip crack to ensure the equine followed suit. These drills were done
with a great deal of patience and reassurance, but they do not return to the stable until
the task is completed.

Once the animal successfully leapt the obstacle while led by reins, then—and only
then— is mounted leaping attempted. If done improperly, the rider may find himself
launched into the air. Horses are polite animals, and they will frequently allow their
rider to cross the ditch or bar first! A mounted rider is required to sit correctly while in
the saddle and ensure their head, back, legs, and feet were in the proper position. This
gave the equestrian a sense of balance and poise. A correctly seated rider also aids his

50   R.L.T. Beale, *History of the Ninth Virginia Cavalry in the War Between the States* (Richmond, VA: B.F.
     Johnson Publishing, 1899) 15-6.
51   John W. Thomason, *J.E.B. Stuart (Lincoln and London:* University of Nebraska Press, 1994.) 79.

mount by using good form, as horses learn to take subtle cues from their rider's posture, leg and heel pressure, and rein position. A poorly seated soldier does not move with the horse but pours all over it, confusing the horse and increasing the wear and tear on the animal's back. Initially, each horse carried little more than the saddle and the trooper. Gradually, as the training progressed, more equipment was added until the animal was ready to carry its full complement, which included the trooper, his carbine, pistol, and his saber.[52] Keeping the animals controlled and in formation, whether that organization be by ranks, columns, or files, was drilled into both man and beast. Turning movements, special maneuvers, saber drills, and mounted and dismounted fighting had to be done with precision at a moment's notice, all of which were directed by bugle calls or verbal orders.

Perhaps one of the most challenging tasks was to desensitize the horses from the "din of battle." Rifles, pistols, and cannon make an incredible amount of noise and can produce a great deal of smoke. Horses, by their very nature, can be easily startled, and if they are not controlled and reassured, the result could be disastrous. Ensuring these animals (and the men who rode them) did not panic required gradual desensitization. The process began with the experienced riders and horses being kept, initially, at a far distance from the unsuspecting recruits, and from this distance, they would begin to fire their pistols or carbines. Great care was given to the new horses; they, at that point, needed to be quieted and reassured if the exercises were to continue. The firing was gradually moved closer and closer to the animals. When desensitizing these creatures, one must allow time for them to relax or decompress. Modern-day horse trainer Warrick Schiller uses the adage, "allow the horse to be a horse." Rest periods where nothing is asked of them is the part that comes naturally to them and allowed for bonding between man and beast.

At last, when the new horses were ready, the troopers would fire weapons while mounted. This process continued until the animals could function and respond to the commands given to them by their masters. Next, they were ridden toward cavalrymen, who were both mounted and dismounted, all the while the firing continued. These drills were always supervised by officers and experienced troopers. Finally, once these animals were accustomed to all manner of firing from atop, around, and toward them, the other noise and stimuli were introduced—Saber drills, the fluttering of flags, bugle calls, cannon firing, the use of lances, and the beating of drums. Today, if one observed modern police horse training, one would see many of the same techniques used. Many recruits were noted to initially complain about the frequency of the drills, but when all was said and done, the rigorous training of both man and beast was appreciated:

> *"Our drills, mounted and dismounted, were incessant. Mutterings of dissatisfaction because of these were loud and unceasing. We could not then understand why we should be compelled to jump our horses over ditches and fences, especially so if we were awkward, and both riders*

---

52   The tack, i.e., saddle, saddle pad, bridle/reins, and all necessary equipment necessary approximately 100 pounds

and horses together fell into the ditches instead of jumping over them. Nor could we see the necessity of our being required to mount with stirrups crossed, nor why we should ride in a circle and cut bags off poles with quick strokes of the saber. These exercises were irksome and were not relished by the officers any more than by the men. We did not then appreciate the value of these drills. But when in the next year we were in the field actively campaigning, every man understood how much he was benefited by having been taught to mount rapidly and to be ready for any demand which required quick action and prompt service."[53]

The artillery utilized horses mainly as beasts of burden. Horses routinely hauled cannon, as well as its limbers, caisson, and forges while on the campaign, and during combat, they maneuvered that equipment into position on the battlefield. For this to occur, the horse was broken to both saddle and harness, and its temperament was to be gentle and docile. The noise and smoke generated by a single cannon can be unnerving to a human, but to an animal, even more so— the sound, smoke, and counterfire of enemy batteries challenged even the best-trained horses to stand their ground. As with cavalry horses, great care, gentle treatment, and reassurance were critical to forming a bond between man and beast.

These animals were harnessed (generally) in teams of six to a gun and limber and six to a caisson. Of the six horses, the left three bore saddles and were ridden by soldiers (near side). This is defined as "riding pillion." The front horse was called the "lead," the second horse was called the "swing," and the last was called the "wheel" horse. Horses on the right side of the piece were called the "offside" and were not customarily ridden. The team of six horses pulling the caisson took this arrangement as well. Members of the battery were sometimes permitted to ride on the limbers or caisson, but care was taken when traversing poor terrain and roads.[54]

One unit that saw extensive action on July 2, 1863 was that of Judson Clark's Battery B 1st NJ Artillery. Michael Hanifen, who wrote of the battery's exploits, describes the duties of the men who rode atop the animals:

"To each gun and caisson were six horses, under care of three drivers, called, respectively, lead, swing and wheel drivers, each mounted on nigh horse, booted and spurred, with whip on right wrist to be used if necessary, on the off horse. Their duty was to care for the horses, feed and water them, and harness them quickly at call of boots and saddles. Every man was made familiar with the duty of every other, whether cannoneer or driver."[55]

---

53   William Brooke Rawle, *History of the Third Pennsylvania Cavalry, Sixteenth Regiment Pennsylvania Volunteers in the American Civil War 1861-1865* (Philadelphia, PA: Franklin Printing Company, 1905) 23.

54   William F. Barry, William H. French, and Henry J. Hunt, *Instruction for Field Artillery, Prepared by the Board of Artillery* (Philadelphia, PA: J.B. Lippincott and Co.,1860) 52.

55   Michael Hanifen, *History of Battery B, First New Jersey Artillery* (Ottawa, IL: Republican-Times Printers, 1905) 9.

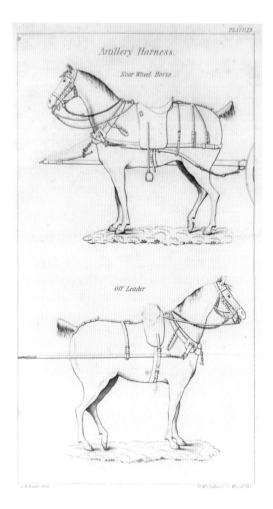

Units like Battery B drilled as frequently as possible. In the Union army, these batteries typically consisted of six guns. They were drilled by an individual gun, by section (two guns), and finally by the entire battery. To place the cannon in the proper positions required the quick action of drivers and horses.

Once the piece arrived at its assigned place, the cannon was unlimbered. The limber and horses then quickly moved to a position behind the trail of the cannon. Horses were generally not unharnessed and remained with the battery. If the unit had to advance, retreat, or quickly reposition, the animals had to be ready to move at a moment's notice. The caisson was positioned behind the limber, and its team also remained harnessed and prepared to maneuver.

Artillery harness. LOC.

Below: Artillery moving into position. Note the drivers are mounted on the left, or near horse. This is defined as "riding pillion." The swing or middle drivers bear a whip in their right hands. Edwin Forbes Collection, LOC.

The spacing for the guns typically was approximately fourteen yards wheel to wheel. The lead horse for the limber was about six yards behind the handspike on the trail of the gun. The lead horse of the caisson about eleven yards behind the limber. Every effort was taken to keep the horses as safe as possible. Should one horse of the limber be killed, wounded, or disabled, the corresponding horse from the caisson was brought up to replace it. Each battery was equipped primarily with draft horses as well as saddle horses for officers and non-commissioned officers. Each Union battery (six cannon) had on average, 175 horses. These included horses for the cannon and limber, caisson, travelling forge, supply wagon, spare horses, and the mounts of the sergeants, buglers and artificers.[56]

Battery and horse formation.
Timothy O'Sullivan, LOC.

The Keystone Battery in formation showing the approximate distance of horses with the cannon. LOC.

---

56   William F. Barry, William H. French, and Henry J Hunt, *Instruction for Field Artillery, Prepared by the Board of Artillery* (Philadelphia, PA: J.B. Lippincott and Co, 1860) 36.

Confederate batteries usually were assigned four cannons (there were exceptions to this rule), and it was not uncommon for these batteries to have different types of cannon. Each gun had a limber and caisson as their Union foes did, as well as a team of six horses for each. While cavalryman in the Confederate army procured their own mounts, the artillery drew horses from the Quartermaster, which obtained its animals through purchase and capture. The theft of horses was forbidden, and any animal not purchased was to be restored to its owner. Also, it was forbidden to buy a horse or mule without first ascertaining the right of the owner to sell the animal.[57] These regulations, however, could be overlooked or broadly interpreted in enemy territory!

The Ordinance Bureau of the Confederacy required its artillery horses to be 'heavy, strong draught horses.' They wanted first-class artillery horses, and by August of 1863, they were willing to pay a standard fee of $350.00 Confederate dollars per animal. One discretionary example was a horse blind in one eye. While this may be an impediment, the animal could still be considered a first-class artillery horse, albeit at a lower purchase price. Horses older than nine years and even up to eighteen years could still be considered for service as a first-class artillery horse, again at a reduced purchasing price.[58]

Horses not only served in direct combat, but also in the rear echelon. Two and four team ambulances carried men from the battlefield to aid stations and field hospitals further to the rear. Supply wagons (by the thousands) pulled by horse and mule ensured the wheels of war continued to turn. By the late spring of 1863 significant battles such as 2nd Bull Run, Antietam, Fredericksburg, and Chancellorsville had claimed the lives of thousands of men and animals. The need for horses and mules continued to grow exponentially, with no end in sight. Implements of war can be replaced, soldiers and equines can also be replaced, but the bond between man and beast cannot be easily duplicated.

Perhaps therein lies the uniqueness and versatility of the horse They are majestic and noble beasts, but they certainly can be intimidating. Their sheer size can be a cause for alarm, and those who work around them understand their physical strength and temperament. As a person gradually learns the animal's behavior, the horse in turn learns his rider's personality and behaviors. Nothing provides more satisfaction than the face of another genuinely happy to see them. The horse, appropriately trained, has this reaction. Once these animals are trained, and in this case, prepared for battle, a bond forms between man and beast. Losing a friend or comrade in arms during a war is traumatic. The experience was no different for man and horse: all trained, all disciplined, all expendable. The days of the battle approached.

---

57 *Regulations for the Army of the Confederate States, 1863, corrected and enlarged with a revised index the only correct edition,* (Richmond, VA: J.W. Randolph, 1863) 77, #764.

58 *General orders from Adjutant and Inspector-General's office, Confederate States army, from January 1862 to December 1863,* (Columbia: Steam Powered Presses of Evans and Cogswell, 1864) 138.

Above: A Civil War ambulance. LOC.

Mule driven supply wagon. Edwin Forbes Collection. LOC.

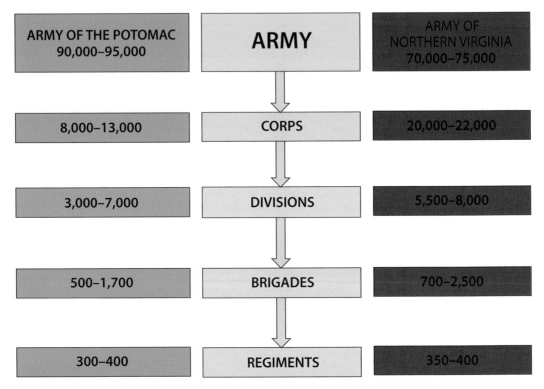

Civil War Army Organization
Representing the Average Number of Soldiers

ARMY OF THE POTOMAC 90,000–95,000	ARMY	ARMY OF NORTHERN VIRGINIA 70,000–75,000
8,000–13,000	CORPS	20,000–22,000
3,000–7,000	DIVISIONS	5,500–8,000
500–1,700	BRIGADES	700–2,500
300–400	REGIMENTS	350–400

The above numbers represent the armies' approximate strengths at the start of the Gettysburg campaign. See Appendix I for the full Union and Confederate Orders of Battle. Illustration by the author.

CHAPTER 4

*"I looked, and there before me was a white horse!
Its rider held a bow, and he was given a crown,
and he rode out as a conqueror bent on conquest."*

BOOK OF REVELATION 6:2

PRELUDE: LEE INVADES THE NORTH

The Gettysburg Campaign began on June 3, 1863 when General Robert E. Lee, commander of the Army of Northern Virginia, began his push north. His 75,000 men and about 29,000 horses gradually trekked from their position at Fredericksburg across the Rappahannock River into Maryland and, finally, into Pennsylvania, covering about 130 miles.[59] Soon after their arrival, his force divided and one-third (about 20,500) of those men, now under the command of Lt. General Richard Ewell, moved north and east to threaten the larger cities of York and Harrisburg, the capital of Pennsylvania. The remainder of Lee's army, under the commands of Lt. General A.P. Hill and Lt. General James Longstreet, remained to the south and west, utilizing the mountain passes and gaps to maneuver further into Pennsylvania. Those same mountains acted as a natural partition, concealing the movements of the Rebels. The Confederate cavalry commander, Major General J.E.B. Stuart, was to gather intelligence concerning the whereabouts of the Army of the Potomac and forage for supplies while causing as much damage to the Union forces as possible. One of Stuart's primary objectives was to inform Lee when the Union Army crossed the Potomac River. Lee hoped that his move into the north would cause the Army of the Potomac to pursue him. The constant communication from Stuart regarding the Federal movements would allow Lee adequate time to formulate and execute plans to engage the Union army on northern soil.

---

59 Blake Magner, *Traveller and Company: The Horses of Gettysburg* (Gettysburg, PA: Farnsworth House Military Impressions, 1995). Manger lists the number of Confederate horses at Gettysburg on p. 47 as nearing 29,000. Whether or not this includes mules and remounts is not specified. This could, in fact, increase the number even higher.

This daunting task placed a great burden on Stuart's shoulders. Stuart's cavalry, like Lee's infantry, was also divided. His cavalry division consisted of some 8,100 troopers, including horse artillery. The 1,179 men of Brigadier General Albert G. Jenkins brigade were detailed to accompany Ewell's Second Corps on its trek toward Harrisburg. The remaining brigades of Colonel John Chambliss, Brigadier General Wade Hampton, and Brigadier General Fitzhugh Lee accompanied Stuart. Stuart's remaining two brigades of Brigadier Generals William E. Jones and Beverly Robertson were left to guard Ashby's and Snicker's Gap.[60] The 35th Virginia Battalion was detached from Jones and sent with the Second Corps of the Army of Northern Virginia.

Since the war's onset in April of 1861, the North had a seemingly inexhaustible resource of men and supplies to keep the gears of war in motion. Most of the battles to this point took place in the South, which left their farmers with few crops to harvest. This disadvantage left Lee's army in want of supplies, food and horses. Through the invasion of the North, his force could subsist on the untouched farms and requisition needed supplies from northern cities and towns. This plan—in theory—allowed the southern farmers to plant and harvest desperately needed crops. The success of this plan required the Northern army to withdraw from Virginia. A large invasion force that threatened Northern livelihood and commerce certainly would prompt a response, if not Lee had the freedom to threaten and capture larger cities such as Harrisburg, Baltimore and even Washington DC. In order to bring an end to the invasion, President Lincoln marshaled the Union army to pursue the Confederates.

The Army of Northern Virginia under Lee's command, with proper concert of action would deliver a crushing defeat to the Federal army on northern soil. Lee deduced that the morale in the north was waning. The Union army, in the eastern theater, had this vital resource dwindle following recent devastating defeats at Lee's hand at battles such as Fredericksburg, Second Manassas, and Chancellorsville. Even during the bloody battle of Antietam (Sharpsburg, Maryland), when it appeared that Lee might be trapped and defeated, the Confederates managed to withdraw to fight another day. If Lee and his army defeated and severely crippled the Federal army on northern soil, the subsequent Southern victory would erode the Northern morale enough to potentially end the war and gain the Confederacy's independence.

The Union Army of the Potomac, numbering some 90,000-95,000 men accompanied by nearly 44,000 horses and mules and under the command of Major General Joseph Hooker, began pursuing Lee's Army. In order to gather intelligence "Fighting Joe Hooker," as he was known, sent Union Cavalry Commander Major General Alfred Pleasonton along with Union infantry across the Rappahannock river at Kelly's and Beverly's Ford. They were to head toward Culpepper Court House in Virginia, which was being used by Lee as a concentration point. Some 7,900 horsemen and 3,000 infantrymen soon engaged J.E.B. Stuart's Cavalry in what became the most significant cavalry engagement of the war—Brandy Station. J.E.B. Stuart had staged a grand review of his near 10,000 horsemen and horse artillery, once on June 5 and then on June 8,

---

60   *War of Rebellion, Official Records of the Union and Confederate Armies*. Series 1. Volume 27. Part 2. Reports (Washington: Government Printing Office,1889.) 315-316, 691-692

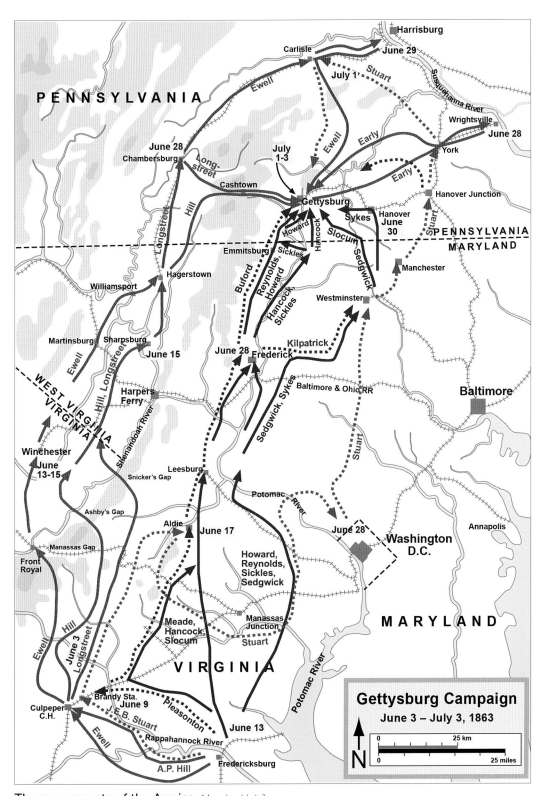

The movements of the Armies. Map by Hal Jespersen.

where none other than Robert E. Lee was the guest of honor. Stuart had been issued orders to begin a movement northward to screen Lee's movements. Near dawn on June 9, 1863, the Confederates were attacked by Federal troopers and infantry. The battle raged for nearly twelve hours.

Both man and beast fell victim to the ravages in this melee. Often the man astride the horse was struck, but sometimes the horses, too, were a target, whether purposefully or as collateral damage. When man or horse is disabled, the other can be as well. Colonel Matthew C. Butler of the 2nd South Carolina Cavalry, attempting to hold his line, was brought reinforcements by Captain Farley of General Stuart's staff. These were the men of the 4th Virginia Cavalry Regiment. As both Butler and Farley surveyed the area, tragedy struck both man and beast:

> *"While in the road, side by side (Butler) with Captain Farley, their horses' heads in opposite directions, a shell from the enemy struck the ground nearby, ricocheted, cut off Butler's right leg above the ankle, passed through his horse, through Farley's horse, and carried away Farley's leg at the knee."* [61]

The campaign trail that led to Gettysburg had barely commenced and the casualties began to mount and only increased as the days continued. In the end, the Federals withdrew, yet one thing was certain—the Union cavalry, decidedly inferior in skill as riders and as a capable fighting unit, had evolved. Their abilities rose, and the grey cavaliers were now matched. Confederate Major Henry B. McClellan writes in his memoirs following the battle of Brandy Station:

> *"One result of incalculable importance certainly did follow this battle, it 'made' the Federal cavalry. Up to that time, confessedly inferior to the Southern horseman, they gained on this day that confidence in themselves and in their commanders, which enabled them to contest so fiercely the subsequent battlefields of June July and October."* [62]

Unfortunately for Lee, the eyes and ears of his army, that is his cavalry, were unable to fulfill the earnest need for surveillance and intelligence. Following the Battle of Brandy Station, Stuart and his cavalry engaged in a series of clashes with Federal troops at Aldie, Middleburg, Upperville, Haymarket, and Fairfax Station in Virginia from June 17 through June 27, 1863. Stuart and his cavalry were separated from the main Confederate body while conducting a raiding mission near Rockville, Maryland on June 28, 1863. During this raid, Stuart captured 125 Union supply wagons. This slowed his movements and resulted in Stuart's inability to rejoin Lee and provide the necessary

61 H.B. McClellan, *The Life and Campaigns of Major General J.E.B. Stuart* (Boston and NY: Houghton Mifflin and Company, 1885) 291.

62 H.B. McClellan, *The Life and Campaigns of Major General J.E.B. Stuart* (New York, NY: Houghton Mifflin and Company, 1885) 294.

intelligence that Lee desperately needed. Stuart now had to take yet another circumventing detour, resulting in a collision at Westminster, Maryland on June 29.

Stuart's cavalry continued north and eastward, riding around the Union army that blocked the path to rejoin Lee. Stuart headed to Hanover, Pennsylvania, but citizens of Hanover were not alone. On June 30th, Federal cavalry were present under the command of Brigadier General Judson Kilpatrick and Brigadier General George Armstrong Custer. A spirited battle ensued resulting in a stalemate, but this engagement forced Stuart's horseman, artillery and wagon trains further northward. Stuart finally arrived in a town thirty-four miles north of Gettysburg, at Carlisle, where he briefly battled Federal troops. This furthered his delay, and while in Carlisle on July 1, he learned Lee had engaged the Union army at Gettysburg. Stuart and his horseman then rode to the point of exhaustion to rejoin Lee's Army. His arrival in the afternoon hours of July 2 left the man who trusted him most—Lee—blind and without proper intelligence of the enemy's movements.

The loss in horseflesh for Stuart's command further reduced their effectiveness.[63] Stuart had missed the first day's action altogether, and his late arrival on July 2 proved too late to provide any useful information on the Federal army's' position and strength. Lee later said after Stuart's death following the Battle of Yellow Tavern in May of 1864, *"he (Stuart) never brought me a false piece of information."*[64] At Gettysburg, Lee received little, if any information, evoking a sharp rebuke from his Commander. Lee was heard to have said, "General Stuart, you are here at last!" The absence of Stuart and his horseman was keenly felt. As stated, without Stuart, Lee was unaware of the swift reaction and movement of the Union Army's pursuit and unaware that the federal troops crossed the Potomac River on June 28, having to rely instead on intelligence provided by a spy named Henry Harrison.[65]

Despite the pursuit of Lee, politics and full control of the Army of the Potomac were hampered from Washington DC. Joe Hooker was unable to wrestle away the additional Federal troops garrisoned at nearby Harpers Ferry from Major General Henry Halleck, General in Chief. As a result, "Fighting Joe" tendered his resignation, which was promptly approved by Halleck and Abraham Lincoln. On June 28, awakened from his sleep near Frederick, Maryland, Major General George Meade received orders that he was now in command of the Army of the Potomac. Meade wasted no time in his duties. His orders, virtually the same as Hooker's—to keep his army between Lee and the nations' capital and Baltimore, and to find Lee and end the invasion. Ironically, Halleck released the Union forces at Harpers Ferry to be utilized as Meade saw fit. Lee soon learned Meade had replaced Hooker. William Shakespeare eloquently wrote, "A horse, a

---

63   Charles Teague, *Gettysburg by the Numbers: The Essential Pocket Compendium of Crucial and Curious Data about the Battle* (Gettysburg, PA: Adams County Historical Society, 2006) 21. Stuart, according to this reference, lost some 2000 horses. The number, while not verified via primary accounts, does illustrate the toll exacted on these animals.

64   Robert Edward Lee Jr., *Recollections and Letters of General Robert E Lee* (New York, NY: Doubleday Page and Company, 1905) 125.

65   *OR.,* Series 1. Volume 27. Part 2. 316.

horse, my kingdom for a horse." Lee, in this moment, needed horses. He also required accurate information from the men who rode them.

Confederates now moved with caution through the Cumberland Valley. Members of the Adam's County Cavalry (later to become the 21st Pennsylvania Cavalry Company B) under the command of Captain Robert Bell patrolled the area. Comprised of men from Gettysburg and Adams County, this independent command had been mustered into six month's service on June 23, 1863. These horsemen performed scouting duties, conducted patrols, and kept watch for the appearance of Confederate troops. Bell's company had two notable members: Sgt William Lightner and Private George Washington Sandoe, each played a role in future events.

Major General Jubal Early's Division arrived in Gettysburg on June 26, 1863. The infantry under the command of Brigadier General John B. Gordon arrived. David Conover of Gettysburg recalled the scene:

> *"We were in the Diamond but a short while when Early's infantry began to arrive. After the Infantry got in, or about that time, they had a large black horse, a very fine animal in the center of the square. One soldier pointing to it said to us. That's Milroy's horse; we captured it from Milroy."[66]*

Soon a cavalry unit, the 35th Virginia Battalion (detached from William E. Jones' Cavalry Brigade), under the command of Lt. Col. Elijah V. White, entered the town. Here, Tillie Pierce, a resident of the town, described the scene:

> *"We were informed they had crossed the State line, then were at Chambersburg, then at Carlisle, then at or near Harrisburg, and would soon have possession of our capital. We had often heard of their taking horses and cattle, carrying off the property, and destroying buildings. A week had hardly elapsed when another alarm beset us. "The Rebels are coming! The Rebels are coming!" was passed from lip to lip, and all was again consternation. We were having our regular literary exercises on Friday afternoon, at our Seminary, when the cry reached our ears. Rushing to the door and standing on the front portico, we beheld in the direction of the Theological Seminary, a dark, dense mass, moving toward town. Our teacher, Mrs. Eyster, at once said: "Children, run home as quickly as you can." It did not require repeating. I am satisfied some of the girls did not reach their homes before the Rebels were in the streets. As for myself, I had scarcely reached the front door, when, on looking up the road, I saw some of the men on horseback. I scrambled in, slammed shut the door, and hastening to the sitting room, peeped out between the shutters. What a horrible sight! There they were, human beings! Clad almost in rags, covered with dust, riding wildly, pell-mell down the hill toward our home! Shouting,*

---

66   "Killing of Geo. W. Sandoe. A Battle Story Told by David A. Conover," *Gettysburg Compiler*, September 27, 1905, p. 2.

*yelling most unearthly, cursing, brandishing their revolvers, and firing right
and left. I was fully persuaded that the Rebels had actually come at last.
What they would do with us was a fearful question to my young mind.
Soon the town was filled with infantry, and then the searching and ran-
sacking began in earnest. They wanted horses, clothing, anything, and
almost everything they could conveniently carry away.*[67]

The Confederates indeed levied demands upon the town and insisted on supplies,
food, and anything that could be made useful. Not specifically on the list were horses,
but many of the townspeople had taken precautions to shelter their animals to prevent
capture. Tillie's family had one equine that was now in danger of capture. She related
her family's efforts to protect this animal:

*"Upon the report of, and just previous to this raid, the citizens had sent
their horses out the Baltimore Pike, as far as the Cemetery. There they
were to be kept until those having the care of them were signaled that
the enemy was about when they were to hasten as fast as possible in the
direction of Baltimore.*

*Along with this party, father sent our horse, in charge of the hired
boy we then had living with us. I was very much attached to the animal,
for she was gentle and very pretty. I had often ridden her. The cavalry referred to above came so suddenly that no signal was given. They
overtook the boys with the horses, captured, and brought them all back
to town she was standing and asked what the matter was, Mother said to
them: "You don't want the boy! He is not our boy; he is only living with
us." One of the men replied: "No we don't want the boy, you can have
him; we are only after the horses."*

*As they were passing our house my mother beckoned to the raid-
ers, and some of them rode over to where*[68] Tillie's father attempted to
appeal the animal's capture directly to White, but came away alone, the
horse still in Confederate hands. *"We frequently saw the Rebels riding
our horse up and down the street, until at last, she became so lame she
could hardly get along. That was the last we saw of her, and I felt that I
had been robbed of a dear friend."*[69]

Sgt William Lightner and Private George Washington Sandoe of Bell's Adams County Cavalry approached from the outskirts of town. They rode their mounts from the
direction of Rock Creek toward the Baltimore Pike, just south of Gettysburg and Cemetery Hill. Due to the brush along a fence line, they did not see Rebel pickets until it
was too late. They were ordered to halt. Lightner managed to jump his steed across

---

67   Tillie Pierce, *At Gettysburg, Or What A Girl Saw and Heard of The Battle* (New York: W. Lake Boreland,
     1889) 20-22.
68   Ibid., 24.
69   Ibid., 27.

the fence and rode down the Pike. Sandoe was not so fortunate. His horse failed to make the jump and Sandoe fell from his mount. While attempting to remount, he fired his pistol at the Confederates but was shot in the head and killed.[70] The Confederate marksman took Sandoe's horse as his trophy. Elizabeth Thorn, who was a caretaker of Evergreen Cemetery[71], related the story from the man who shot Sandoe:

> *"They rode around the house on the pavement to the window and asked for bread and butter and buttermilk...My mother went and got them all she had for them, and just then a rebel rode up the pike and had another horse beside his. The ones who were eating said to him: "Oh, you have another one." and the one who came up the pike said: "yes, the -- -- shot at me, but he did not hit me, and I shot at him and blowed (sic) him down like nothing, and here I got his horse, and he lays down the pike." The man whom the rebel had killed was Sandoe, who had composed a company in Gettysburg."[72]*

David Conover also recollected and seemingly confirmed Thorn's Account:

> *"Sometime before leaving town I was standing in front of the Mclean Residence on Baltimore Street, now the Geo. E. Stock home. There were some officers on horseback very near to the pavement, right in front of where I was. A cavalryman came riding up leading a horse. I heard him say, here is the horse, I've shot the rider. I am sorry, but I had to do it in self-defense. As no other person was known to have been shot on that day I've always believed he referred to Sandoe and had his horse."[73]*

Monument to the 21st PA Cavalry. This monument is located along the Baltimore Pike. Photograph by the author.

At right: The secondary monument of the 21st PA Cavalry denotes the approximate location where Sandoe was killed on June 26, 1863. It is also located along the Baltimore Pike. Photograph by the author.

70   John, B Horner, *Sgt Hugh Paxton Bigham Lincoln's Guard at Gettysburg* (Gettysburg, PA: Horner Enterprises, 1994) 17.

71   Evergreen Cemetery is located atop Cemetery Hill.

72   "Woman Keeper of Cemetery in 1863, Describes the Battle," *Gettysburg Times*, July 2, 1938, p. 3.

73   "Killing of Geo. W. Sandoe. A Battle Story Told by David A. Conover," *Gettysburg Compiler*, September 27, 1905, p. 2.

The Confederates soon departed Gettysburg, but a tide of events ensured their return. Lee's army was now situated southwest of the town, with portions of his commands heading north and northeast. By June 29, the Army of the Potomac was in Maryland along with some cavalry units in Pennsylvania. Lee learned of the Federal movements on July 29 from the spy, Harrison, and he now shifted and changed his movements to concentrate his army. Gettysburg, with its road network, provided the logistical means to reunite his men. No less than ten roads intersect the town, which made it an ideal location. Also, on June 29, Lee recalled Richard Ewell's 20,500 men. Their new directives called for them to concentrate toward Gettysburg or Cashtown (eight miles westward) as circumstances dictated. Harrisburg and the city of York remained safe from further threats.

June 30, 1863 proved to be a day of consternation for the citizens of Gettysburg. Confederates under the command of Brigadier General Johnston Pettigrew's brigade of nearly 2,600 men approached Gettysburg from the west along the Chambersburg Pike. They sought supplies as well as scouted for enemy troops. Pettigrew had specific orders from Lee to avoid any engagement with enemy troops until the Army of Northern Virginia concentrated its full force. As he and his infantry approached the town, they spied Federal cavalry in the distance, who rode northward along the Emmitsburg Road. These Union troopers belonged to John Buford's 1st Division of Cavalry. They, too, observed the Confederates approach the town and moved with haste toward the city. Pettigrew dutifully obeyed Lee's order and withdrew his men westward toward Cashtown, where he reported this new intelligence. Buford and his troopers had been ordered to Gettysburg by Major General Alfred Pleasonton, the Cavalry Corps Commander.[74] The townspeople, relieved at their arrival, lined Washington Street as nearly 2,700 troopers and six artillery pieces arrived. Tillie Pierce wrote of the scene she witnessed:

"A little before noon on Tuesday, June 30th, a great number of Union cavalry began to arrive in the town. They passed northwardly along Washington Street, turned toward the west on reaching Chambersburg Street, and passed out in the direction of the Theological Seminary. It was to me a novel and grand sight. I had never seen so many soldiers at one time. They were Union soldiers, and that was enough for me, for I then knew we had protection, and I felt they were our dearest friends. I afterward learned that these men were Buford's cavalry, numbering about six thousand men.[75] A crowd of "us girls" were standing on the corner of Washington and High Streets as these soldiers passed by. Desiring to encourage them, who, as we were told, would before long be in battle, my sister started to sing the old war song "Our Union Forever." As some of us did not know the whole of the piece, we kept repeating the chorus. Thus, we sought to cheer our brave men; and we felt amply repaid when we saw that our efforts were appreciated. Their countenances brightened,

---

74   *OR.*, Series I. Volume 27. Part 3. 400.
75   Buford's Cavalry consisted of just over 4000 troopers. Only two brigades were in Gettysburg on June 30th and on the first day's battle, numbering around 2700 men.

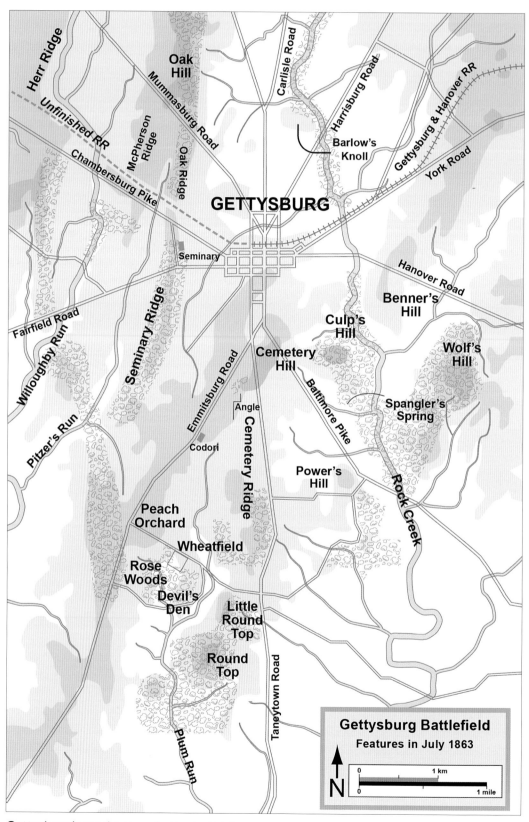

Gettysburg's road network. Map by Hal Jespersen.

and we received their thanks and cheers. After the battle, some of these soldiers told us that the singing was very good, but that they would have liked to have heard more than the chorus."[76]

"Young boys eager to see the spectacle were witnessed running alongside the Cavalry horses and spent a better part of the days remainder helping with menial chores such as watering the horses.[77] One such lad was Hugh Zeigler, who, with other boys in the town were permitted to ride the soldier's horses to water."[78]

Members of the 6th New York Cavalry also painted a similar picture of the events as Pettigrew's Confederates encroached upon the town:

"Gettysburg was a flourishing town of about 5000 inhabitants[79], about forty miles from Baltimore and eleven from Emmitsburg. The rebels had invaded it a few days prior, but their welcome was cold; they did considerable damage in and about town, burned the railroad bridge and a train of cars, and seized what horses they could find and took goods from the stores, their main object being to secure shoes and clothing. About ten o'clock, Pettigrew's Confederate brigade of Heth's division made its appearance in the western suburbs of the town and halted, their pickets advancing close to the residences on the outskirts. They had come with instructions to search the town for army supplies, shoes, etc. They did not enter the town, however, but examined it with their field-glasses. Learning of the approach of Meade's advance guard, they withdrew toward Cashtown, leaving their pickets about four miles from Gettysburg. The Sixth New York Cavalry reached Gettysburg at 11 a.m. but found the enemy had fallen back from the town. The citizens, already in a state of terror and excitement over the great invasion, gazed with interest and satisfaction as the long column of veteran troopers, with trampling horses and fluttering guidons, moved through their streets. The troops were highly welcomed; such enthusiasm and loyalty were seldom witnessed."[80]

76   Tillie Pierce, *At Gettysburg, Or What A Girl Saw and Heard of The Battle* (New York: Lake Boreland. 1889) 28-29.

77   Gerald R. Bennett, *Days of Uncertainty and Dread,* (Camp Hill, PA: Plank's Suburban Press, 1994) 17.

78   Hugh McClain Zeigler, *Reminiscence of Hugh M. Zeigler of the Battle of Gettysburg Which Occurred on the First, Second, and Third Days of July 1863.* Adams County Historical Society Archives.

79   Gettysburg was in fact a town of about 2400 people. The 1860 census officially placed the population at 2390.

80   Hillman A. Hall, H, W.B. Besley, Gilbert G. Wood, *History of the Sixth New York Cavalry (Second Ira Harris Guard) Second Brigade - First Division - Cavalry Corps, Army of the Potomac, 1861*-1865 (Worcester, Mass: The Blanchard Press, 1908) 133-134.

Captain W.C. Hazleton of the 8th Illinois Cavalry related a similar scene:

> *"The enthusiastic reception which the people of Gettysburg gave our cavalry as we reached the city on the day before the fight, and the wonderful reception on our troops. Men, women, and children crowded the sidewalks and vied with each other in demonstrations of joyous welcome. Hands were reached up eagerly to clasp the hands of your bronzed and dusty troopers. Cake, beer, milk, and wine were passed up to the moving column as we marched slowly along the crowded streets, doors, windows, and balconies were filled with ladies waving their handkerchiefs; Bright eyes and smiling faces looked down from open window upon the troopers; Then a matron trying to smile through her tears, as she remembers her own boy in the army. Altogether it was one of the most touching, spontaneous, and heartfelt demonstrations my eyes ever witnessed."*[81]

The sudden rush of the citizens toward men and beast displayed the firm control and discipline these units possessed. In many cases, a sudden onslaught of people toward horses is not the safest choice, but the mere presence of these animals and their riders provided some measure of hope that the town remained safe. This desire was to last but a short time and was described in Brigadier General John Buford's relayed message to Major General Alfred Pleasonton, Cavalry Corps Commander:

> *"I entered this place today at 11 am. Found everyone in a terrible state of excitement on account of the enemy's advance upon this place. He had approached to within a one-half mile of the town when the head of my column entered. My men and horses are fagged out. I have not been able to get any grain yet. It is all in the country, and the people talk instead of working. Facilities for shoeing are nothing. Early's people seized every shoe and nail they could find."*[82]

This message confirmed that Buford, his men and their horses endured the deprivations and hardships of war. The campaign up to this point had been grueling. Each army since early June covered nearly 130 miles. The men and their animals were exhausted. The weather before this had been a mixture of rain and sunshine, so while initially the roads were in reasonable condition, the mire and mud soon took its toll on Buford's troopers and their mounts. Vigilant care of these animals was necessary to keep the grueling pace. Wet, muddy conditions are known to pull the horseshoes from these animals. By this time, many of these animals needed shoeing. The constant march through rain and muddy roadways further decreased the animals' constitution.

---

81   "The People of Gettysburg. An Address made at the Regimental Reunion by W.C. Hazelton." *Gettysburg Star and Sentinel*, September 1, 1891. Adams County Historical Society.

82   *OR*. Series 1. Volume 27. Part 1. 923.

Buford relayed more information. To Major General John F. Reynolds, who commanded not only the First Corps but also the "left-wing" of the Army of the Potomac that consisted of his Corps as well as that of the Eleventh and Third Corps, he wrote:

General Reynolds
Major-General, Commanding.
Gettysburg, June 30, 1863—10.30 p. m.

The Reserve Brigade, under General Merritt, is at Mechanicstown with my trains. General Pleasonton wrote he would inform me when he relieved it. Today I received instructions saying it would picket toward Hagerstown and south. I am satisfied that A. P. Hill's Corps is massed just back of Cashtown, about 9 miles from this place. Pender's division of this (Hill's) Corps came up to-day— of which I advised you, saying, "The enemy in my front is increased." The enemy's pickets (infantry and artillery) are within 4 miles of this place, on the Cashtown road. My parties have returned that went north, northwest, and northeast, after crossing the road from Cashtown to Oxford in several places. They heard nothing of any force having passed over it lately. The road, however, is terribly infested with prowling cavalry parties. Near Heidlersburg today, one of my parties captured a courier of Lee's. Nothing was found on him. He says Ewell's Corps is crossing the mountains from Carlisle, Rodes' division being at Petersburg in advance. Long-street, from all I can learn, is still behind Hill. I have many rumors and reports of the enemy advancing upon me from toward York. I have to pay attention to some of them, which causes me to overwork my horses and men. I can get no forage nor rations; am out of both. The people give and sell the men something to eat, but I can't stand that way of subsisting; it causes dreadful straggling. Should I have to fall back, advise me by what route.
    Respectfully,
    JNO. BUFORD.

To Major General Alfred Pleasonton, the Cavalry Corps Commander, he sent a dispatch that contained similar information a few minutes later:

General Pleasonton
Gettysburg, June 30—10.40 p. m.

I have the honor to state the following facts: A. P. Hill's Corps, composed of Anderson, Heth, and Pender, is massed back of Cashtown, 9 miles from this place. His pickets, composed of infantry and artillery, are in sight of mine. There is a road from Cashtown running through Mummasburg and Hunterstown on to York pike at Oxford, which is terribly infested with rov-

ing detachments of cavalry. Rumor says Ewell is coming over the moun-
tains from Carlisle. One of his escorts was captured to-day near Heidlers-
burg. He says Rodes, commanding a division of Ewell's, has already
crossed the mountains from Carlisle. When will the reserve be relieved,
and where are my wagons? I have no need of them, as I can find no for-
age. I have kept General Reynolds informed of all that has transpired.
  I am, very respectfully, your obedient servant,
  JNO. BUFORD, Brigadier-General of Volunteers.[83]

Only a brief respite occurred after they arrived in Gettysburg. The evening of June 30, Buford placed mounted videttes (mounted patrols or sentries who are primarily tasked to give an early warning of the advance of enemy troops) west and north of Gettysburg. These troopers patrolled the roads that Confederates were likely to use the next day. This required one or two mounted cavalrymen spaced about every one-hundred to two-hundred yards in an arc from the Fairfield Road to the York Pike. Behind this front line around 400-500 yards, a reserve of additional mounted men provided periodic relief and rest. Approximately 1,000 yards behind the reserve sat the Grand guard. Buford took great care placing his men on the evening of June 30. He specifically utilized the horses' versatility and the skill of their riders to communicate any encroachment by their foe. The constant motion along the front vidette line, as well as the back-and-forth communication, continued to fatigue both man and beast. The horses, too, were equally tired and in need of rest. The weight of the trooper and his saddle, the trooper's equipment, and the constant mounting and dismounting caused chaffing and sores to develop on the horses' backs.[84]

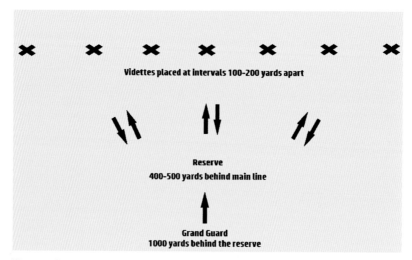

Videttes placed at intervals 100-200 yards apart

Reserve
400-500 yards behind main line

Grand Guard
1000 yards behind the reserve

Illustration of vidette placement, according to the McClellan Manual. Illustration by the author.

---

83 *OR.* Series 1. Volume 27. Part 1. 923-924.

84 The amount of equipment that each trooper carried, in many cases, approached one hundred pounds. This included the saddle, bridle, blankets, weaponry, and other necessary equipment. All of this equipment, including the weight of the trooper, neared two hundred forty pounds.

That evening, Colonel Thomas Devin, one of Buford's brigade commanders balked at an early arrival by Confederate forces. Buford offered a stern warning of the grim future events:

> *"On the night of the 30th, General Buford spent some hours with Colonel Devin of the Sixth New York (who was in command of the Second Brigade). While commenting on the information brought in by Devin 's scouts, Buford remarked that the battle would be fought at that point, and he was afraid it would be commenced in the morning before the infantry would get up. Devin, who did not believe in so early an advance of the enemy, said that he would take care of all that would attack his front during the ensuing twenty-four hours. Buford answered, 'No, you won't. They will attack you in the morning, and they will come 'booming,' skirmishers three deep. You will have to fight like the devil to hold your own until supports arrive. The enemy must know the importance of this position and will strain every nerve to secure it, and if we are able to hold it, we shall do well.' "*[85]

A significant concern that troubled Buford was the timely arrival of infantry support. If the high command of the Army of the Potomac ordered the defense of this town and its road network, Buford, along with his brigades, required reinforcements. Without them, failure was a foregone conclusion. Approximately 4:00 am on July 1, Major General John F. Reynolds, commander of the left wing of the Army of the Potomac, ordered into motion the movement of Union infantry from the First Corps toward Gettysburg with the Eleventh and Third Corps in close support.[86]

Brigadier General Johnston Pettigrew, the commander of the raiding party on June 30, reported the presence of Union troopers in Gettysburg to his immediate commander Major General Henry Heth. Lt. General A.P. Hill, commander of the Army of Northern Virginia's Third Corps, also learned of this reconnaissance. Neither commander took Pettigrew's information to heart. Instead, they believed only a small militia or perhaps a detachment of cavalry lay in their path. Lee's Army, in desperate need of supplies (especially want of shoes) ensured the Confederates return, thereby testing the issued order not to start a significant engagement until the Confederates were concentrated. The tale of "shoes" and in ample supply has been cited as the cause of this battle. Even though Rebel forces picked the town clean of any useful items on June 26, the rumor of the presence of shoes was the stated catalyst for their return on July 1. Perhaps there were shoes at Gettysburg; indeed, there were! Roughly 2,750 pairs of cavalry boots and thousands of horseshoes, all being utilized by Buford's troopers and horses. What better way to force your enemy to reveal his hand than to return the next day, a reconnaissance in force.

85 *Hillman A. Hall, H, W.B. Besley, Gilbert G. Wood, History of the Sixth New York Cavalry (Second Ira Harris Guard) Second Brigade - First Division - Cavalry Corps, Army of the Potomac, 1861-1865 (Worcester, Mass: The Blanchard Press, 1908)136.*

86 *Ibid., 134.*

That evening, Lt. Marcellus E. Jones of the 8th Illinois Cavalry and the troopers of his command advanced westward along the Chambersburg Pike to a ridge a short distance from the town known as Herr's Ridge, the location where Herr's Tavern sat. Here, Lt. Jones made his headquarters. He then advanced about thirty-five men under his command. He posted these men one-mile further west. He then moved forward about one hundred rods and stationed his main picket line (videttes) on the crest of a ridge (Knoxlyn's Ridge). This line extended both to left and the right of the Chambersburg Pike.[87] Attempting to gain a few hours sleep, Jones and his men dismounted and used their saddles as pillows.[88] July 1 had arrived. Just past dawn, Confederate infantry began their march eastward toward Gettysburg. Soon a fired carbine rang out and broke the quiet dawn. The devil would now have his due, as Buford predicted.

Major General George Gordon Meade (above), Major General John Fulton Reynolds, and Brigadier General John Buford. LOC.

---

87 *1 rod is the equivalent of 5½ yards.*

88 *Marcellus E. Jones, The Marcellus E. Jones Journal (Chicago: Peregrine, Stime, Newman, Ritzman and Bruckner Ltd.1897) ALBG Library Files.*

Colonels William Gamble
(above) and Thomas Devin.
LOC.

General Robert Edward Lee and Major General Henry Heth. LOC.

CHAPTER 5

"Then another horse came out, a fiery red one. Its rider was given power to take peace from the earth and to make people kill each other. To him was given a large sword."

BOOK OF REVELATION 6:4

JULY 1, 1863: THE FIRST DAY OF BATTLE

"OPENING THE BALL"

The roar of artillery and musketry did not start the Battle of Gettysburg; rather, it was a solitary shot. Officer Lt. Marcellus E. Jones is often cited as firing the first shot, but he left the picket line—not to carry out orders or deliver vital information, but rather to procure something to eat. He purchased a loaf of bread and butter, and while in the midst of a brief respite, he saw Private George Heim gallop toward him at full speed. Heim delivered a message that Sergeant Levi Shaffer wished to see Jones at once. Jones mounted his horse and galloped toward Shaffer atop Knoxlyn's Ridge and near the home of Ephraim Whisler. Jones spied a dust cloud moving gradually toward his position. This information was then relayed to Major Beveridge, Jones' regimental commander. "Boots and Saddles" bugle call was sounded, alerting the rest of the command to prepare. Horses that were not ready were immediately bridled and saddled. Jones then asked for Shaffer's Sharps carbine, took aim at a Confederate officer who was mounted on a light gray horse, and fired. [89]Jones is credited with "opening the ball," or firing the first shot that started this bloody battle around 7:30 am on July 1, 1863. The Rebel officer who was fired upon by Jones was not hit by the shot. Confederates under the commands of Brigadier Generals James Archer and Joe Davis deployed their skirmishers and advanced, attempting to reveal the identity and number of their assailants.

---

89   Marcellus E. Jones, *The Marcellus E. Jones Journal* (Chicago: Peregrine, Stime, Newman, Ritzman and Bruckner Ltd.1897) ALBG Library Files.

Before the Civil War, mounted soldiers were known as "Dragoons." These soldiers were trained to fight not only from horseback but also on the ground. They utilized sabers, pistols, lancets, and rifles with a shorter barrel, which were conducive to mounted operations. This elite group eventually was designated as cavalry, and their operations and purpose evolved over time to include reconnaissance missions that utilized the horse's speed and versatility to deliver intelligence to army commanders. The cavalry also served as combat troops and like their predecessors fought mounted and dismounted. They also provided 'screening' by keeping their numbers between themselves and the enemy. Today's notion of 'civil war cavalry' is still synonymous with the 'charge'—the firing of weapons, drawing sabers, and even using the horse as a battering ram striking other horses and unfortunate persons caught in their path.

Disadvantaged numerically, Buford and the approximately 2,700 troopers and 6 cannon of 2nd U.S. Artillery Battery A, under the command of Lt. John Calef, faced nearly 7,400 men of Confederate Major General Henry Heth's division of infantry and artillery. Buford now dismounted his troopers, who were armed with breech-loading Sharps carbines that provided a superior rate of fire (five to six shots per minute as compared to the two to three rounds with a muzzle-loading musket).[90]

Buford utilized the terrain, enhanced fire power, and the horses' speed to maneuver his troopers. This was Buford's intent from the beginning—to delay the Confederate advance and purchase time for the arrival of infantry support. The presence of the horse further diminished the number of men available for combat. One out of every four troopers now held and tended the mounts of the three cavalrymen on the firing line and reduced his overall strength by 25%. Horses even when well trained, remain "flight animals," and if left unattended, the soldier's sole means of retreat or falling back may indeed be absent when needed the most. Those troopers that held the horses of their comrades required sound horse handling skills to alleviate their mounts fears and natural instincts to flee.

With the early warning of approaching Confederates given, the videttes accomplished their mission and fell back from Knoxlyn's Ridge to Herr's Ridge. Along Herr's Ridge sat a more substantial portion of 8th Illinois, who were now joined by the returning videttes. They delayed the Confederates as long as possible and fell back where the majority of Colonel William Gamble's and a small portion of Colonel Thomas Devin's brigades (part of the 6th NY and 17th PA Cavalry units) sat deployed along McPherson's Ridge north and south of the Chambersburg/Cashtown Pike. The remainder of Devin's brigade covered the northern approaches of Gettysburg.

Buford intermittently utilized the cupola of the Lutheran Theological Seminary as a point in which to observe the conflict unfold. He turned his attention from the action west and north of the Seminary to the south and hoped for the timely arrival of Major General John F. Reynolds of the First Corps, and with him, the promised Union infantry.

---

90 A Sharps carbine loads its rounds from the rear of the barrel or breech. Carbine barrels were shorter in length and more conducive for cavalry operations.

BUFORD'S CAVALRY OPPOSING THE
CONFEDERATE ADVANCE UPON GETTYSBURG.

Buford's men fighting dismounted on July 1ˢᵗ, 1863. Note the trooper tending to horses of his comrades. Battles and Leaders of the Civil War (contributions by US & CSA officers, based upon "the Century War Series") JOHNSON and BUEL.

The Lutheran Theological Seminary atop Seminary Ridge. Brigadier General John Buford intermittently utilized the building's cupola to observe his Federal cavalry engage Confederates on the morning of July 1, 1863. Photograph by the author.

Around 9:30-10:00 am, Buford received welcomed news. John Reynolds and the infantry were quickly approaching the town of Gettysburg along the Emmitsburg Road. The constant training and drills that the once "green" troopers complained about so fiercely had paid off, as the Union cavalry delayed the Confederates and held them in check. Captain Stephen Weld of Reynold's staff related the following scene:

> *"General Reynolds came in and woke us up this morning, as he has frequently had to do, but we little thought that it would be the last time that he would do so, or that he had passed his last night on this earth. We moved off at 8 a.m., the weather still being muggy and disagreeable, and making the roads very bad in some places. When we reached the outskirts of Gettysburg, a man told us that the rebels were driving in our cavalry pickets, and immediately General Reynolds went into the town on a fast gallop, through it, and a mile out on the other side, where he found General Buford and the cavalry engaging the enemy, who were advancing in strong force. He immediately sent me to General Meade, 13 or 14 miles off, to say that the enemy were coming on in strong force, and that he was afraid they would get the heights on the other side of the town before he could; that he would fight them all through the town, however, and keep them back as long as possible. I delivered the message to General Meade at 11:20, having been an hour and twenty minutes on my way."[91]*

Weld was to ride with the greatest speed, even if it meant killing his horse. And if he did, he was to take his orderly's animal.[92] It seemed cruel to ride an animal until it collapsed, yet other officers reluctantly adopted the same philosophy. Charles Francis Adams of the 1st Massachusetts Cavalry wrote with empathy as well as determination:

> *"I do my best for my horses and am sorry for them; but all war is cruel and it is my business to bring every man I can into the presence of the enemy, and so make war short. So I have but one rule, a horse must go until he can't be spurred any further, and then the rider must get another horse as soon as he can seize on one."[93]*

How far and how fast can an animal travel when given an order such as the one Weld was given? It depends on several factors: The weight of the rider, the distance the horse must travel, the overall health and stamina of the horse, and the breed of horse. Thoroughbreds are known for their hardy constitutions, but even they would be hard pressed to gallop at a speed of twenty-five or thirty miles per hour for more than

91   Stephen, M. Weld, *War Diaries and Letters of Stephen Minot Weld: 1861-1865* (Cambridge: The Riverside Press, 1912) 229.

92   Ibid., 232.

93   Worthington C. Ford, *A Cycle of Adams Letters 1861-1865* (New York, NY: Kraus Reprint Company, 1969) vol. 1, p. 4. US Army Education and Heritage Center, Carlisle PA.

two miles without becoming fatigued. Some consideration and 'horse' sense were needed to plan a trip of this distance. A horse simply cannot race indefinitely at maximum speeds over long distances without collapsing. Weld had the ability to alternate between a trot (seven to ten miles per hour) and a canter (ten to seventeen miles per hour), which is more beneficial to both horse and rider. If Weld did alternate between a trot and a canter—perhaps even including some brief gallops—his mount may have indeed completed its mission and survived.

THE DEATH OF REYNOLDS

Buford mounted his horse named Grey Eagle and met Reynolds, who was mounted on a black stallion named Fancy, and for a few moments, they discussed the unfolding events. Once the infantry had taken the place of the cavalry, Buford pulled his tired horseman to the flanks. Colonel Devin guarded the approaches to the north while Colonel Gamble's troopers were posted to the left near the Fairfield road. Reynolds led the troops of Lysander Cutler's Brigade of infantry and James Hall's 2nd Maine Battery of artillery to the northern side of the Chambersburg Pike to confront the Confederate infantry of Brigadier General Joe Davis' Brigade. Once these dispositions were complete, he then turned his attention to the area of Herbst's Woods. He placed the Iron Brigade, under the command of Brigadier General Solomon Meredith, into position to stem the advance of Brigadier General James Archer's brigade of Confederate infantry. It was here that Reynold's met his fate. Mounted at the time of his death, he exhorted the Iron Brigade with his last words, "Forward men for God's sake forward" and "Drive those fellows out of that wood!" It is documented that:

> *"Reynold's turned to look for his supporting columns and to hasten them on, and as he reached the point of woods, he was struck by a ball fired, and was fatally wounded; his horse carried him a few rods towards the open, and he fell on the ground dead."*[94]

Point of woods where Reynolds fell. Matthew Brady. LOC.

94   Joseph G. Rosengarten, *William Reynolds Rear Admiral, John Fulton Reynolds, Major General USV, Colonel 5th US Infantry, A Memoir,* (Philadelphia, PA: J.B. Lippencott and Co. Philadelphia: 1880) 19.

The tree where Reynolds fell. LOC.

Modern-day monument located on Reynolds Ave. Note the difference in the appearance of the "woods." Photograph by the author.

The death of Reynolds. Alfred Waud. LOC.

Equestrian Statue of Major General John F. Reynolds located along modern-day Route 30.
Photograph by the author.

Equestrian statues located on the battlefield are masterful works of art. They are also the source of one of the biggest Gettysburg myths. According to the legend, if all four hooves are firmly placed on the ground, the rider survived the battle unharmed. One raised hoof indicated the rider was wounded, and two raised hooves indicated the rider was killed. This is an inaccurate way to interpret the meaning of the horse's position when considering the sculpture.

Henry Kirke Bush-Brown, a skilled and noted sculptor and lover of horses, created three equestrian statues: Generals Meade, Reynolds, and Sedgwick. In 1915, with the unsubstantiated explanation gaining momentum, William C. Storrick, then the Superintendent of Guides, interviewed Brown about the stance of the horse in the sculptures, whereby Brown discounted this theory. The position of the horse's hooves, in Reynolds' case, did not to correspond his fate.[95] On July 1, 1863, Reynolds and his mount were in constant motion. He rode from one melee to the next and oversaw the placement of the troops to the north of the Chambersburg Pike when his attention shifted to the woods that bear his name today. Reynolds saw the advancement of the Confederate forces under Brigadier General James Archer and quickly spurred Fancy into motion.

---

95   W.C. Storrick to Frederick Tilbert, National Park Historian, March 28, 1939. Gettysburg National Military Park Library Files. See also Gettysburg Compiler, February 8th, 1898.

Brigadier Solomon Meredith, who commanded the Iron Brigade, was also wounded like many men that day. Meredith's nickname was "Long Sol" because he stood six foot and seven inches tall. Meredith was mounted at the time of his wounding. An individual of that height while mounted made an impressive target, but more impressive was his mount, a large roan named Tom. Meredith was struck upon the head by a piece of a shell that fractured his skull. This was but the first of two insults. His mount was also hit and wounded. As the animal toppled, it fell on top of Meredith, fracturing the General's ribs and injuring his right leg.[96] Meredith's son, Lt. Samuel Meredith, was also present at Gettysburg as an officer with the 19th Indiana Infantry. He was mounted on "Barney," a saddlebred. Barney had the distinct honor of being the sole horse of the Iron Brigade to escape uninjured.[97]

With the death of Reynolds, Major General Oliver Otis Howard assumed command of the Federal Army. Howard had commanded the Eleventh Corps, and now the responsibility to stem the Confederate advance was placed upon his shoulders. The Eleventh Corps now came under the command of Major General Carl Schurz. As the Eleventh Corps arrived at approximately 11:30 am, it pushed northward through Gettysburg toward Oak Hill, which was a large prominent terrain feature that lay north and slightly west of the town.

About this same time, Major General Robert Rodes Confederate division also approached Gettysburg from the north. As the Eleventh Corps moved through Gettysburg, two divisions totaling approximately 5,500 men moved northward to confront Confederates whose troops now threatened to seize Oak Hill. It was within reach, each side now raced to occupy this high ground. The lead elements of Major General Robert Rode's division of infantry arrived before the Federal troops and seized control of Oak Hill.

The last of the Eleventh Corps three divisions under the command of Brigadier General Adolph von Steinwehr received orders from Howard to take possession and secure Cemetery Hill. This prominent hill provided clear views of the surrounding terrain, and once fortified, served as a rallying point if Federal forces were compelled to retreat. It proved to be a sound decision. The First Corps now commanded by Major General Abner Doubleday was situated to the west along McPherson's Ridge (south of the Chambersburg Pike), as well as north of the Pike along the tree line of Shead's Woods and Oak Ridge. With the occupation of Oak Hill by Confederate forces, the Union army now attempted to connect the left of Eleventh Corps to the right of the First Corps on Oak Ridge. Unfortunately, this placed the Union soldiers north of the town in a large exposed flat parcel of land with little cover or concealment.

Near noon on July 1, the infantry engagements waned, except for some artillery fire. This mid-day lull lasted approximately two hours. The Union army had held its own, for the moment. The First and the Eleventh Corps of Union infantry and artillery, plus the troopers of Buford's command, were all that were available until the evening hours. To the west, additional Confederates of Major General Henry Heth's division and

---

96   Frederick Whitford, Andrew Martin, Phyllis Mattheis, *The Queen of American Agriculture a Biography of Virginia Claypool Meredith,* (West Lafayette, Indiana: Purdue University Press, 2008) 43.

97   Ibid., 43.

that of Major General Dorsey Pender now arrived and were poised to attack. At approximately 2:00 pm, the attacks renewed not only west of Gettysburg, but also to the north. To the northeast, Confederate General Jubal Early's division approached Gettysburg about 2:30 pm, and their subsequent attack at approximately 3:30 pm upon the right flank of the Eleventh Corps was keenly felt.

BARLOW'S KNOLL

To the North of the town, Brigadier General Francis Barlow moved his division to a modestly sized knoll, which today bears his name.[98] Barlow had observed this area as a potential threat to his command. If Confederates seized control, it could be utilized as an artillery platform to quickly shell the Eleventh Corps, most of whom were positioned with little or no cover and concealment. Among the Union soldiers ordered to hold this area was nineteen-year-old Lt. Bayard Wilkeson, commanding Battery "G" 4th U.S. Artillery.

Battery "G" 4th U.S. Artillery. Lt. Bayard Wilkeson Commanding. Alfred Waud. LOC.

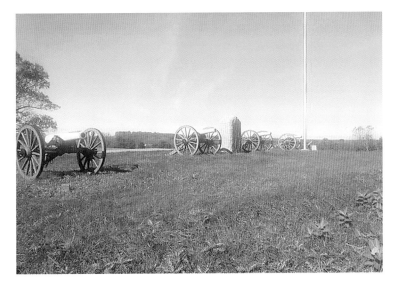

Battery "G" 4th US Artillery, Howard Ave.

Photograph by the author.

---

98   At the time of the battle, it was known as Blocher's Knoll.

"Wilkeson, his intelligence extraordinary, had a genius for command. He took exceptional care of his men, horses, and equipment, even to the mending of the nosebags and patching blankets.[99] It was the first of the Eleventh Corps artillery to gallop through Gettysburg on the 1st of July 1863. The guns were thrown into battery on the extreme front of the now historic field, and Wilkeson, mounted, after speaking a few words of warning with a loaded revolver in his hand to some of the drivers and some distrusted cannoneers, walked his horse to a position much to the front of his guns and ordered to open fire on Ewell's advancing Corps. He could see but one way to hold his men to their ground without flinching and make their work effectively, and that was to sit still on his horse in their front and direct the fire of the six pieces from his saddle."[100]

Wilkeson and his artillery supported by two Union infantry brigades bore the full force of Confederate Brigadier Generals George Dole's and John B. Gordon's Georgian brigades. Gordon, who was present at the second Battle of Winchester, obtained an ample reward from that engagement, a horse re-named "Milroy." This animal was a coal-black stallion, and it was the first time he rode this animal into battle. Confederate John Stiles gave a vivid description of Gordon mounted on Milroy:

"Gordon was the most glorious and inspiring thing I ever looked upon. He was riding a beautiful coal-black stallion, captured at Winchester, that belonged to one of the Federal Generals in Milroy's army- a majestic animal, whose neck was clothed with thunder. I never saw a horse's neck so arched, his eye so fierce, his nostril so dilated. He followed in a trot, close upon the heels of the battle line, his head right in among the slanting barrels and bayonets, the reins loose upon his neck, his rider standing in his stirrups, bareheaded, hat in hand, arms extended, and in a voice like a trumpet, exhorting his men. It was superb; absolutely thrilling. I recall the feeling that I would not give so much as a dime to ensure the independence of the Confederacy."[101]

While the above description equates to the 'Glory of War,' sometimes other snippets of the story are omitted. The fire breathing mount, which only lacked the wings of Pegasus, had never been ridden into battle by Gordon. Gordon's version of events paints a similar picture, though without the fanfare and with a different outcome: *"He behaved well at first under artillery fire, but later encountering a fierce fire of musketry, he turned tail and bolted to the rear a hundred yards or more."[102]* The fact that Milroy

99   A nosebag is simply a feedbag for horses.
100 Author Unknown. Handwritten description of Bayard Wilkeson. Association of Licensed Battlefield Guides Library Files, Gettysburg, PA.
101 Robert Stiles, *Four Years Under Marse Robert*, (NY and Washington: Neale Publishing Company, 1904) 211.
102 Ibid., 211.

was captured and was the mount of Major General Robert Milroy begs the question—had this animal ever been trained and utilized? And, more specifically, had he been de-sensitized to the chaos of battle? Apparently, "Milroy" did have a breaking point, which he and Gordon found.

The Eleventh Corps blocked Gordon's path into Gettysburg. In addition to the musketry of the Federal infantry, Wilkeson's battery was firmly planted. Gordon saw the gallant lieutenant mounted on his horse, projecting a source of leadership as he sat like a statue on his mount. In order to spare his own troops, and because of the shot and shell fired from Battery G, Gordon surmised to target the man and the animal. Lt. Colonel Hilary Jones' battalion of artillery posted along the Harrisburg Road opened fire upon the knoll. One round found its mark and nearly tore Wilkeson's leg from his body. The animal, too, went down. Wilkeson applied a tourniquet to his shattered leg then was carried to the Adam's County poor house. According to later (unsubstantiated) stories, he finished the job the shell had begun by amputating the remains of his leg with a pocketknife. He later died of his wounds.[103]

Gordon had predicted correctly; his Georgia brigade, supported by more infantry under the command of Brigadier General George Doles and Louisiana troops under the command of Brigadier General Harry Hays, wrested control of the knoll and began a push toward the town of Gettysburg in pursuit of the retreating Federal soldiers. In a letter to Wilkeson' sister, John Wilkeson, Bayard's father, described his son's demise briefly: *"Bayard was on his horse in command of his battery, giving special attention to his right section, a long shell struck the horse and passed through it hit him on his right leg below the knee, crushing it shockingly."*[104] Officers such as Wilkeson and Gordon, when mounted in the heat of battle, provided a source of inspiration, courage and leadership to their men.

Looking to the northeast, the open terrain and the Brigade Marker of Brigadier General John B. Gordon's Georgians located on Howard Ave.
Photograph by the author.

---

103 Author Unknown. Handwritten description of Bayard Wilkeson. Source Files: of the Library of the Association of Licensed Battlefield Guides, Gettysburg, PA.

104 John Wilkeson, A Letter to His Daughter. Buffalo. July 6th, Monday, 1863. ALBG Library Files.

The horse accepts the leadership of its rider (or lack of leadership) and each are readily distinguished by fellow soldiers. Enter the tale of Colonel Seraphim Meyer, the commanding officer of the 107th Ohio Volunteer Infantry, also located atop Barlow's Knoll. Meyer, based on eyewitness descriptions, was not the most skilled rider. He spoke German and broken English, which made his orders a challenge to understand due to his accent and high-pitched voice, especially in the heat of battle. Meyer had a habit, while mounted, to crouch low, placing his chest to the animal's neck as if to hug it. This appearance did not inspire confidence or courage but, rather, quite the opposite. In addition, Meyer issued haphazard orders that resulted in the incorrect placement of the soldiers under his command. When the Federal troops withdrew through the town and arrived upon Cemetery Hill, Meyer still mounted with his sword in its scabbard, did little to rally his men. Meyer's peculiarities and actions did not go unnoticed. Brigadier General Adelbert Ames, who was Meyer's brigade commander, later relieved him of duty and subsequently had the Colonel arrested and court-martialed. He was later acquitted and resigned.[105] The Eleventh Corps began to give way under the heavy Confederate attacks, around 4:00 pm, they carried out a hard-fought retreat toward and through the town of Gettysburg to the heights beyond it, Cemetery Hill.

The renewed attacks by Confederates, with fresh reinforcements and the collapse and withdrawal of the Eleventh Corps, set into motion a chain reaction that compelled the Union lines both north and south of the Chambersburg Pike to also retreat. Those Federal soldiers to the north of the pike, despite inflicting heavy casualties, fell back toward Cemetery Hill. The Union troops south of the Pike fell back to Seminary Ridge and made a final attempt to stem the Confederate advance. Even with a stubborn defense, the remainder of the Union forces withdrew and retreated toward Cemetery Hill. This left Seminary Ridge in Confederate hands. Despite overwhelming numbers, Federal troops had other challenges that prompted withdrawal—the availability of needed ammunition.

A CHANCE MEETING ON THE HILL

Typically, infantrymen carried sixty rounds of ammunition into action, which can be expended in a short amount of time. It was on July 1 that Union Sergeant Jerome A. Watrous found himself, his wagons, and his mule teams heading westward toward the action along Seminary Ridge with a delivery of vitally needed ammunition. Watrous and his wagons not only arrived, but they also distributed the ammunition and returned to Cemetery Hill. Upon, their return Watrous recalled his encounter with Major General Winfield Scott Hancock, who was dispatched to Gettysburg by General Meade to appraise the tactical situation. Hancock arrived on Cemetery Hill around 4:30 pm,

---

105 Brian Matthew Jordan, "The Unfortunate Colonel," *Civil War Monitor*, 6 No. 4. Winter 2016. 62. See also Richard A. Baumgartner, *Buckeye Blood, Ohio at Gettysburg* (Huntington, West Virginia: Blue Acorn Press, 2003) 47.

and after conferring with Howard and surveying the surrounding hills and ridges as a strong position, he selected the ground at Gettysburg to make their stand. While Hancock was busy directing and rallying the retreating remnants of the Federal First and Eleventh Corps, Watrous asked Hancock for orders. Hancock was known for his temper and initially replied:

"Great God, what have you got here? What have you got a wagon here for? You haven't been out into the action?"

"Yes, Sir, just came back with the rear guard," Watrous replied.

Hancock questioned him further. *"Did you lose all of your ammunition?"*

"No sir distributed nearly all of it," Watrous answered.

"Lose any of your wagons?"

"Well, I got back with some of them," said Watrous.

And Hancock, known for his temper and command of profane language, congratulated Watrous, *"You did well, Sergeant, just move your wagons down there and report to me in half an hour."*[106]

Mules were not used, under normal circumstances, in battle. The skittish nature of this animal, its stubbornness, and disposition to flee served as a source of bewilderment and perhaps amusement to Hancock. Watrous and his team took upon themselves the initiative to aid their comrades. The fact they made it to the front and back stymied perhaps even Watrous.

Hancock's Equestrian Statue, located atop the eastern portion of Cemetery Hill, was dedicated on the afternoon of June 5, 1896. Sculpted by Frank Edwin Elwell, it portrays Hancock mounted and gesturing with his hand, communicating to the retreating Union troops to stop, rally, and stand their ground, calming a scene of confusion and chaos. Through his leadership and that of many others, the Union army maintained its control over the high ground, namely Cemetery Hill and subsequently Culp's Hill. This monument, along with Reynolds, also served to perpetuate the "hoof myth," as Hancock sustained a wound on July 3—it happens to be a coincidence that the animal's front leg and hoof are raised.

Located adjacent to Hancock is the Equestrian Statue of Major General Oliver Otis Howard which was sculpted by Robert Aitken and dedicated November 12, 1932. Howard is credited with identifying the tactical importance of Cemetery Hill and wisely assigning troops to secure it as a fallback position.

---

106 J.A. Watrous, *Commandry of the State of Wisconsin, Military Order of the Loyal Legion of the United States. Volume 1*(Milwaukee: Burdick, Armitage and Allen, 1891) 299-300. Watrous was a Sergeant in the 6th Wisconsin Volunteer Infantry Regiment Company E.

Equestrian Statue of Major General Winfield Scott Hancock. Located on East Cemetery Hill along the Baltimore Pike. Photograph by the author.

The Equestrian Statue of Major General Oliver Otis Howard. Sculpted by Robert Ingersoll Aitken and dedicated in 1932. Located on East Cemetery Hill. Photograph by the author.

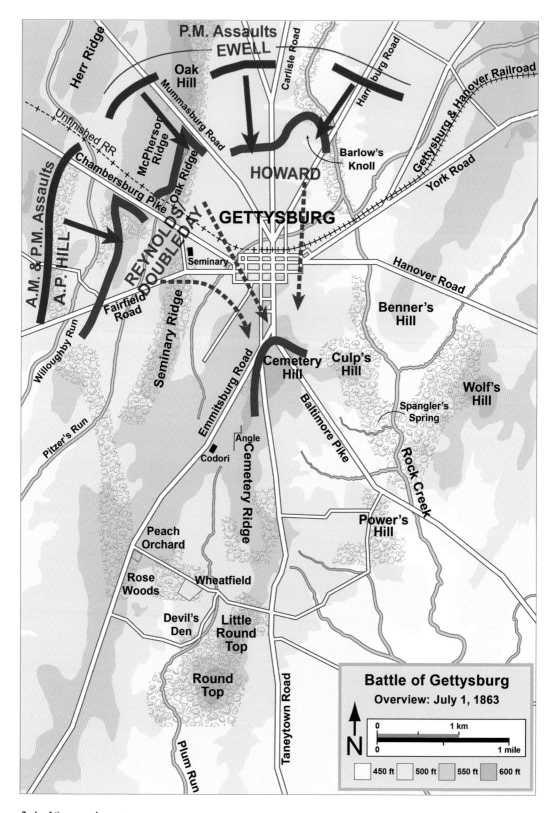

July 1st overview. Map by Hal Jespersen.

Lee's army had performed well, but the victory he sought was incomplete. Lee, who arrived to witness his victorious army gain another victory also witnessed the retreating Federal army massing on Cemetery Hill. Adjacent to this sat another formidable imposing elevation called Culp's Hill. To ensure the complete victory Lee desired, those heights must be taken. Despite the danger, Lee navigated Traveller through the streets of Gettysburg seeking to press his advantage. Liberty Hollinger, a sixteen-year-old girl at the time who lived in a home at the intersection of the Hanover Road and the York Pike, witnessed General Lee astride Traveller with other mounted staff officers in front of her family's house. To this young girl, the sight of the famous General and his mount left an impression in which she recalled:

> *"I very well remember his face and striking appearance on his splendid warhorse Traveller. They were in front of our house for some time, which General Lee was observing through his glasses the hills south of the town which General Howard had taken refuge. After careful examination I heard him say something like this 'Those hills all around are natural fortresses, wonderful, wonderful! It will be difficult to capture them or dislodge the troops holding them.'"[107]*

Lee issued orders to Lieutenant General Richard Ewell, commander of the Second Corps for the Army of Northern Virginia, to use the momentum of the victory and take Cemetery Hill and/or Culp's Hill. Lee issued the order using the words "if practicable" as well as "avoid bringing on a general engagement." Ewell utilized his judgment and discretion that day. Due to the many factors—worn troops wearied by marching and fighting, inadequate availability of an artillery platform, uncoordinated efforts through an unfamiliar town, the presence of Federals on Cemetery and Culp's Hill, and lack of cooperation/support from A.P. Hill's Corps— Ewell did not press the attacks any further.

By the early evening hours, the Union army now held the heights of Cemetery and Culp's Hill. Lee lamented even more the absence of his trusted but still missing Cavalry Commander J.E.B. Stuart and the intelligence he typically provided, namely the location and strength of the Yankee army. Lt. General James Longstreet, commander of the First Corps of the Army of Northern Virginia, arrived riding Hero that evening and joined Lee. Longstreet was Lee's second in command and the one to whom Lee referred to as my "Old Warhorse." Longstreet and Lee surveyed the area mounted, Lee atop Traveller and Longstreet on Hero. After the visual survey, Longstreet proposed pulling out of the town altogether and moving around the left of the Union army, and eventually interpose the Army of Northern Virginia between Washington D.C. and the Army of the Potomac.

The result Longstreet hoped for was the withdraw of the Federal army from Gettysburg and the eventual pursuit of the Rebel army. This afforded the Confederates, according to Longstreet's estimation, the ability to pick better ground on which to

107 Jacob A Clutz, Liberty Hollinger. *Some Personal Recollections of the Battle of Gettysburg.* Adams County Historical Society.

engage the Union army while simultaneously threatening the nation's capital. Long-street saw the strength of the Union position, but to his dismay, Lee was determined to continue the fight on the next day. The remaining elements of Lee's army began to arrive into the vicinity of Gettysburg throughout the night of July 1 and encamped near the town.

The Union army began to reach the area that evening, and eventually the Union position began to take the shape of a fishhook. Included amongst these units were the newly appointed commander of the Army of the Potomac, Major General George Gordon Meade. Meade rode from Taneytown and arrived on the field shortly after midnight. Sometime after his arrival and before dawn, he, along with Generals Oliver Howard, Brigadier General Henry Hunt, and engineer Captain William H. Paine, set out for a nighttime ride to reconnoiter the field. Their journey took them south along Cemetery Ridge toward Little Round Top and to the vicinity of Rock Creek and Culps Hill. The full moon on that journey certainly helped the party traverse the terrain, but the horses excellent night vision was also to their benefit. Considering horses are prey animals, their senses are more acute. Their view on a moonlit night would be on par with a human's during the day.[108] Baldy and his equine companions saw the rocks and the changes in the terrain well before General Meade and his staff, who kept their reins loosened to aid their animals' vision. Perhaps the party suffered some disorientation, relying on their mounts surefootedness to negotiate the obstacles. A map of the area was formulated based upon this reconnaissance, as well as the selection of General Meade's headquarters, the home of Lydia Leister which sat along the Taneytown Road.

The combined casualties on July 1 exceeded 15,000 men killed, wounded, missing, and captured. The loss in horseflesh killed, injured, and exposure also continued to climb.

---

108   Christine Barakat, "Your Horse's Night Vision." *Equus*. September 10th, 2003.

CHAPTER 6

*"I looked, and there before me was a black horse!
Its rider was holding a pair of scales in his hand."*

BOOK OF REVELATION 6:5

JULY 2, 1863: THE BLOODIEST DAY

LEE AND LONGSTREET

On the morning of July 2, Lee still had little information on which to base an attack. The now heavily fortified Cemetery Hill and the steep wooded and rocky Culp's Hill afforded his army poor prospects. Lee turned his attention toward the southern end of the field. Lee dispatched one of his engineers named Captain Samuel Johnston and Major John Clarke of Longstreet's staff, with a contingency of approximately six total men to reconnoiter this area of the field.

They left mounted at perhaps 4:00 am on July 2. Lee desired information to formulate a plan of battle that afforded his commanders the best opportunity for success. Johnston and his party were to scout the left of the Union army.[109] The terrain, at least initially, was not treacherous on horseback, however, once across the Emmitsburg Road, the ground became rockier and wooded with the terminus of Warfield Ridge and the steep slopes of Big and Little Round Top. Johnston and his party claim to have *"got up the slopes of round top that was occupied by General Hood, and later on a cavalry fight."* Johnston and his party found no Union forces. He returned to report his findings, cautiously passing and avoiding, according to him, only four Union cavalrymen. [110]

Johnston and his small entourage needed to carefully maneuver and control their mounts during this mission. The smaller number of animals made for a smaller chance

---

109 David, A Powell, "A Reconnaissance Gone Awry: Captain Samuel R. Johnston's Fateful Trip to Little Round Top." *Gettysburg Magazine*, 23. June 2000.

110 Ibid.

of detection, as the rustling of trees and bramble, the generation of dust, and the neighing and whinnying were kept to a minimum. Thus, a smaller group sufficed. Upon his return at approximately 7:30 am, Johnston submitted the gathered intelligence. He indicated to Lee that he indeed made it to the summit of "Round Top" without encountering enemy troops. The route which Johnston took is still debated, as is where he decided to end his mission and return. At that time, John Buford's cavalry was posted in the vicinity of the Peach Orchard and along the Emmitsburg Road. At the time, Union infantry was also located, at the very minimum, on the northern slopes of Little Round Top. How Johnston managed to ride so far without spying thousands of enemy troops remains a mystery. What is not a mystery is the decision Lee made based upon this report—to attack an area "void" of Union troops, the left of the Union army.

Lee met with Longstreet, two of Longstreet's divisional commanders Major Generals Hood and McLaws, as well as Lt. General A.P. Hill, commander of the Third Corps of the Army of Northern Virginia, where Lee issued orders for the attack. Lee then mounted Traveller and rode to the left of his line near the base of Culp's Hill to review the battle plans with Lt. General Richard Ewell. The overall strategy of the assault entailed Longstreet attacking "up" the Emmitsburg Road, utilizing it as a guide to strike Cemetery Ridge and Cemetery Hill. General Hill was ordered to send his infantry toward Cemetery Ridge in coordination with Longstreet and to prevent the Federal troops from sending reinforcements and exploit any breakthrough. Upon the commencement of this attack, General Ewell was to simultaneously "demonstrate" against Culp's Hill/Cemetery Hill. By shelling this area, it gave the appearance that an all-encompassing assault was to be launched, thus keeping Union forces pinned down. Ewell received an additional discretionary order to convert his demonstration into an all-out attack "if" he was able to seize Culp's Hill and Cemetery Hill. This plan of attack placed a three-pronged assault that encompassed the Union army and, if coordinated and properly executed, would give Lee the victory he sought.

Lee had hoped for the attacks to begin as soon as possible, but logistics, the arrival of reinforcements, and marching nearly 15,000 men and artillery pieces over unfamiliar territory without detection served to delay this plan. The artillery pieces numbered nearly seventy in total. With six horses to pull one cannon and its limber, along with an additional six for the caisson, the march included at least 840 animals. Longstreet, who wished that Lee maneuver his army to better ground rather than attack, was less than enthusiastic, and many placed his lack of zeal as a cause of the Confederacy's defeat at Gettysburg. One must not overlook the fact that Stuart's cavalry did not arrive until the mid-afternoon hours on that day, too late to reconnoiter not only the left of the Union line, but also its right. Longstreet began his march to the launch point around noon. Once they arrived, the intelligence initially provided had changed. Federal soldiers were now present in great force.

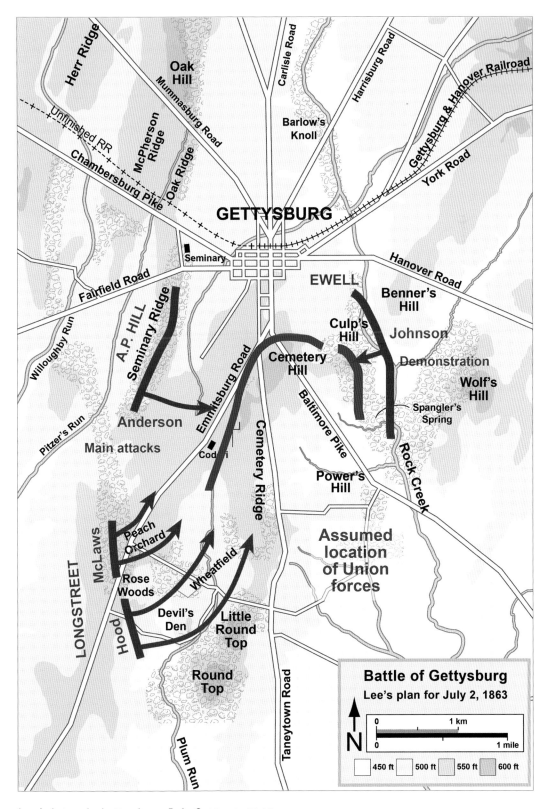

Lee's intended attack on July 2. Map by Hal Jespersen.

MEADE AND SICKLES

The early and mid-morning hours of July 2 came as a relief for George Meade. Each hour that passed without an enemy attack only cemented the strength of his line, which now encompassed Culp's Hill, Cemetery Hill, and Cemetery Ridge southward toward the northern slopes of Little Round Top. Union reinforcements continued to arrive and were positioned where they were most needed. Major General Daniel Edgar Sickles commanded the Union Third Corps. His near 10,600 men were ordered by Meade to be situated along Cemetery Ridge. Sickles was ordered to connect with the Union Second Corps (on his right) and extend his line southward (toward the left) and occupy, at the minimum, the northern slopes of Little Roundtop. In the early morning hours of July 2, the Union Twelfth Corps began its move from the base of Little Round Top toward Culp's Hill. The Third Corps was to assume the position the Twelfth Corps had vacated, creating a solid line connecting with the Second Corps on his right as well as anchoring Little Round Top.[111] The middle of Sickles' line, however, sat lower in respect to that of the flanks of his assigned position. He observed an elevated area to his front, a Peach Orchard, and a ridge under the Emmitsburg Road. The ridgeline that ran under the Emmitsburg road now blocked his line of sight and the view of Seminary Ridge. This left Sickles with an uneasy feeling. If the Confederates seized this "higher" ground, it "could" be, in turn, used as an artillery platform to shell his line. The occupation of this higher ground by his Corps generated (in Sickles mind) a better position for his infantry and artillery, with clear fields of fire and an unobstructed view of Seminary Ridge.

General Sickles sought to clarify his orders and his assigned position with Meade, only to be told to maintain the line he was appointed. These clarifications were carried via horseback by Meade's son and an aide, Captain George Meade Jr. Sickles requested the assistance of Brigadier General Gouverneur Warren, the Chief of Engineers, to inspect the potential merits of his proposal to move his troops forward. Instead of Warren, who was occupied with "other duties," Meade relented, and at Sickles' request sent Brigadier General Henry Hunt the Chief of Artillery. Hunt and Sickles inspected the proposed terrain. While Hunt found some advantages the prospective site, he pointed out the difficulty of maintaining such a long line without

Major General Daniel Edgar Sickles. Third Corps Commander. Matthew Brady, LOC.

---

111 The topic of Dan Sickles' assigned position on July 2nd is the catalyst of many debates. The official report has Brigadier General David Birney placing his division of Sickles' Corps along Cemetery Ridge and anchoring the end of his line on Sugar Loaf Mountain, another name for Little Round Top.

reinforcements. Hunt cautioned Sickles that he was not to move on Hunt's authority, but instead, he was to wait for the order to come from Meade.

Sickles was also troubled by the uneasy feeling that the Confederates may try to move around his left flank. Under the suggestion from Hunt, Sickles dispatched a unit of about 300 men that consisted of 100 men of the First United States Sharpshooters and 200 men of the 3rd Maine Infantry Regiment. Their mission was to reconnoiter the area along Seminary Ridge in the vicinity of Pitzer's Woods. They crossed the Emmitsburg Road and entered the woods. Soon after, they encountered the Rebel skirmish line of Cadmus Wilcox's Alabama brigade, and that resulted in a brief engagement.

The Union soldiers withdrew and reported their findings to General Sickles, which served as a catalyst for his next decision. At approximately 2:00 pm, Sickles, without orders, moved his entire Corps and posted it along the Emmitsburg Road, occupying the Peach Orchard. It was here that his line bent back at an acute angle and passed the southern edge of a wheatfield, finally coming to rest in the giant boulders of Devil's Den. The point of his line that angled toward the Wheatfield from the Peach Orchard created a "salient," or an area that can be assailed from multiple directions. Today, it is called Sickles' Salient. Henry Hunt's observation proved correct. Sickles' newly formed line created a three-quarter of a mile gap between Cemetery Ridge and his new position. It was undermanned, thin, and in need of reinforcements.

Approximately 3:00 pm, General Meade learned of this unauthorized movement as Sickles rode to a council of war located at the Leister house. He was met by an irritated Meade and told not to dismount. Sickles was to return to his command, and Meade soon followed to see for himself what his subordinate had done. Baldy, Meade's mount, was not readily available. Meade accepted the offer of Major General Alfred Pleasonton, the Cavalry Corps commander, the use of his mount, who was named "Slicky." Meade quickly rode to Sickles' position and curtly explained to his subordinate that he was too far forward. Sickles offered to withdraw his men, but it was too late, and a short time after 3:00 pm, the Confederates emerged from the tree line along Seminary Ridge and prepared to fire their artillery. As Meade promised infantry support and allowed Sickles to draw upon the artillery reserve for assistance, the Confederate artillery opened fire, and a shell that passed overhead ended the meeting. Major Henry Tremain, a staff officer and aide for General Sickles, recounted the scene.

> General Sickles saluted with a polite observation, and General Meade said:
> "General Sickles, I am afraid you are too far out." General Sickles responded: I will withdraw if you wish, sir. General Meade replied: I think it is too late. The enemy will not allow you. If you need more artillery call on the reserve artillery. (Bang! a single gun sounded.) The Fifth Corps — and a division of Hancock's —will support you. His last sentence was caught with difficulty. It was interrupted. It came out in jerks, in sections; between the acts, to speak literally. The conference was not concluded. The conversation could not be continued. Neither the noise nor any destruction had arrested it. Attracted by the group, it was a shot at them

*from the battery I have mentioned. The great ball went high and harm-
lessly struck the ground beyond. But the whizzing missile had frightened
the charger of General Meade into an uncontrollable frenzy. He reared,
he plunged. He could not be quieted; nothing was possible to be done
with such a beast except to let him run; and run he would and run he
did. The staff straggled after him; and so General Meade, against his own
will, as I then believed and afterwards ascertained to be the fact, was apparently ingloriously and involuntarily carried temporarily from the front
at the formal opening of the furious engagement of July 2, 1863. There
can be no question that for a time that frenzied horse was running away.
But he bore his rider safely, and a sad misfortune under all the circumstances was happily averted."*[112]

Cavalry Corps Commander Major General Alfred Pleasonton. It is unknown if this is Slicky,
his horse. LOC.

---

112 Henry Edwin Tremain. *Two days of war, a Gettysburg narrative, and other excursions,* (New York: Bonnell, Silver and Bowers, 1905.) 63.

To an inexperienced rider, it may seem as if one horse is no different than the next, but nothing could be further from the truth. Every animal has its own personality and responds differently to commands and startling threats. Experienced riders recognize the potential difficulties and danger in riding and controlling a horse to which you are not accustomed. During an armed conflict, there is little time to ask if the horse has any vices, such as how it may startle or respond to certain cues and equipment. In this case, Meade was on a "borrowed" mount. A shell bursting nearby could startle any animal, but as he found out, abrupt actions and movements to regain control of the horse only caused matters to worsen. Tremain elaborated on the potential cause of Meade's misfortune:

> *"In relating this incident to General Pleasonton, the Cavalry Corps commander then tarrying at the army headquarters, he told me that there was a simple explanation of the horse feature of this affair. General Meade had sent for his own horse and was impatient at the delay in bringing it to him. He had ordered it instantly. Pleasonton, who was standing near, said: 'Take my horse, general. He is right here." With minds preoccupied in a battle neither general stopped to" talk horse." General Pleasonton never thought to caution General Meade not to use his curb rein. The men of the old regular army habitually used the curb. This was General Meade's habit. This animal was bridled with a peculiar curb, which, as Pleasonton narrates, he seldom, if ever, used on this horse, reining him only by the snaffle. So, it was probable that at his initial fright from the passing missile this horse suddenly felt an involuntary twitch of the curb (he was not accustomed to the feel of a curb bit) as the rider (Meade) may have carelessly seized his rein and so the spirited animal made off with him. There was no particular harm done by or to anybody in the whole affair, as far as I ever learned."*[113]

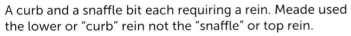

A curb and a snaffle bit each requiring a rein. Meade used the lower or "curb" rein not the "snaffle" or top rein.
Photograph by the author. GNMP.

113 Ibid., 64-65.

Modern day "snaffle" bit. Pictured "Polo." Photograph by and courtesy of Terry Latschar.

A curb bit with one set of reins. Virginia State Memorial. Photograph by the author. GNMP.

UP THE EMMITSBURG ROAD

Upon emerging from Seminary Ridge, Longstreet quickly became aware of how the situation had changed. The presumed unoccupied ground now had 10,600 men of General Sickles' Third Corps obstructing their path. The attacks were not called off. Longstreet's infantry and artillery had their work cut out for them and now had to sweep the Union infantry and artillery from their positions to strike their intended target, Cemetery Ridge. Major General John Bell Hood, one of Longstreet's divisional commanders, made several appeals to Longstreet to allow a turning (flanking) movement to the right of the Confederate line. His objections were centered on not only the

Union infantry and artillery with which he had to contend, but also the daunting terrain upon which his men needed to cross. Hood recounted *"immense boulders of stone, so massed together as to form narrow openings, which would break our ranks and cause the men to scatter whilst climbing up the rocky precipice."*[114] Marching over difficult ground was hazardous with the effects of the shot, shell, and musketry, but on horseback, the adversity and frustration multiplied. Hood's appeals were denied, with the final words coming from Longstreet himself stating *"attack up the Emmitsburg Road"* and *"we must obey the orders of General Lee."*

Major General John Bell Hood, CSA. LOC.

---

114 John B. Hood, *Advance and Retreat. Personal Experiences in the United States and Confederate States Armies.* Edited by Richard N. Current, (Bloomington: Indiana University Press, 1959) 58-59.

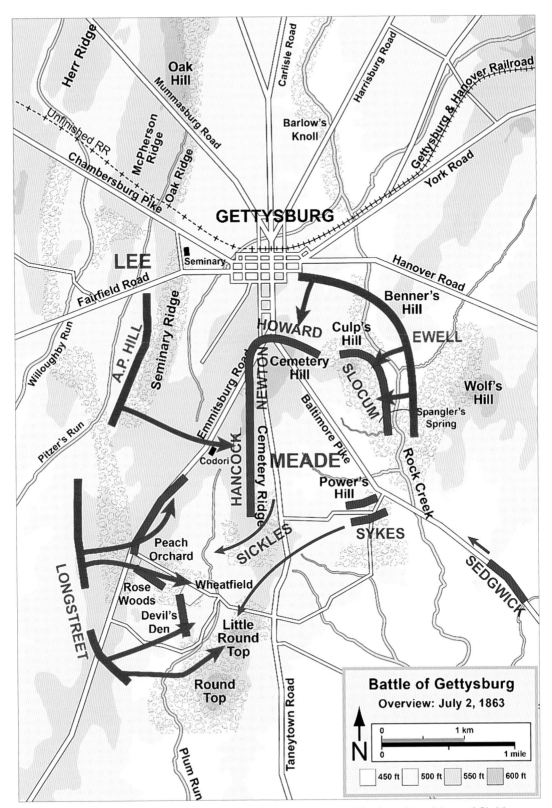

The attacks of July 2nd as they occurred. The forward and isolated position of Sickles Third Corps along the Emmitsburg Road, Peach Orchard, Wheatfield and Devil's Den.
Map by Hal Jespersen.

The attacks started with Hood's division and progressed sequentially from the Confederate right to the left (en-echelon). Each brigade's successive attack gave way to the next. They struck the Union line and did not allow the Federal troops the opportunity to shuffle their men or call upon neighboring regiments for reinforcements. Hood was mounted at the time the attacks began:

"I saw General Hood on horseback about 300-400 yards obliquely to my left, just out of direct range of the battery fire, in the edge of the timber. He took off his hat. Held it above him in his right hand, rose to his full height in his stirrups, and shouted in a stentorian voice, 'Forward! Steady! Forward!'[115]

Hood then relayed what happened soon after: *"I then rode forward with my line under heavy fire. In about 20 minutes, after reaching the peach orchard, I was severely wounded in the arm and borne from the field."*[116]

As Hood surged forward, so did the brigade of Brigadier General Evander Law, followed shortly by Brigadier General Jerome Robertson's brigade that consisted of men from Texas and Arkansas. They were assailed not only by shot and shell but also the forward elements of the 2nd United States Sharpshooters regiment. The alignment of the Confederates was altered due to this, the uneven, rocky terrain, and the wounding of Robertson[117]. Maintaining their alignment became problematic and resulted in the separation of Law's brigade of Alabamians and Robertson's brigade. The 4th and 5th Texas crossed what is now the "Slaughter Pen" and eventually assaulted the southern slope of Little Round Top with Law's Alabamians, who also traversed the Slaughter Pen and slopes of Big Round Top. The 1st Texas and 3rd Arkansas now moved toward Devil's Den and the woods adjacent to it.

Visitors to the field today may walk the ground from either the Union or Confederate perspective. They quickly learn that looks can be deceiving. The land is uneven and filled with rocks of all sizes, and traversing it requires sure footing and attention to obstacles. Possessing good stamina is also recommended. The visitor is free to choose his or her own path and rest when needed. The most significant advantage—no one is trying to kill you. Imagine yourself on horseback seven to eight feet above the terrain attempting to control your mount as you descend and climb your way through this labyrinth.

As a human on horseback, you can see what is before you well. But, what of the creature carrying you? Can this animal see what you see? After all, you must trust each other, but the answer is no, your horse does not see what you see, since human vision differs from that of a horse. Human eyes are forward facing and on the front of the head, allowing for binocular or stereoscopic vision. Peripheral vision is limited, in this

---

115 Benjamin Joseph Polley, *Hood's Texas Brigade*, (Dayton, Ohio: Morning Side Bookshop, 1988) 177. Taken from the letters of John C. West, Company E 4th Texas.

116 John B. Hood, *Advance and Retreat. Personal Experiences in the United States and Confederate States Armies.* Edited by Richard N. Current, (Bloomington: Indiana University Press, 1959) 58-59. Hood's wounding does not place him in the Peach Orchard assailed by Barksdale's Brigade of Mississippians, rather the orchard located at the Bushman Farm.

117 OR., Series 1. Vol 27. Part 2. Robertson stated he was wounded when night closed.

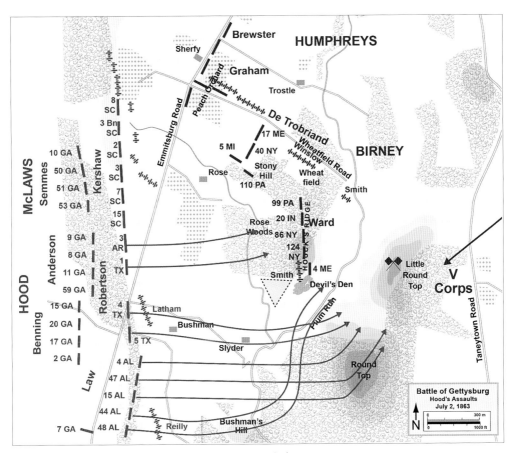

The late afternoon opening assault on July 2nd. Map by Hal Jespersen.

case. People see in color, and in the best of cases, our 20/20 vision allows the eyes to accommodate to objects near and far. During the night or in limited light, the pupil will dilate to allow as much light to enter the eye as possible. Horses, on the other hand, are prey and not predator, and they compensate for this with eyesight. The horse's eyes are located laterally (more to the side of the head). This gives them both monocular and binocular vision with a field of view that spans around 350 degrees. In other words, horses have excellent peripheral vision. Seeing movement in one eye (monocular vision), the animal will lift its head and look directly at the point of interest and focus both eyes upon it (binocular vision). For this to occur, the animal must be able to lift or lower its head. They have one of the largest eyes of land-based animals and can see very well in the dark and are thought to have dichromatic vision, seeing in shades of mainly green and yellow (think grass and hay). They do, however, have blind spots. One is located directly behind the tail. Therefore, one should use caution by approaching a horse from an angle so they can see you coming. The second blind spot is to the horse's front, from the base of the eyes to the ground and out to about six feet. The animal can compensate for this by moving its head to bring an area into its field of vision.[118] [119]

118 Janet L. Jones, "How Your Horse's Vision Differs From Yours." *Equus Magazine*. January 29, 2016.
119 Les Sellnow, "The Equine Eye." *The Horse: Your Guide to Equine Health Care*. October 15, 2001.

The Bushman Farm with Little Round Top in the distance. The terrain is manageable in the foreground, but beyond it becomes more precarious. It was near the orchard in the foreground that General Hood was to have been wounded on July 2nd. Photograph by the author.

The Slyder Farm in the distance. Looming behind it, the slopes of Little Round Top and Devil's Den. Photograph by the author.

Longstreet at Gettysburg July 2nd.
H.A. Ogden, LOC.

The rocks between Devils Den and Big Round Top are known as the Slaughter Pen. Photograph by the author.

The Slaughter Pen. Looking east soon after the battle. LOC.

Looking southward, the tree line in the far distance is that of Warfield Ridge, where General Hood's Division began its attack on July 2nd. Photograph by the author.

With this in mind, after viewing the preceding terrain pictures (and particularly when one visits the field in person) it becomes clear the difficulty these equines had. A horse kept on a tight rein will have minimal movement of its head and neck. This may seem as if the rider is keeping his mount under control when, in practical terms, it only further limits his visual field. To negotiate the treacherous terrain, these animals must be able to lift and lower their heads. On July 2, there are some accounts of mounted Confederates attempting to negotiate this terrain while mounted. Hood and his staff and couriers were mounted. Few, if any, of the men of Brigadier George T. Anderson's Brigade of Georgians mention horses. The field and staff officers of Brigadier General Joseph B. Kershaw's Brigade of South Carolinians were dismounted due to the many obstacles in the way.[120] The Union army, however, rode their animals across this terrain, From Cemetery Ridge to the contested ground, including the steep slopes of Little Round Top and the boulders of Devils Den.

LITTLE ROUND TOP

Soon after the shelling began, Meade dispatched Brigadier General Gouverneur Warren, Chief of Engineers of the Army of the Potomac, to the summit of Little Round Top to investigate the hill and situation. When Warren arrived with members of his staff, which included Lieutenant Ranald Mackenzie, he was shocked only to find a small detachment of signalman. The hill was void of any infantry or artillery. The western face of Little Round Top had been cleared of its trees well before the battle and revealed a steep slope strewn with boulders. The cleared area also provided an excellent view south, west, and north of its location. Men on horseback attempted to ride up this slope only to find it impossible. The eastern slope of the hill was still wooded, and its northern slopes afforded a marginally better path.

Warren sent Mackenzie to Sickles to inform him of the situation and to deploy troops to come to the defense of the hill. Sickles replied that he was unable to do so, requiring his entire Corps to defend his front. Mackenzie then found Major General George Sykes, the commander of the Union Fifth Corps. Sykes, under orders from Meade, was en-route to bolster the defenses and hold the ground. Mackenzie informed Sykes of the situation. General Sykes recognized the importance of the hill and dispatched a courier to General Barnes, instructing him to send a brigade to Little Round Top. Before he could reach Barnes, he was intercepted by Colonel Strong Vincent of Barnes' 3rd brigade—*"What are your orders?"* Vincent asked, but when the messenger inquired about the location of General Barnes, he asked again, *"What are your orders? Give me your orders."*

Upon hearing them, Vincent took the initiative and responsibility to lead his men toward the south end of the hill.[121] Vincent and his orderly, Private Oliver Norton, spurred their horses and attempted to scale the western face of the hill, but found it

---

120 Joseph B. Kershaw, *Kershaw's Brigade at Gettysburg*. Gettysburg National Military Park Library Files.
121 Oliver W. Norton, *The Attack and Defense of Little Round Top. Gettysburg, July 2, 1863*, (Gettysburg, PA: Stan Clark Military Books, 1913/1992) 292-295.

too rocky and steep. They turned and instead climbed the eastern (rear) slopes. As they arrived, their brigade flag attracted the Confederates' attention as shells burst nearby. This prompted Vincent to order Norton to get behind the rocks. Both men dismounted, and Vincent gave "Old Jim's" (Vincent's mount) reins to Private Norton.

Vincent's brigade consisted of about 1300 men who arrived soon after, and Vincent's regimental commanders rode to this destination as well. All dismounted then handed their mounts to their orderlies, who then took them to the rear of the ledge.[122] Vincent had dismounted in such haste that he neglected to unstrap his sword from Old Jim. Instead of a sword, his wife's riding crop became his symbol of command.[123] His brigade arrived with only a few moments to spare before Confederates assailed the southern slopes of Little Round Top.

Brigadier General Gouverneur K. Warren. Matthew Brady Collection. LOC.

---

122 James H. Nevins and William B Styles, *What Death More Glorious. A Biography of General Strong Vincent,* (New Jersey: Belle Grove Publishing, 1997) 72-73.

123 Ibid., 111.

The Western face of Little Round Top. Note the mass of rocks and boulders that made it impossible to climb on horseback. Photograph by the author.

Little Round Top (left) and Big Round Top (right). LOC.

Colonel Strong Vincent. LOC.

Atop Little Round Top looking northwest. Photograph by the author.

Little Round Top looking southwest. The boulders of Devil's Den visible in the distance. The 16th Michigan Volunteer Infantry's monument in the foreground. Photograph by the author.

Warren mounted his gray horse and rode as rapidly as possible to locate additional reinforcements. He found the 140th NY Infantry regiment under the Command of Colonel Patrick O'Rorke. Captain Joseph M. Leeper of the 140th NY recalled that Warren was seen riding rapidly down the right base of Little Round Top. He ordered O'Rorke to take his men and go to the aid of Colonel Vincent and form on his right. O'Rorke complied and arrived atop the hill at the moment when they were needed most.[124] Vincent saw the right of his line begin to waiver, he climbed atop a large boulder, and with his wife's little riding crop in his hand, he exhorted his men *do not give them an inch of ground!* Moments later, he fell with a groin wound that proved to be mortal, dying on July 7, 1863. Warren ordered O'Rorke immediately into action. O'Rorke and the 140th NY blunted the Confederate attack. O'Rorke was killed in action soon after.

Also impressed to defend the hill was the remainder of Brigadier General Stephen Weed's brigade as well as Battery "D" 5th US Artillery under the command of Lieutenant Charles Hazlett. The artillery ascended the hill using the eastern side at a trot with *"whips and spurs vigorously applied. Each man and horse trying to pull the whole battery by himself."*[125] Lieutenant Rittenhouse of Battery D described the ground as a place no rider would go, yet there was Hazlett, mounted and placing his artillery while wearing a white hat. Rittenhouse later related the following events:

> *"Corporal Taylor while still working his piece, called to me, "General Weed is shot." I ran to him where he was lying alone, in rear of Taylor; (he was shot and paralyzed below the shoulders), and he said, "I am cut in two; I want to see Hazlett." He was called; he dismounted and ran to Weed's side. After giving him directions about the payment of two or three small debts he owed his brother officers, held him closer to him, to give, as I supposed, a confidential message, when a ball struck Hazlett in the head, and he never spoke again. Hazlett wore a white hat and it cost him his life. I heard a ball strike and as I looked to my right I saw, at my very elbow Corporal Taylor holding Hazlett in his arms. The scene of Hazlett on horseback with his white hat on, are fresh in my mind today."*[126]

Confederates stormed the southern slopes of the hill in successive waves, but ultimately were deprived possession of the hill. Little Round Top remained in Union hands.

---

124 John B. Bachelder, David L. Ladd, Audrey J. Ladd, and Richard Allen Sauers, *The Bachelder papers: Gettysburg in Their Own Words.* (Dayton, Ohio: Morningside House, Inc. 1994) 896. Letter of Captain Joseph M. Leeper 140th NY Volunteers.

125 Military Order of the Loyal Legion of the United States, *War papers: being papers read before the Commandery of the District of Columbia, Military Order of the Loyal Legion of the United States.* (Wilmington, N.C.: Broadfoot, 1993) 37. The Battle of Gettysburg as seen from Little Round Top. Captain B.F. Rittenhouse.

126 Ibid., 39-40.

THE DEVIL'S DEN

The 1st Texas moved through a triangular shaped field toward Devils Den with the 3rd Arkansas to their left. The ground in this area is inhospitable and the terrain is littered from one end to another with large rocks and boulders. Like granite, these are indigenous to the area and known as diabase or Gettysburg sill.[127] Their mere presence makes the ground difficult to cross on foot, and even more so on horseback.

The fighting in the area of the Triangular Field pitted men of the 1st Texas against those of the 124th NY infantry regiment commanded by Colonel Augustus Van Horn Ellis. The Texans made slow progress as they ascended the slopes that lead to Devil's Den. Major James Cromwell approached Ellis and urged a charge of the 124th toward the Texans. This request was denied twice by Ellis, but then their horses were brought forward. Cromwell and Ellis mounted. Captain Silliman witnessed the officers on horseback amid this struggle, remonstrated them for making themselves the perfect target:

> *"The Major's only reply is, "The men must see us today," and he rides slowly to and wheels his horse about in the rear of the center of the left wing; wherewith drawn sword and eyes fixed on the Colonel, he impatiently awaits his superior's pleasure. Presently Ellis by a simple nod gives*

The Triangular Field, over which Ellis, Cromwell and the 124th NY charged. Photograph by the author.

---

127 Gary Adelman and Timothy Smith, *Devil's Den A History and Guide*, (Gettysburg, PA.: Thomas Publications, 1997) 1.

the desired permission; at which Cromwell waves his sword twice above his head, makes a lunge forward, shouts the charge, and putting spurs to his horse, dashes forward through the lines. The men cease firing for a minute and with ready bayonets rush after him. Ellis sits still in his saddle and looks on as if in proud admiration of both his loved Major and gallant sons of Orange, until the regiment is fairly underway, and then rushes with them into the thickest of the fray. The conflict at this point defies description. Roaring cannon, crashing riflery, screeching shots, bursting shells, hissing bullets, cheers, shouts, shrieks, and groans were the notes of the song of death which greeted the grim reaper, as with mighty sweeps he leveled down the richest field of scarlet human grain ever garnered on this continent. The enemy's line, unable to withstand our fierce onset, broke and fled, and Cromwell his noble face flushed with victory, and his extended right arm waving his flashing saber — uttered a shout of triumph. But it had barely escaped his lips when the second line of the foe poured into us a terrible fire which seemed in an instant to bring down a full quarter of our number. Once more we hear our loved Cromwell's shout, and once again we see, amid the fire and smoke, his noble form and flashing blade; but the next instant his brave heart is pierced by a rebel bullet, his right arm drops powerless, his lifeless body falls backward from his saddle and loud above the din of battle we hear Ellis shout, " My God! My God, men! Your Major's down; save him! save him." Again, the onset of Orange County's sons becomes irresistible, and the second line of the foe wavers and falls back; but another and solid line takes its place, whose fresh fire falls with frightful effect on our now skeleton ranks. So terrible is it that two-thirds of the artillerymen in our rear are either killed or wounded, and the balance driven from their guns, by the shells and bullets which pass over and through our line. But our brave Ellis yet remains, now seen in bold relief, now lost amid the clouds of powder smoke. A moment longer the central figure, he directs his regiment. Again the rebel line begins to waver, and we see his proud form rise in his stirrups ; his long sharp sword is extended upward, a half uttered order escapes his lips, when suddenly his trusty blade falls point downward, his chin drops on his breast, and his body with a weave pitches forward, head foremost among the rocks ; at which his wounded beast rears and with a mad plunge dashes away, staggering blindly through the ranks of the foe, who is now giving ground again, firing wildly as he goes. But we are too weak to follow him, yet with the desperate effort, the Orange Blossoms struggle forward and gather up such as they may of the wounded, and with them and the bodies of Ellis and Cromwell."[128]

128 Charles H. Weygant, *History of the One Hundred and Twenty-fourth Regiment, N.Y.S.V.,* (Newburgh, N.Y.: Journal Printing House, 1877) 175-177.

The Texans that assailed this area described the same scenario above from their point of view:

"The Federals were led by splendid officers and made a noble charge: but when they met the murderous fire from behind the rocks where we crouched, they faltered. Only for a moment, though, and on they came right up to the rocks. Again, they faltered, for now, most of their officers were down. Again, it was, but for a second and cheered on by some of the bravest men I have ever seen, they rallied in the very face of death and charged right up to the muzzles of our guns. There was one officer, a major, who won our admiration by his courage and gallantry. He was a very handsome man and rode a beautiful, high-spirited gray horse. The animal seemed to partake of the spirit of the rider, and as he came on with a free, graceful stride into that hell of death and carnage, head erect and ears pointed, horse and man offered a picture such as is seldom seen. The two seemed the very impersonation of heroic courage. As the withering, scathing volleys from behind' the rocks cut into the ranks of the regiment the major led, and his gallant men went down like grain before a scythe, he followed close at their heels, and when, time and again, they stopped and would have fled the merciless fire, each time he rallied them as if his puissant arm alone could stay the storm. But his efforts were, in the end, unavailing; the pluck of himself and his men only made the carnage the more dreadful, for the Lone Star banner and the flag of Georgia continued floating from the hill, showing who stood, defiant and unyielding, beneath their folds. In the last and most determined charge they made on us, the gallant officer made his supreme effort. Riding into our very midst, seeming to bear a charmed life, he sat proudly on the noble gray, and still cheered on his men. ' Don't shoot at him don't kill him,' our boys shouted to each other; ' he is too brave a man to die shoot his horse and capture the man. But it could not be. In a second or two, horse and rider went down together, pierced by a dozen balls. Thus, died a hero one of the most gallant men that ever gave up his life on the red field of carnage. Though it was that of an enemy, we honored the dead body as if it had been that of one of our own men. Such courage belongs not to any one army or country, but to mankind."[129]

It is thought provoking how opposing sides viewed horses as noble, gallant, as well as the bravery and skill of the rider, yet did not hesitate to bring down one or both in the midst of battle.

---

129 Benjamin Joseph Polley, *Hood's Texas Brigade*, (Dayton, Ohio: Morning Side Bookshop, 1988) 170-171.

Devil's Den. Photograph by the author.

The most skilled rider and the sure-footed horse would find this terrain challenging in peaceful times; now, in a storm of shot, shell and musketry rode Confederate William Barbee. Barbee served as a courier for General Hood, but when the action started, he was not easily kept from a fight. Barbee approached his comrades of the 1st Texas, waving his hat while riding his sorrel horse as fast as it took him. Eventually, at that pace over this ground, the animal was bound to lose his footing, and he did. The fate of his animal is not known—Barbee did not stop to check. Instead, he hit the ground running, grabbed his rifle and entered the fray.[130] It is a reasonable probability that Barbee's animal wasn't the only one spurred into action and lost its footing.

Further to the west in the area between Devils Den and the Wheatfield, the 20th Indiana attempted to stop the advance Brigadier General George T. Anderson's Brigade of Georgians and the 3rd Arkansas Infantry regiment. Colonel Joseph Wheeler, the Hoosier's commanding officer, was mounted at the onset. He was shot through the temple during the first volley and fell from his horse. Command eventually fell to Captain Erasmus Gilbreath. Gilbreath attempted to mount Wheeler's horse, but the animal became so restive that he could not hold him. Gilbreath abandoned the attempt and let the creature go.[131] Gilbreath tried to mount an animal which he was not familiar; the horse had been pushed passed its breaking point and put into flight mode. The sudden vol-

---

130 Ibid., 172.

131 Erasmus, C. Gilbreath, Company I 20th Indiana. U.S. Army History Institute, Carlisle Barracks, PA. ALBG Library Files.

ley, the fall of his master, coupled with a total stranger attempting to mount during the confusion and noise quickly taxed even the most disciplined and well-trained steed.

Adjacent to the 20th Indiana sat the Wheatfield of farmer John Rose.[132] Over the course of the late afternoon and evening hours, thousands of soldiers from both armies attempted to wrest control from the other. Like waves crashing on a shore, attack and counterattack led Confederates to reform their battle lines, while Union reinforcements hurried to stem their advance. By the end of July 2, this twenty-six-acre enclosure of golden ripe wheat was trampled and stained with blood. The 116th Pennsylvania Infantry regiment, while en route, observed something not commonly seen—a woman on horseback. Major St. Clair Mulholland related the scene:

"The solid shot falling on the soft ground of a newly plowed field threw the earth in showers over the men. While passing the Trossell (sic) house a woman on horseback and in uniform galloped back from the line of battle asked for some information and returned to the front again. She was a nurse of the Third Corps, Anna Etheridge[133] and was directing the removal of the wounded. She was cool and self-possessed and did not seem to mind the fire."[134]

Anna Etheridge. LOC.

Anna Ethridge.[135] By John Sartain.

132 The Rose Farm at the time of the battle was owned by George Rose. His brother, John, lived in the house and worked the farm including the Wheatfield.
133 Anna Etheridge hailed from Detroit Michigan and at Gettysburg served with the 3rd Michigan Infantry as a Vivandière. This position entailed among other tasks nursing duties.
134 St. Clair A. Mulholland, *The Story of the 116th Regiment Pennsylvania Volunteers in the War of the Rebellion. Record of a Gallant Command*, (Philadelphia: F. McManus Jr. and Co., 1903) 135.
135 L.P. Brockett and Mary C. Vaughn, *Woman's Work in the Civil War. A Record*, (Philadelphia: Zeigler, Mcurdy and Company, 1867) 746.

The illustration of Etheridge on horseback, while dramatized, perhaps is not too far from what Mulholland described. Was Etheridge sitting astride her mount, with both feet in stirrups? In the illustration, it appears she is riding side-saddle. Riding sidesaddle allowed women in dresses to sit upon a horse with a degree of poise and modesty. Specialized saddles have been made for this method of riding. It involved placing the left foot into the stirrup, and the right leg placed around an upright pommel, which is used for support. With the proper practice, posture, and balance, it is possible to ride the animal as if one were riding the traditional way.

THE PEACH ORCHARD, THE TROSTLE FARM, AND THE EMMITSBURG ROAD

What information Etheridge sought remains unclear. What is known, however, is the location of the 3rd Michigan infantry, the Peach Orchard of Joseph Sherfy. Sickles' line ran north to south along the Emmitsburg Road. It started in the vicinity of the Codori Farm. The Peach Orchard sat along the Emmitsburg Road at the intersection of the Wheatfield Road. This orchard became the southernmost extent of Sickles' line before it bent southeast at near right angles. Sickles' line nearly doubled in length. The disposition of his troops created a vulnerable and isolated position. As Longstreet's July 2 assault progressed from his right to left, it was only a matter of time before Confederates assaulted the Peach Orchard on several fronts. Cannon already boomed forth shot and shell toward the orchard. One Confederate battery of twelve-pound Howitzers, the "Brooks Artillery" under the command of Lieutenant Stephen Gilbert, positioned itself along the outskirts of the woods (Seminary Ridge). At about 4:00 pm, they opened fire. Gilbert recalled that this *"commenced one of the most terrible fires of artillery ever heard. Men and horses falling on every hand."*[136] Behind Gilbert and his cannon waited Brigadier General William Barksdale and his Mississippians. Just over 1600 men now lay as they awaited the order to advance— their target, the Peach Orchard.

Barksdale and his brigade endured this cannonade while they watched the brigade of Brigadier General Joseph B. Kershaw's South Carolinians assail Stony Hill as well as the southern end of the Peach Orchard. Barksdale grew restless and appealed directly to Longstreet to unleash his troops. When the order finally came, Barksdale's face was radiant with joy. He rode his mount down the line, which now formed for battle. He took his position at the front of his command. The instructions Barksdale issued called for an advance and a swing to the left. The General described as a *"large rather heavily built man of blonde complexion, with thin light hair. He was not a graceful horseman, though his forward, impetuous bearing, especially in battle, overshadowed and more than made up for such deficiencies."*[137] The field officers, in Kershaw's Brigade, had

---

136 A.P. Prince, *Brooks Artillery, Rhett's Battery*. Columbia, SC.: South Carolina Department of Archives and History, 1898. Gettysburg National Military Park Library Files.

137 Mississippi Historical Society, and Franklin L. Riley, *Publications of the Mississippi Historical Society. Volume XIV*, (Oxford, Mississippi: The Society, 1914) 336. Gettysburg National Military Park Library Files.

received orders that *"no officers below the rank of Brigadier or Acting Brigadier-General should ride into battle, because of the fact that the government had a great deal of difficulty in replacing the killed horses."[138]* Perhaps a sentiment of President Abraham Lincoln silently echoed through both armies, *"I can make more generals, but horses cost money!"*

Brigadier General William Barksdale. LOC

Below: The initial assault of the Peach Orchard.
Map by Hall Jespersen..

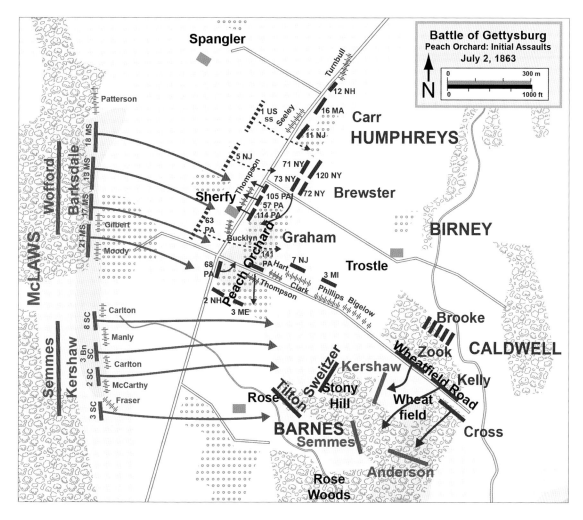

138 Ibid., 237-238. The quote is from Major George B. Gerald of the 18th Mississippi.

Captain George Randolph, Sickles' Chief of Artillery, dispatched an aid to locate additional artillery units to bolster the line. He found Lieutenant Colonel Freeman McGilvery and the 1st Volunteer Artillery Brigade. Soon McGilvery, Battery C and F of the Pennsylvania Light Artillery, the 15th NY Artillery, and the 5th and 9th Massachusetts Artillery were hurried toward the front lines. While en route, Captain John Bigelow of the 9th Massachusetts noted that they halted briefly near the Trostle House and re-membered:

> *"A spirited military spectacle lay before us; General Sickles was standing beneath a tree close by, staff officers and orderlies coming and going in all directions; at the Famous Peach Orchard angle on rising ground, along the Emmetsburg (sic) Road about 500 yards in our front, white smoke was curling up from the rapid and crashing volleys of Graham's Third Corps Infantry, and the deep-toned booming of Randolph's guns as they tried to repel the furious assault of Longstreet with Kershaw's and Barksdale's Brigades."[139]*

9TH MASS. BATTERY.

A sketch by Charles Reed of the 9th Mass shows the deployment toward the Peach Orchard. The right background tree shows a group of dismounted men, that of General Sickles and his staff. LOC.

---

139 John Bigelow, *The Peach Orchard Gettysburg July 2nd, 1863 Explained by Official Reports and Maps*, (Minneapolis: Kimball-Storer Co., 1910) 52.

Battery C and F took positions in the Peach Orchard, while the remaining batteries took positions near the Wheatfield Road, which runs perpendicular to the Emmitsburg Road and intersects at the Peach Orchard. They faced south toward the farm and home of George Rose. It is here that the Federal artillerists came under fire. Some of these batteries began losing men and horses before they were able to fire a shot. Union cannons engaged the Confederate batteries. Men and horses fell as casualties started to mount. Horses had to be cut from their harnesses and replaced.[140]

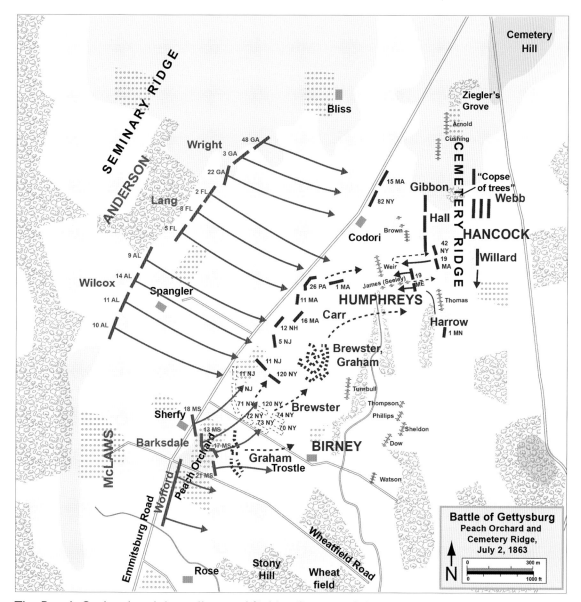

The Peach Orchard and the collapse of Sickles Corps and the subsequent strike of Cemetery Ridge. Map by Hal Jespersen.

---

140 Ibid., 53.

The distance from the Confederate lines to the Peach Orchard is approximately six hundred yards. It was not long before the area was hit. Union Brigadier General Charles Graham commanded a brigade and remained mounted through the ordeal until his animal was shot. *"His horse was wounded and pitched the General over his head, leaving him in a dazed state of mind."*[141] The attacks upon the Peach Orchard were launched approximately 5:30 pm, and by 6:00 pm, the Union forces, despite desperate attempts to hold their positions, began to retreat. The collapse of the Peach Orchard soon saw Sickles' line slowly yield to Confederate forces. As they were overrun, the Federal infantry withdrew in an organized manner as was possible.

The artillery, however, did not have the ability to leave in the same way. The cannon had to be limbered or attached to the wagon that the horses pulled. Many of the artillery horses were killed or wounded, due to their proximity to the fighting. Many times, they were collateral damage, and sometimes, they were explicitly targeted. When enough horses had been killed or disabled, cannon were more likely to be captured. For an artillery commander, there was no greater disgrace than the loss of your guns and ammunition. Casper R. Carlisle, assigned to Battery F of the Pennsylvania Independent Light Artillery, under the command of Captain James Thompson found themselves in precisely this predicament. Carlisle quickly went back to rescue one of the cannons from capture, where he found the drivers wounded. The lead and swing horses (front and middle) were dead. One of the wheel horses was alive and the other near-death, which made this brave act even more perilous. Carlisle, assisted by Thompson, cut the dead animals from the limber and helped to pull the gun and the two remaining horses to safety near Cemetery Ridge. As they neared the ridge, the mortally wounded animal succumbed and perished. Carlisle was later awarded the Medal of Honor for his actions.[142] [143]

Battery F. Pennsylvania Light Artillery. Located in the Peach Orchard.
Photograph by the author.

141 Mississippi Historical Society, and Franklin L. Riley, *Publications of the Mississippi Historical Society. Volume XIV*, (Oxford, Mississippi: The Society, 1914) 336. Gettysburg National Military Park Library. Page 337.

142 Charles Hanna, *Gettysburg Medal of Honor Recipients*, (Springville, Utah: Bonneville Books, 2010) 51-52

143 B.T. Arlington, *The Medal of Honor at Gettysburg*, (Gettysburg, PA.: Thomas Publications, 1996) 11.

General Sickles watched from his position adjacent to the Trostle Farm barn, where his headquarters was located nearby. He was atop his horse[144] when a solid shot cannonball struck him just below the right knee. Surprisingly, the animal was not injured. Dan Sickles felt sudden dampness around his leg and, upon inspection, viewed the remains of his shattered limb. He was helped to dismount and eventually transported from the field to a makeshift hospital, where doctors later amputated his shattered extremity.

General Sickles. LOC.

DAN.E.SICKLES

Wounding marker of General Sickles. To the right of the marker, the Trostle Farm barn. Photograph by the author.

144 Sickles had two notable mounts. Tammany and Grand Old Cannister and Grape.

With the collapse of the Peach Orchard, the Union line along the Emmitsburg Road was unable to stem the Confederates' advance. Federal infantry and artillery began to withdraw toward Cemetery Ridge. Lt. Colonel McGilvery issued orders for the 9th Mass. to withdraw. Captain Bigelow not only had the 21st Mississippi coming toward his front but sharpshooters to his left front. The men and horses of the 9th Mass. had never seen combat prior to this day, and it was a baptism by fire for both man and beast. Bigelow determined that the only reasonable recourse was to retire by "prolonge." A prolonge is simply a long heavy rope that served a variety of functions. One such task allowed the cannon to be pulled and fired without the need to limber and unlimber (attach and detach) the gun. At the end of the gun's trail is an eyelet called a lunette. The cannon is faced toward the enemy. One end of the rope is attached to the lunette and the other to a "hitch" called a "pintle." Once the cannon is fired, the recoil, along with the horses moving at a walk or slow trot, can pull the piece to its next position. While it moved, the gun crew reloaded and fired as needed. This slowed the Confederate advancement from the front and allowed protection of the flanks.

Unfortunately, like Battery F, the 9th Mass. suffered severe casualties in men and especially horses. Their numbers dwindled and required the gun crews to serve as beasts of burden. As the guns fired, the recoil of the cannon augmented with the pulling effort of the artillerists augmented by the surviving equines, allowed them to continue to retreat and maintain their alignment. Bigelow spied an exit in a stone wall near the

The forward position of the 9th Mass located along the Wheatfield Road. In the distance behind the center stone monument lies a large tree (Witness Tree), and to its right, the roof of the Trostle Farm barn. It is across this field that Bigelow's men, guns, and the surviving animals retreated firing by prolonge. Photograph by the author.

Trostle house and proceeded to retire toward it, firing as they fell back. Bigelow recalled the action:

> *"No friendly supports, of any kind, were in sight; but Johnnie Rebs in great numbers. Bullets were coming into our midst from many directions and a Confederate battery added to our difficulties. Still prolonges were fixed and we withdrew the—the left section keeping Kershaw's skirmishers back with cannister, and the other two sections bowling solid shot towards Barksdale's men. We moved slowly, the recoil of the guns retiring them, while the prolonges enabled us to keep alignment; but the loss in men and horses was severe."* [145]

Bigelow and the survivors now hoped to limber their guns and proceed through the exit and toward the Union line along Cemetery Ridge. Lt. Col. McGilvery spurred his mount to the scene and issued new orders. McGilvery, whose own horse was riddled with bullets, ordered the 9th Mass. to stand its ground. The confusion and lack of support along Cemetery Ridge required time to repair and reorganize. Infantry and artillery had to be located and placed to plug the gap vacated by Sickles. Bigelow's battery now purchased some time for McGilvery to fortify Cemetery Ridge with a defensive artillery line.[146]

The noise one cannon generates is deafening. Today, firing demonstrations are a common occurrence at Gettysburg National Military Park but the artillery reenactors use far less gun powder than what was required during the battle. Still, these demonstrations are ear-piercing, causing the ground to shake and visitors to feel a concussive wave that literally passes through your body.

Bigelow's stand adjacent to the Trostle Farm. The tree line to the left were filled with Joseph Kershaw's South Carolinians. Looking south toward the Wheatfield.
Photograph by the author.

145 John Bigelow, *The Peach Orchard Gettysburg July 2nd, 1863 Explained by Official Reports and Maps,* (Minneapolis: Kimball-Storer Co., 1910) 56.

146 John B. Bachelder, David L. Ladd, Audrey J. Ladd, and Richard Allen Sauers, *The Bachelder papers: Gettysburg in Their Own Words Volume 1,* (Dayton, Ohio: Morningside House, Inc. 1994) 176. Account of Captain Bigelow.

The 9th Mass. view forward shows the grassy rise from which 21st Mississippi Infantry approached. Looking southwest toward the Peach Orchard (beyond the rise).
Photograph by the author.

Trostle Barn   Cemetery Ridge   9th Massachusetts approximate location

Trostle House

Witness Tree

Terrain from the advancing Confederate's perspective.
Photograph by the author.

Approximate Path of the 21st Mississippi Infantry

The 9th Mass monument located along present-day United States Ave. The Trostle Farm and house lie behind the guns. These guns were situated across the road in the fields, which show the tree line to the left and the grassy rise.
Photograph by the author.

Imagine how the noise affected the horse, whose sense of hearing is acute. This is a defense mechanism that allows them to hear the approach of a predator. An equine's ear can rotate 180 degrees and do so independently of the other ear. While riding an animal, a person may notice that the horse's ears seem to move in all directions. One may point forward, while the other points to the side. If the horse hears a suspicious noise e.g., rustling of leaves or a stick snap, it will lift or focus their head, ears and eyes to see if a threat exists, while the ears point forward directly toward the source. The horse may even stop walking in order to investigate the situation. When in the company of a horse, you can bet that your horse hears and sees something that you do not. This explains a horse's reactive behavior and why they can startle so easily.[147]

Carrying soldiers and cannon into battle exposed these animals to a great deal of stimuli, and all of it the horse disliked. Musketry, booming cannon, the spewing of smoke from each, the yells and groans of soldiers in the heat of battle, the shaking ground, the shrieks of frightened animals, and the ensuing chaos provided the perfect ingredients for a complete system overload. How did these animals cope with the "din" of battle? Desensitization during training exercises certainly aids this process, but even that is not 100 percent reliable. Artillery horses were required to be more docile and, to a degree, easier to manage. The other portion of the equation lies with the bond of trust between horse and soldier and the training that both endured.

As the melee continued, Bigelow's artillerists and horses, in essence, penned in and formed a semi-circle before the stone wall. Eventually, the left two guns were unable to be serviced and were ordered to withdraw. The remaining four stood their ground until approximately 6:30 pm. Soon after, the Confederates forced the 9th from its position and captured four of the guns. This resulted in 28 men out of 104 and 80 out of 88 horses to become casualties. The 21st Mississippi sustained 139 casualties out of 424 men. In later years, Bigelow recounted several stories regarding this action as told by his men. They all mention man and horse:

> *"The right gun, the fifth, horses all killed and left 50 yards up the slope;*
> *One driver killed, sergeant and gunner wounded and gone; two cannon-*
> *eers wounded and one lying under the gun. The next gun, all but one*
> *horse killed; sergeant wounded twice; one cannoneer shot through the*
> *body lying in the enemy's lines."*

He recounted the death of Lt. Christopher Erickson:

> *"I saw Lt. Erickson as he passed near me, reeling in his saddle. (He had*
> *been shot through the lungs early in the engagement but refused to*
> *leave his guns). He asked me for some water, drank nearly a canteen*
> *full. He afterwards saw the right piece some distance to the rear and in*
> *danger of capture; Rode up to it, and was shot through the head, indeed*
> *riddled with bullets: fell dead, his horse passing into the enemy's lines."*

---

147 Kathleen Lundberg "Horses' sensitive hearing makes them more reactive to loud sounds—like fire-works." *The Ann Arbor News*, June 22nd, 2011.

Undeniably, many other similar stories are told, but perhaps the most notable of these concerned Captain Bigelow and bugler Corporal Charles W. Reed. Bigelow re-membered:

> *"I sat on my horse calling the men, when my bugler, on my right, drew his horse back on his haunches, as he saw six sharpshooters on our left taking deliberate aim at us. I stopped two and my horse two more of their bullets. My orderly was nearby, and, dismounting raised me from the ground. I fell within 50 feet of the stone wall. I was lifted on my or-derly's horse and taken back to the hospital by bugler Reed at a walk."*

Cemetery Ridge was now reinforced with artillery. The Union cannoneers along the ridge attempted to hasten the pair's pace to minimize the risk of friendly shell-fire. Bigelow had been hit in the side and hand; he was unable to ride at any speed faster than a walk. Reed not only managed his own mount, but also his commanding offi-cer's, despite continual firing from Confederates:

> *"Bugler Reed's nerve, however, did not fail him. He did not hasten his horse's movement, a single step, but he guided on both horses with one hand, holding me on mine with the other."*

For his actions on July 2, Reed was awarded the Medal of Honor. [148]

BUGLER REED SAVING HIS CAPTAIN AT GETTYSBURG.

Corporal Charles W. Reed leads Captain John Bigelow to safety. Charles Reed collection. LOC.

148 John Bigelow, *The Peach Orchard Gettys-burg July 2nd, 1863 Explained by Official Re-ports and Maps,* (Minneapolis: Kimball-Stor-er Co., 1910) 56-65.

Dead horses on the Trostle Farm property after the battle. LOC.

The Trostle Farmhouse. Numerous dead horses litter the ground. To the right of the house, a limber with its hitching pole pointing upward can be seen. LOC

Dead artillery horse with its limber post battle. LOC

Modern views of the Trostle barn and farmhouse. The 9th Mass. Monument in foreground. Photograph by the author.

As the 21st Mississippi engaged Bigelow, the remaining Mississippi regiments under Barksdale's command crossed the Emmitsburg Road and moved northward toward Cemetery Ridge. It is near a thicket of vegetation along the small stream of Plum Run that his attacks lost their momentum, and Barksdale was brought down with a mortal wound. Through all of this, Barksdale remained mounted. A large man (Barksdale) on a horse presented a target of opportunity when most others were on foot. Yet, he managed to push the Federal forces from their positions until confronted by Union reinforcements. J. C. Lloyd of the 13th Mississippi recounted Barksdale's demise:

> *"A divergence to the left and we run over and capture a battery. Then a divergence to the right to face a force not yet driven back. Then on an on until no enemy was seen in our front. Then still on to the Plum river. And did our gallant Barksdale ride into our midst and still say, "Forward through the bushes" Did I hear him make a sound and see men rush to him and see taken off his horse and started off the field? I turn again to*

the front and see the enemy bursting through the bushes and firing on us. They had come out from the top of the hill and fresh."[149]

The Mississippians found themselves isolated and faced the fresh Union Infantry under the command of Colonel George Willard. The volley of musketry delivered by Willard's men brought down Barksdale and stemmed his advance. After Barksdale's brigade attacked, the next units to advance were that of Brigadier General Cadmus Wilcox's Alabamians and Col. David Lang's Floridians. Union Soldiers along the Emmitsburg Road now faced Confederates that attacked from their left but also directly to their front.

Lieutenant John G. Turnbull commanded the 3rd U.S. Artillery, Batteries F and K. His six bronze Napoleon cannons sat just north of the Daniel Klingel Farm along the Emmitsburg Road. They now were in the path of both the Alabamians and Floridians. Like Bigelow, and many other artillery units that day, Turnbull stood his ground until the sheer numbers and momentum drove him back toward Cemetery Ridge. Turnbull, like Bigelow, retreated and fired with prolong, utilizing recoil and horse to pull back his guns. He lost 45 animals on July 2. Writing of his experiences that day, he said:

> *"Soon enemy infantry of Wilcox advanced upon them, when they opened with cannister, and as they advanced the battery limbered up and retreated firing with prolong. The firing with cannister continued until exhausted; but the enemy came down in force and killed so many of the horses that four guns were left on the field."*[150]

Colonel Hilary A. Herbert of the 8th Alabama Infantry also attacked along and eventually across the Emmitsburg Road. He wrote of an attack made against Union cannon positioned there:

> *"Some of these pieces were defended very gallantly, firing grape at us within 50 yards or less. One brave little fellow apparently not more than 14-15 years old sat erect on the lead horse of a caisson looking straight to the front, trying to whip his horse forward to save his charge until our line was upon him. The two-wheel horses had been shot down, but he did not know this. While admiring him as the very personification of Casabianca (sic), Some excited Confederate from behind to my inexpressible regret, shot him down."*[151]

149 Mississippi Historical Society, and Franklin L. Riley, *Publications of the Mississippi Historical Society. Volume XIV*, (Oxford, Mississippi: The Society, 1914) 239.

150 John B. Bachelder. David L. Ladd, Audrey J. Ladd, and Richard Allen Sauers, *The Bachelder papers: Gettysburg in Their Own Words Volume 1*, (Dayton, Ohio: Morningside House, Inc. 1994) 284. Letter from John Turnbull to John Bachelder,

151 John B. Bachelder. David L. Ladd, Audrey J. Ladd, and Richard Allen Sauers, *The Bachelder papers: Gettysburg in Their Own Words Volume 2*, (Dayton, Ohio: Morningside House, Inc. 1994) 1057.

The limber and cannon of one of Turnbull's or Bigelow's guns weighed in excess of 3800 pounds fully loaded with ammunition. The caisson also approached the same weight.[152] Evenly distributed, each animal was required to pull approximately 630-650 pounds. Colonel Herbert's description of the above incident perhaps shed some light on the subject. One solitary horse out of six remained to pull a caisson. No manner of whipping or kicking can change what the animal physically cannot do. A full complement of six horses completed this task and makes it evident why these animals were targeted, as well as the soldiers who drove them.

As Wilcox's Alabamians moved toward Cemetery Ridge, Union General Winfield Scott Hancock observed a gap in the line, and Wilcox moved toward it, threatening a breakthrough. With Federal reinforcements en route, Hancock needed to buy time. He came upon the 1st Minnesota Volunteer Infantry. While only 262 men strong, Colonel William Covill received his orders. He was to *"advance and take those colors."* The charge of the Minnesota troops was made over the gently sloped Cemetery Ridge, toward a thicket of brush along the banks of Plum Run. Covill realized the critical nature of the order and dismounted along with the other officers. Their horses placed to the right and rear of the regiment. They were spared this day, but as for the 1st Minnesota, they suffered 67 percent casualties in a span of 15 minutes. Wilcox's momentum was halted.[153]

The time was now after 7:00 pm. Confederates under the command of Brigadier Ambrose Wright managed a breakthrough along Cemetery Ridge. With waning daylight and a lack of reinforcements, Wright was unable to hold the gains he had made. On the western portion of Cemetery Ridge, the fighting slowly came to a halt. Lee had made some gains. He captured Devils Den and the Peach Orchard, but the Union line held. The July 2 plans of General Lee, however, called for coordinated attacks on different locations of the field. Lt. General Richard Ewell was to "demonstrate" or feign assaults on Culps Hill, and if an opportunity presented to convert this into an all-out attack and progress toward the eastern, northern and northwestern portions of Cemetery Hill. Ewell placed his artillery in an area that threatened the formidable defenses of Cemetery Hill. Once set, he waited for Longstreet's attack to commence and then joined into the fray.

BENNER'S HILL, EAST CEMETERY HILL, AND CULP'S HILL

The defenses of Cemetery and Culps Hill were formidable. Culps Hill, with its steep heavily wooded slopes, now had the entire Twelfth Corps plus part of the First, protected behind entrenchments and breastworks. The eastern slopes of Cemetery Hill had numerous artillery pieces placed and infantry along its lower slopes. The Confederate artillery barrage not only needed to convince the Federals that an imminent all-out attack was soon to be launched, but also needed to do as much damage as

---

152 Phillip M. Cole, *Civil War Artillery at Gettysburg*, (Ortanna, PA.: Colecraft Industries, 2002) 103.

153 John B. Bachelder. David L. Ladd, Audrey J. Ladd, and Richard Allen Sauers, *The Bachelder papers: Gettysburg in Their Own Words Volume 1*, (Dayton, Ohio: Morningside House, Inc. 1994) 285.

possible to support an infantry assault. Finding a hill of sufficient elevation for Lee's artillery proved difficult. The nearby heights failed to match that of the Union position. The closest was a hill east of Cemetery Hill called Benner's Hill, which sat approximately three-quarters of a mile away. The hill sat in the open and offered little if any concealment or protection.

Major Joseph W. Latimer, the 19-year-old known as the "Boy Major" of the Second Corps of the Army of Northern Virginia placed his artillery battalion atop Benner's Hill. The Confederate Division of Major General Edward Johnson sat poised to assault Culp's Hill if the opportunity presented. To the northeast, Major General Jubal Early's Division also awaited orders to join the melee and launch an attack on the northern and eastern portion of Cemetery Hill. Now they anticipated the sound of Longstreet's guns. In the mid-afternoon hours, the distant booming of Longstreet's guns announced that the attacks had commenced. At 4:00 pm, Issac Seymor, an Adjutant in Brigadier General Harry Hay's Louisiana Brigade recalled:

> *"One of our artillery battalions appeared on a high hill in the rear of the left-wing of our Division, and boldly opened upon the powerful Yankee batteries in out front. The contest was a very unequal one, the Federals bringing at least fifty guns to bear on our eighteen guns. Their guns were protected by earthworks, while ours were placed on the bald top of a hill, with no covering of any kind to guns or men. But the gallant commander of the Confederate batteries, Major Latimer, maintained the fight for fully one hour, though suffering terribly in men and horses, and being terribly wounded himself."*[154]

On the evening of July 1, two Confederate brigades (Brigadier Generals John Gordon and William Smith) were dispatched to the extreme left of the Army of Northern Virginia. Their mission, to scout the area and guard the left flank against a presumed large body of Union soldiers that had been seen in the area. On July 2, Lee's overdue cavalry commander Major General J.E.B. Stuart arrived at Gettysburg. Lee dispatched Stuart to the extreme left of his army. Word needed to be sent to Johnson that his "left flank" was secure. Man and horse again were required to carry this information a distance of about two miles. Robert Stiles volunteered for this mission, which took him into the direct path of the artillery contest that now took place between Benner's Hill and East Cemetery Hill. He later wrote in his memoirs and painted a unique picture of man and beast:

> *"For the first few hundred yards, as above suggested, the configuration of the ground was such that the fire was entirely cut off--not so much as even one stray shell whistled above my head. But in a few moments, as I rose a hill and my course veered to the left, I struck a well-defined aerial*

---

154 Issac Seymour, *Issac Seymour Journal (Adjutant, Hay's Brigade),* William Clements Library, University of Michigan. Transcript by K. R. George. October 1984. Gettysburg National Military Park Library Files.

current, a meteoric stream, of projectiles and explosions, and I felt my little horse shudder and squat under me, and then he made one frantic effort to turn and fly. I pulled him fiercely back against the iron torrent until he breasted it squarely and then, seeming to realize the requirements of the position, he elongated and flattened himself as much as possible, while I lay as close to him as I could, and we fairly devoured the way."[155]

As Stiles rode toward his objective, he related three distinct impressions that were imprinted in his memory; the first was the ride itself:

"The first is a silhouette of my little horse and me as we sped on our perilous way. I put him first because he did it, I only endured. After his first shy he never shrank or swerved again but held to his course straight and swift as a greyhound; nay, as an arrow flies. He seemed to be possessed, whether intelligently or instinctively, of the double purpose of making himself small and getting there. His figure was that of a running hare--low to the ground, with ears laid flat and every limb stretched--while I was nothing but the smallest possible projection above his back and along his flanks."[156]

The second scene was recorded upon reaching Benner's Hill, where Latimer's cannon dueled with the Union artillery not more than three-quarters of a mile distant:

"Never, before or after, did I see fifteen or twenty guns in such a condition of wreck and destruction as this battalion was. It had been hurled backward, as it were, by the very weight and impact of metal, from the position it had occupied on the crest of a little ridge, into a saucer-shaped depression behind it; and such a scene as it presented--guns dismounted and disabled, carriages splintered and crushed, ammunition chests exploded, limbers upset, wounded horses plunging and kicking, dashing out the brains of men tangled in the harness; while cannoneers with pistols were crawling around through the wreck shooting the struggling horses to save the lives of the wounded men. I said the little horse did not again swerve from his course. He was compelled to do so at this point, as it was impracticable to ride through the battalion, which lay directly in our track; but we had a full view of it as we followed the higher ground from which it had been driven."[157]

Indeed, Stiles description was on target with Issac Seymour's account:

---

155 Robert Stiles, *Major of Artillery in the Army of Northern Virginia. Four Years Under Marse Robert*, (New York and Washington: The Neale Publishing Company, 1904) 216.

156 Ibid., 217

157 Ibid., 218.

"The roar of the guns was continuous and deafening; the shot and shell could be seen tearing through the hostile batteries, dismounting guns, killing and wounding men and horses, while ever and anon, an ammunition chest would explode, sending a bright column of smoke far up towards the heavens. I saw the brave little Latimer (he was only 21 years old)[158], sitting quietly on his horse amid this tempest of shot and shell, calmly directing the fire of his guns; but alas a shell presently explodes over him and down go horse and rider, the first dead and the other wounded. The Major's leg being caught under the prostrate horse and pinned to the earth, he would not permit the cannoneers to leave their pieces to extricate him, but cooly (sic) lay there giving his orders, until seeing the futility of prolonging the fight commanded his batteries to retire."[159]

Finally, Stiles reached General Johnson and delivered the message from Gordon that the left flank was secure from any Federal threat. At that point, both he and his mount were exhausted:

"The third and last picture connected with my desperate ride is of the finish and of the doughty division commander in whose behalf I had taken it. He was sometimes called "Alleghany Johnson" and "Fence-Rail Johnson," because of his having been wounded at the battle of Alleghany, and, in consequence, walking with a very perceptible limp and aiding the process with a staff about as long as a rail and almost as thick as the club of Giant Despair. He was a heavy, thick-set man, and when I saw him was on foot and hobbling along with the help of this gigantic walking-cane. It was toward the gloaming and I did not see him very distinctly, but remember that when I gasped out the message I bore from Gordon, he simply growled back, "Very well, sir"--and, my responsibility discharged, I dropped from the saddle to the ground, the last thing I remember being my little horse standing over me, his sides heaving and panting and his head drooping and sinking until his muzzle almost touched my body. How long I lay and he stood there, or where we went after we recovered breath and motion, I have not the faintest recollection."[160]

Riding a horse on a trail is and should be a relaxing way to spend any day. A well trained and respectful horse meanders through trees, up and down hills and through open fields, trusting the rider upon its back. The rider likewise trusts and respects the horse to obey cues and commands. This relationship is built and earned, never bestowed. Even the most well-trained horse on a peaceful trail can startle and, like us,

---

158 Latimer was 19. Born August 27th, 1843 and died August 1st, 1863.

159 Issac Seymour, *Issac Seymour Journal (Adjutant, Hay's Brigade),* William Clements Library, University of Michigan. Transcript by K. R. George. October 1984. Gettysburg National Military Park Library Files.

160 Robert Stiles, *Major of Artillery in the Army of Northern Virginia. Four Years Under Marse Robert,* (New York and Washington: The Neale Publishing Company, 1904) 218.

make mistakes. It is simply how we both learn. Stiles' situation was entirely different— The artillery shells whistling overhead and the subsequent explosions un-nerved Stiles' animal, and it attempted to bolt away. It experienced a complete system overload, which puts the animal's fight or flight instincts on high alert. This can cause the animal to run first and ask questions later. The sensation of a startled horse under the saddle that attempts to bolt can shock any rider. Stiles' horse was, at the very least, at a cantor or a gallop. An animal going from 20 plus miles per hour to an abrupt stop and shifting directions requires the rider to have a great deal of situational awareness, balance and control. How the rider reacts in that moment, when every muscle in the animal's body tenses and then suddenly shifts in another direction, determines in many cases if the rider will remain in the saddle or be sent flying out of it. With the proper application of aids and cues, Stiles and his mount carried out their mission.

During Longstreet's assault on July 2, Culp's Hill was nearly left abandoned. General Meade shifted approximately 7,700 men toward the vicinity of the Round Tops, leaving Culp's Hill defended by 1,400 Union infantrymen. These men from the state of New York were under the command of Brigadier General George Greene. At approximately 7:00 pm, Johnson's Confederates crossed Rock Creek and began to scale the steep wooded slopes of the hill. Their assault continued well after sunset. In the evening darkness, the Rebel soldiers managed to capture the lower portion of Culp's Hill. The upper part remained in Union hands.

Cemetery Hill also came under attack. Around 8:00 pm, Confederates of Major General Jubal Early's Division (about 2500 men) assaulted the eastern slopes of the hill. Colonel Isaac Avery led a brigade of North Carolinians along with a brigade of Louisianans commanded by Brigadier General Harry T. Hays. It was Avery, however, who stood out, as he was mounted on a horse crossing the gently sloping fields ahead of his troops. Avery and his aide Lt. John A. McPherson at the onset of the attacks were both mounted. Avery then decided to go in on foot, and McPherson dismounted. Again, Avery changed his mind and stayed in the saddle. The evening twilight coupled with the smoke of battle diminished the visual acuity of both north and south. McPherson did not see his commander fall. A round found its mark and struck Avery in the neck and toppled him from his mount.[161] Avery did not survive his wound.

With the evening darkness and lack of additional supports, the attacks on July 2, 1863, ended. The day had been even more deadly than July 1. The Union position had held, and despite Sickles' unauthorized move, the Federal forces met threat after threat and blunted Confederate attempts to wrestle Meade from his position. Lee gained some ground, but the crushing defeat of the Army of the Potomac he sought still eluded him. The toll on both men and beast was keenly felt. All tried to rest amid the moans and groans of the wounded. The final day soon arrived at dawn, the last day of battle.

---

161 Avery Family of North Carolina Papers #33, Southern Historical Collection, Wilson Library, University of North Carolina at Chapel Hill. Folder #26. https://web.lib.unc.edu/civilwar/index.php/2013/09/03/3-september-1863/

CHAPTER 7

"I looked, and there before me was a pale horse! Its rider was named Death, and Hades was following close behind him. They were given power over a fourth of the earth to kill by sword, famine and plague, and by the wild beasts of the earth."

BOOK OF REVELATION 6:8

JULY 3, 1863: THE DIE IS CAST

General George Meade and the Army of the Potomac endured the events of July 2, and despite some loss of ground, the Federal army deprived Lee of the crushing victory he sought. This came at a significant cost to both armies. Known for his temper and referred to as an "old snapping turtle," Meade perhaps felt one casualty hit close to home. Baldy, his mount in the waning hours of July 2, carried Meade to the front and left center of his line as reinforcements were hurried into place. A bullet passed through Meade's right trouser leg then through the flap of his saddle and passed into Baldy's body. The horse came to a standstill, and Meade was unable to coax his companion to move on. Meade remarked that *"Baldy is done for this time."* It was the first time the animal refused to go in under fire. Meade, supplied with another animal, continued the day as "Old Baldy" was led to the rear. This was the sixth and final time Baldy had been wounded (twice at 1st Bull Run, once at 2nd Bull Run, Antietam, Fredericksburg and Gettysburg).[162]

Despite the wounding of his mount, Meade, who narrowly escaped a wound himself, had other pressing matters to attend. Meade received a boon in the late afternoon hours, as the Sixth Corps of the Army of the Potomac arrived after a grueling thirty-four-mile march. These soldiers, under the command of Major General John Sedgwick, added nearly 14,000 men to the Federal army. The Union army reached its peak. Around 9:00 pm that evening, Meade called his senior Corps Commanders to his headquarters

---

162 Meade, George. Letter to the Commander of George G. Meade Post No.1 Dept of Penna. G.A.R. Dated March 12th, 1883. The letter was written to clarify Old Baldy's history with Meade. Baldy did recover from his wounding, but never again saw active duty. He was sent to Philadelphia and into the care of Captain Samuel Ringwalt in the spring of 1864. Following the war upon his return home, Meade found his trusted friend in good condition. Old Baldy outlived his master by 10 years and died in 1882.

to discuss the status of the Federal army. At its conclusion, it was resolutely determined that the Army of the Potomac should stand their ground and await an attack by Lee. The meeting dispersed near midnight and the Federal troops of the Twelfth Corps were ordered to return and reoccupy Culp's Hill. They found Confederates held the lower hill, and subsequently orders were issued to retake the lost ground at dawn.

The Equestrian Statue of Major General John Sedgwick, commander of the Sixth Corps, Army of the Potomac. Sedgwick is atop his mount "Handsome Joe." His arrival in the late afternoon hours of July 2nd gave the Federal army nearly 14,000 additional troops at a time when they were most needed. Sculptor: Henry Kirke Bush-Brown. Dedicated in 1913. Located on **Sedgwick Avenue.** Photograph by the author.

Equestrian Statue of Major General Henry Slocum commander of the Twelfth Corps, Army of the Potomac. Sculptor: Edward Clark Potter. Dedicated September 1902. This monument is located atop Steven's Knoll. Located on Slocum Avenue, between Culp's Hill and East Cemetery Hill. Photograph by the author.

Robert E. Lee also had important decisions to make. If he and his army left Gettysburg after two days of combat without a victory, they had fought and suffered casualties that included both man, beast, and supplies all for naught. Any subsequent engagements either made by or forced upon the Confederate army could place Lee at a disadvantage. If Lee remained at Gettysburg, he must decide whether to stay on the offensive or switch to a defensive posture. To remain in Gettysburg in a defensive position and wait for an undetermined period only served to expend valuable supplies, food, forage, and water in enemy territory. There existed the possibility that the Union army may attempt to interrupt Lee's supply trains and retreat routes. Lee determined the only acceptable solution was to continue the offensive. Perhaps if the assault were better coordinated and executed, the victory he sought would come to fruition.

Lee formulated an attack plan. This called for Lt. General Richard Ewell to again assail Culp's Hill while Lt. General James Longstreet and his First Corps—augmented in strength by the arrival of Major General George Pickett's Division (approximately 5500 men)— were to assault Cemetery Ridge and Cemetery Hill, driving the Federals from their position. Lee also planned for a bombardment using every artillery piece available to shell Cemetery Ridge and Hill in an effort to demoralize and force the Union defenders and their artillery from the target.

The first misfortune for Lee's army occurred at dawn (4:30 am) on July 3. The Union Twelfth Corps attempted to wrest control of the lower portion of Culp's Hill lost on July 2. The Federals shelled the lower portion of the hill and followed with an infantry assault. This attack resulted in the longest sustained combat of the battle as Union and Confederate Infantry fought for nearly seven hours. In the end, the Union army prevailed and seized full control of Culp's Hill as the melee slowly waned around 11:00 am.

The plan Lee developed had suffered its first setback. While the Union army began its push to wrest control of Culp's Hill, Confederates, too, began deadly harassment directed toward Cemetery Hill. Major Eugene Blackford, who commanded a battalion of Rebel sharpshooters, received orders to move his men as close to the Federal lines (Cemetery Hill) as possible. At daybreak, he and his marksman were to annoy them with all their power, taking careful aim directed toward Union targets of opportunity, which included their horses. Blackford wrote in his memoirs:

> *"The Day (July 3rd) broke clear, and as soon as it was light there lay before us on the slope of the hill a battery of six Napoleons; they were not more than 400 yards off. Men and horses were all there, standing as if on parade. One signal from my bugle and that battery was utterly destroyed. The few survivors ran back to their trenches on up the hill. The poor horses were all killed."[163]*

At that hour of the day, the animals most likely received their morning care and feed. Soldiers of the battery who stood close to them ensured both man and beast became targets. Without artillerists and horses, the guns were rendered unserviceable. Blackford mused: *"The guns did us no good as we could not get there, but they could not be used against our men and that was a great deal."[164]*

Lee soon found Longstreet, who was less than enthusiastic regarding continued engagements and hoped to maneuver from Gettysburg and force the Union army's pursuit. Lee desired that Longstreet and his command assault the Federal lines on Cemetery Ridge, despite the heavy casualties sustained the previous day. But this also left Longstreet's right flank open to counterattack. After some deliberation, Lee amended his orders and patched together the fresh Division of Major General George Pickett's Virginians, who arrived in the mid-afternoon hours of July 2 and were not utilized in the attacks. Major General Henry Heth's Division, now commanded by Brigadier General Johnston Pettigrew (Heth was wounded July 1) and a final division under the command of Major General Isaac Trimble previously under the command of Major General Dorsey Pender (who was mortally wounded on July 2), completed the assault force. This "improvised Corps" was placed under Longstreet's overall command, who saw the inherent problems of marching 12,500 infantry nearly one mile over open ground. Longstreet vigorously protested the poor prospects of success and subsequent needless loss of life. Despite these protests, Lee remained resolute in his plans and ordered the attack. Longstreet obeyed and planned the attack.[165] This attack is known by several names: Longstreet's Assault, the Pickett Pettigrew Trimble Charge, and lastly, and more notably Pickett's Charge.

---

163 Noah Andre Trudeau, "Eugene Blackford." *America's Civil War*, July 2001. 50-51.
164 Ibid., 51.
165 The controversy surrounding the attack plans on July 3rd to this very day generates heated debates. Many blame Longstreet for its failure, citing the orders were issued to attack as early as possible. A host of variables make this topic the subject matter of numerous publications readers and students can explore and formulate their own opinions.

On the opposite page: July 3rd, 1863. Longstreet's Assault (Pickett's Charge).

Map by Hal Jespersen.

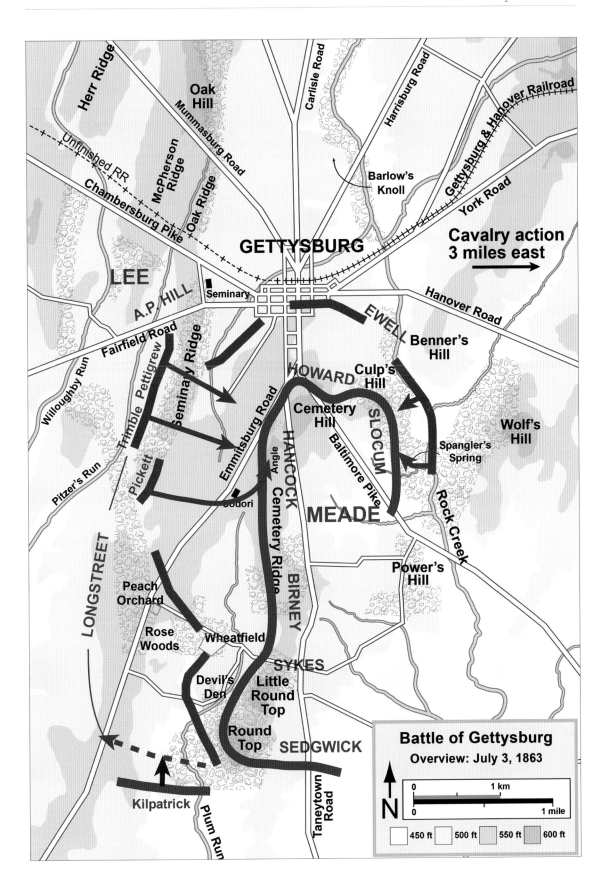

Battle of Gettysburg
Overview: July 3, 1863

July 3 proved to be the hottest day of the battle. By the afternoon hours, the temperature reached a scorching eighty-seven degrees. The oppressive humidity and the lack of any breeze added to the misery of man and equine, and both required rest and shelter from the sweltering heat. Some fortunate individuals can sleep in many adverse conditions if fatigued enough, and horses, like people, need time to rest and decompress.

Horses are unique creatures, as they can survive and function on about three hours of sleep per day. These animals also have a unique ability to sleep standing up. This is due to a "stay apparatus" inherent to these animals, which allows their limbs to lock. Often a person might see an equine standing with his eyes closed, with one hoof bent, which indicates the horse is probably sleeping. If the horse is in a relaxed non-threatening environment, it may often lie down and, also like humans, may enter a deeper sleep which is known as REM (rapid eye movement or dream state). Unfortunately, the noise and chaos of battle constantly loomed and frequent troop deployments required the service of the horse. These situations added to the wear and tear these animals endured and deprived them any opportunity for proper rest.

The large number of dead and wounded attracted flies that served to annoy each army and their mounts. One insect, the "horse-fly," whose bite makes even the stoutest horse cry out in pain, thrives in hot weather. These insects feed upon the blood of horses and can grow over an inch in size. Equipped with claw-like structures, they grasp onto the animal coat and skin and utilize their serrated mandibles to saw into the animal's flesh, which causes severe pain, in order to extract the blood on which they feast. The horse can use its tail, hooves, or it's vigorous shake reaction to drive these pests away, but once bitten, they may bolt or roll on the ground in a frenzy to rid themselves of this nuisance. Mounted persons then and now vigilantly watch and listen for these pests and work hard to repel or kill them. The equine, in most cases, does not mind the vigorous slap needed to destroy them; in fact, they often look at its master with an expression of gratitude.

The extreme summer heat increased the need for potable water, and the vast number of soldiers and horses taxed every local well. Many of the local streams, which provided water in large quantities, ran foul with blood and corpses. The amount of water needed for these animals approached a minimum of 400,000-800,000 gallons of water daily.[166] Horses and mules also require the proper number of calories, and they supplement their diets by grazing. In one day, if these equines received the appropriate ration of oats, corn, or barley, the amount needed equates to 960,000 pounds per day.[167] Horses and mules also require fodder for supportive nutrition as well as proper digestion. Hay can be supplied but grass also suffices. The armies allotted fourteen pounds per day per animal. This amounts to 1.12 million pounds per day. It is easy to see why Lee was unable to sit idle for a substantial period.

---

166 80,000 horses and mules requiring 5-10 gallons of water per day. 80,000 is an estimated number. This includes personal mounts, artillery, cavalry, remounts and wagons as well as mules. The amount of water required by horses like humans increases with activity and perspiration. Water is also critical in order to maintain proper digestion.

167 80,000 animals at 14 pounds per day.

In addition to the heat and humidity, rifle fire from both Union and Rebel troops emanated from the farm of William Bliss. The Bliss Farm sat on the western side of the Emmitsburg Road, almost an equal distance from Seminary Ridge and Cemetery Ridge. Possession of this area allowed the North and South to utilize the barn and house as a platform in which to sharp shoot (snipe) at their enemy. This farm exchanged hands several times since the afternoon hours on July 2. By the late morning hours, the Union army along Cemetery Ridge (both infantry and artillery) began to incur increased casualties and annoyance from the farm. The time came to rid the field of this contended site. Major General Winfield Scott Hancock gave permission to destroy the buildings if necessary. Now Colonel Thomas Smyth needed a volunteer to deliver the message to set the building ablaze. Captain James P. Postles of the 1st Delaware Infantry volunteered to deliver the message. He mounted his horse and directed the animal toward the barn.

For Postles, this ride was wrought with danger. A lone mounted soldier galloping in an open field presents as a target of opportunity. Horses naturally shy away from danger, so now Postles' mount faced a dilemma. Fired shots came from both his front and rear. Union forces returned fire when fired upon, and so it was with Confederate troops. It takes a great deal of courage to turn yourself a target, but Postles placed his mount in the same predicament, an animal that instinctively desired the opposite. The actions and cues Postles gave to his mount must be precise and properly timed. The animal must be kept in a constant state of movement in order to hamper the aim of enemy soldiers; to stop for any reason or length of time allowed Rebel marksman to find their mark. Postles recounted the events:

> *"I at once threw the reins over my horses head, mounted and rode off slowly down the lane, passed the little frame building in which the rebels were and crossed the Emmitsburg Road; and on reaching the field beyond, I put my horse into a gentle lope. As soon as I crossed the Emmitsburg Road, the enemy in the house opened fire on me, which grew hotter and hotter as I drew nearer to them, till it was a constant wonder and surprise to me that none of the bullets which I heard whistling around and so close to me, had hit me. I speedily concluded that the reason they did not hit me was that I was on horseback and in motion."*[168]

Horses respond to pressure and cues. Once they perform what is asked, the pressure is released. For example, if Postles wanted his horse to stop, he simply exerted pressure onto the bit and pulled the reins back. Once the animal came to a stop, he released the pressure and relaxed the reins. If Postles continued to pull back the reins, he is now cueing the animal to go backward. Simple enough. Moving the reins slightly forward with the application of leg, heel or spur pressure tells the animal to move forward. If done simultaneously—rein backward and vigorous application of spurs into the

---

168 W.F. Beyer and O.F. Keydel, *Medal of Honor: A History of Our Country's Recent Wars,* (Detroit, Michigan: The Perrien-Keydel Company, 1905) 228-229.

animal's sides—it immediately sends conflicting instructions, and in theory, the animal will stay in motion but confined to a smaller space. This is precisely what Postles did:

> *"It immediately flashed upon me that my only chance of safety was keeping my horse in motion, not letting him stand. So as I rode up in front of the barn, I threw my whole weight on the bridle rein, and at the same time raising both heels, sank my spurs deep into the horse's side and held them there. The poor brute, his sides torn up by my spurs and his mouth lacerated and bleeding from the cruel curb-bit, reared kicked and plunged, so that I was as bad a mark as though in full gallop."*[169]

Once the orders were delivered, Postles simply redirected his mount toward Cemetery Ridge, relaxed the reins while he kept the spurs dug into his animal, and they were quickly off to the relative safety of Union lines. Neither Postles nor his mount suffered injury. Captain James Parke Postles was later awarded the Medal of Honor for his actions that day.

Horseman galloping across a battlefield. 1860. Alfred Waud. LOC.

---

169 Ibid., 229.

With the Bliss Farm now engulfed in flames, an eerie calm came over the field. Final preparations for the Confederate bombardment and infantry assault slowly concluded. Soldiers and animals now tried to find time for a brief respite from the scorching heat and humidity.

LONGSTREET'S ASSAULT

General Lee issued orders that officers were to make the assault while dismounted to avoid unnecessary exposure to enemy fire.[170] The staff officers of Major General George Pickett's Division, Major Charles Pickett, Captain Baird, Captain Symington, and Captain Robert Bright were occupied as they delivered the orders to the Brigade commanders. Captain Robert Bright recalled the specific orders issued to Brigadier General James Kemper, which stated officers were to make the assault on foot, not horseback. There were several officers who did not heed these orders for various reasons. One was Kemper, who made the charge mounted. Colonel Lewis Williams of the 1st Virginia claimed to be unwell and unable to walk, so he rode his mare that day. Similar orders delivered to Brigadier General Richard B. Garnett's brigade also went unheeded by two officers: Colonel Eppa Hunton of the 8th Virginia, and Garnett. Both men were unwell and unable to negotiate the terrain on foot.[171]

Richard Garnett, prior to the Battle of Gettysburg, suffered a kick to his leg from a horse. In a letter dated June 21, 1863 to a Miss Dandridge, Garnett explained that *"I am partially hors de combat (out of combat) from a kick by a horse in the leg."*[172] In another letter to Miss Dandridge, dated June 25, 1863, he gave a brief update on the injury he sustained. *"I cannot ride on horseback yet and fear that I will not be able to do so for a week or more."*[173] It proved to be an accurate assessment, as Garnett still suffered from the effects of his injury on July 3. Whether a seasoned rider or novice, one of the greatest fears is to be "kicked." Whether or not the horse is trained, respect and caution are needed when entering the animal's personal space. A well-placed kick can prove fatal to people and even other horses. These injuries can break bones, lacerate skin, and cause trauma to soft tissue. In Garnett's case, he happened to be in the wrong place at the right time. It is not known whether the horse that injured his leg was his own mount or an animal whose path he crossed.

Many Confederates disregarded Lee's order. During this assault, the men who were known to be mounted were Major General George Pickett and his staff of Major Charles Pickett, Captain Baird, Captain Symington, and Captain Robert Bright, Brigadier

---

170 Eppa Hunton, *Autobiography of Eppa Hunton,* (Richmond Virginia: The William Byrd Press, Inc., 1933) 91.

171 Southern Historical Society *and* R.A. Brock, Southern Historical Society *Papers Vol. 31,* (Richmond, Virginia, 1903) Robert A. Bright Pickett's Charge. The Story of It as Told by a Member of His Staff. 229-230.

172 Letter from General Richard B. Garnett to Miss Dandridge June 21st, 1863. Bedinger-Dandridge Family Correspondence. Duke University. Courtesy Gettysburg National Military Park Library Files.

173 Letter from General Richard B. Garnett to Miss Dandridge June 25th, 1863. Bedinger-Dandridge Family Correspondence. Duke University. Courtesy Gettysburg National Military Park Library Files.

James Kemper, Brigadier General Richard B. Garnett, Colonel Lewis Williams, Colonel Eppa Hunton, Major General Issac Trimble, and Brigadier General Johnston Pettigrew. If we add into the equation staff officers of other commands who were charged with delivering orders and communications, that number climbed higher.[174] While Lee nor Longstreet participated directly in the charge, they were also mounted at various times.

As the hour approached 1:00 pm, the artillery was in position and the infantry utilized the tree line along Seminary Ridge, as well as its slopes for cover and concealment. With preparations completed, they awaited the inevitable bombardment and assault. Along Cemetery Ridge, Union soldiers rested and kept watch. General Meade, along with other officers and staff, finished lunch when two cannons fired from the vicinity of the Peach Orchard. Moments later, Confederate cannons numbering over 150 opened fire. The bombardment designed to weaken, demoralize, and drive away Federal troops from Cemetery Ridge and Hill had begun. Approximately eighty Union artillery pieces responded in turn as the largest artillery duel on American soil commenced.

The weather conditions did not aid either side; the smoke generated from these artillery pieces was enormous. The heat, humidity, and lack of any breeze ensured the smoke lingered like a dense morning fog and obscured the vision and fields of fire. Unable to properly sight and range their guns, the artillerists began to miss their targets. Confederate fire, in many cases, flew over its intended targets only to wreak havoc in the rear of the Union army along the Taneytown Road. Union cannons overshot their mark as well. This resulted in hundreds of casualties as the shells landed where the Rebel infantry had taken shelter. Sergeant Frederick Fuger of Battery, "A" 4th US Artillery, recalled the scene:

> *"The very earth shook beneath our very feet, and the hills and works seemed to reel like a drunken man. For one hour and a half this terrible firing was continued, during which time the shrieking of shells, the fragments of rocks flying through the air shattered from a stone fence in front of Battery "A"; The splash of bursting shells and shrapnel and the fierce neighing of wounded artillery horses, made a picture terrible, grand and sublime."*
>
> *Sergeant Fuger noted the loss in the Battery's horses was 83 out of 90.*[175]

While the storm of shot and shell fell upon both sides of the field, separate accounts of two generals, one North and one South, seemed to mirror the other. The first described Lt. General James Longstreet, in a letter penned by Brigadier General James Kemper in a post-war correspondence to General Edward Porter Alexander, in which he wrote:

---

174 James A. Hessler, Wayne E. Motts and Steven A. Stanley, *Pickett's Charge at Gettysburg. A Guide to the most Famous Attack in American History*, (El Dorado Hills, CA.: Savas Beatie LLC., 2015) 126. The number of mounted Confederates is listed as at least 15.

175 Fred Fuger, *Battle of Gettysburg and Personal Recollections of that Battle*, (Alexander S. Webb Papers, Yale University) 22-25. ALBG Library Files.

"During the firing of the artillery, (which yet reminds me of Milton's description of the war of artillery between the contending host of Heaven) I made my men lie flat down on the ground, a precaution which poorly protected them for the enemy's hail of shot pelted them and ploughed (sic) through them, and sometimes the fragments of a dozen mangled men were thrown in and about the trench left by a single missile. While this was going on, Longstreet rode slowly and alone immediately in front of our entire line. He sat his large charger with a magnificent grace and composure I never before beheld. This bearing was to me the grandest moral spectacle of the war. I expected to see him fall every instant. Still he moved on, slowly and majestically, with an inspiriting confidence, composure, self-possession and repressed power, in every movement and look, that fascinated me."[176]

Today the Equestrian Statue of Lt. General James Longstreet can be seen along West Confederate Avenue adjacent to Pitzer's Woods. Sculpted by Gary Casteel and dedicated on July 3, 1998, it depicts Longstreet similarly as James Kemper did, alone and isolated and intently viewing the field over which his men crossed. Longstreet's mount was named "Hero." The Longstreet memorial is incredibly unique in that is does not sit on a pedestal. This was by design. It allows visitors to get an "up close" look at the monument and allows for convenient maintenance.

What many visitors initially notice are the horse's hoofs, which perpetuates the myth and fate of the rider. Note that Longstreet not only survived the battle, he did so without injury, yet we see that Hero has not one but one-and-a-half hooves "up." What appears to be an apparent error is not an error at all, considering the myth of the horses' hoofs had been dispelled long ago.

Many visitors remark on the small stature of this animal compared to Longstreet's large frame. Lee's "Old Warhorse" was a large man standing roughly 6'2" and weighed at least 220 pounds. The animal that served as a model for "Hero" was a quarter horse Belgian mix, named "Summer," that stood over 15.5 hands in height. Mr. Casteel took measurements and weights to ensure the accuracy of the animal's appearance. The scene portrayed displays the animal reigned back from its forward movement as he and Longstreet slowed and turned toward the Union lines. These actions cause the neck, barrel, and hindquarters to have an "accordion-like effect" and gives some the illusion that the animal is smaller than average.[177]

---

176 James L. Kemper Letter to General E.P. Alexander. September 20th, 1869. Transcribed by Fred Tilberg. Dearborn Collection of Confederate Civil War Papers. Houghton Library, Harvard University. ALBG Library Files.

177 Gary Casteel, *It's About Time. The Sculpting of the General James Longstreet Memoria,* (Gettysburg, PA.: Four Winds Studio, 1998) Also an Interview with Gary Casteel by the author.

The Equestrian Statue of Lieutenant General James Longstreet. Photograph by the author.

A similar scenario occurred along Cemetery Ridge that involved Major General Winfield Scott Hancock. When the bombardment began, Hancock mounted his horse and rode along Cemetery Ridge, not only to help steady his men's resolve, but also to set an example. It was from this scene that Hancock was told by staff not to needlessly risk his life. Hancock then retorted, *"There are times when a Corps Commander's life does not count!"* While it was a memorable scene from the movie "Gettysburg," sometimes what is depicted and what happened are two entirely different accounts. Following Hancock's death in 1886, his wife, Almira, wrote "Reminiscences." It painted a somewhat different viewpoint:

> *"General Hancock rode along the line to encourage the men and see that everything was in a state of preparation. It was quite remarkable that the General's favorite horse, one he had ridden in many battles, became so terrified by the roar of artillery that he seemed utterly powerless and could not be moved by the severest spurring. The General was, therefore, obliged to borrow a horse from one of his staff-Captain Brownson. This horse was a very tall, light bay with a white nose, the General was riding when he was wounded."[178]*

---

178 Almira Hancock, *Reminiscences of Winfield Scott Hancock by His Wife,* (New York: Charles L. Webster and Company, 1887) 209.

Any animal that becomes unmanageable can put the rider and others at risk. Hancock recognized this as well as the potential effects on troop morale that "could" have happened had he not dismounted. In such situations, there is no shame in dismounting and procuring another mount.

For the next two hours, the cannonade continued. The Confederate bombardment did not have the desired effect. It caused some damage to the Union line along Cemetery Ridge, and many disabled cannons were withdrawn only to be replaced. The Union infantry sustained casualties as well, but not on the scale Lee envisioned. As a result, some 6000 Federal troops remained in command of the ridge, with thousands more in reserve. Later in the duel, the Federal artillery purposely slowed their rate of fire to give the impression that the Confederate plan had succeeded, but after nearly two hours, Rebel artillerists began to run low on the long-range ordinance. If they halted and attempted to replenish their store of ammunition, this also allowed the Federal Army to do the same, negating any gains made. When confronted with this information, James Longstreet silently nodded when asked by George Pickett if the assault was to commence. It was now 3:00 pm. The smoke began to lift. From the Union position on Cemetery Ridge, the spectacle was a grand sight to behold. 12,000 Confederate soldiers formed into a battle line nearly a mile wide, ranks dressed in parade-like precision.

From Seminary Ridge, the Confederates set their sights on a small cluster of trees, or "copse." This small copse of trees aided in guiding the assaulting columns. Their eventual goal—to turn northward with Cemetery Hill as the target. The terrain between Seminary and Cemetery Ridges has gentle rolling slopes and helped to shield Confederates as they advanced. The slopes provided a brief respite from the shells that boomed from Union gunners and allowed the Confederates to close and reform their ranks.

As they neared the Emmitsburg Road, however, Rebel troops began to lose the advantage the terrain provided. They were met with small arms fire from the advanced skirmish lines of Union soldiers. In Pickett's Division, the commander of the 8th Virginia, Colonel Eppa Hunton, sustained a wound to his right leg near the Codori House. The animal Hunton rode at that time received a wound that proved fatal. Hunton and his courier witnessed the suffering of this animal, which caused his courier to deliver the "coup de grace." Hunton's courier *"took the horse by the bridle and led him to the rear. Before he got beyond the range of musketry, he assisted father from the horse and shot the horse to put him out of his agony."*[179] Fortunately for Hunton the horse he rode that day was not his "personal" horse, who was named "Morgan." Morgan survived the battle and was utilized to pull a buggy that carried Hunton back to Virginia.[180]

---

179 Hunton, Eppa. Autobiography of Eppa Hunton. 1933. The William Byrd Press, Inc. Richmond, Virginia. Page 91. This work was dictated by the then 82-year-old veteran to his son, Eppa Hunton Jr.

180 Ibid., 101.

The Codori house and barn along the Emmitsburg Road. Seminary Ridge is the tree line in the background. Photo by the author.

William Tipton photograph of the "Copse of Trees" (far right side of the photo) as seen from the Emmitsburg Road. 1879. LOC.

Brigadier General James Kemper soon became a casualty as well. Kemper recalled that he *"got near enough to the first line of the enemy to distinguish features in the faces of the men in it, when I was shot from my horse."*[181] Despite the severity of his wound, Kemper survived the battle and was captured. Ironically, in a prisoner exchange that followed sometime after the battle, Kemper was exchanged for a Union General who also fell wounded from his mount in the Peach Orchard, and subsequently was captured by Confederates—Brigadier General Charles K. Graham.

---

181 James L. Kemper, Letter to General E.P. Alexander. September 20th, 1869. Transcribed by Fred Tilberg. Dearborn Collection of Confederate Civil War Papers. Houghton Library, Harvard University. ALBG Library Files.

Climbing the slope of Cemetery Ridge, the Copse of Trees visible to the right. The tree to the left marks the "Angle." Photograph by the author.

Brigadier General Richard B. Garnett neared the Union lines as he rode behind his men to help maintain their formation. Mounted on a bay Thoroughbred named "Red Eye," he presented like Kemper, a tempting target. Garnett was killed in action, but Red Eye is thought to have survived and bolted riderless to the rear. Garnett's body was never identified nor recovered following the battle. One individual, R.H. Irvine of the 19th Virginia Regiment, who was detailed as a courier to Garnett during the charge and witnessed his demise, shed light on this event:

> "I was quickly back at his (Garnett's) side, finding him within fifteen or twenty paces of the rock wall, a little to the right of the angle known as the "bloody angle "as we faced the enemy. Just as the General turned his horse's head to the left, he was struck in the head by a rifle or musket ball and fell dead from his horse, and almost at the same moment, a cannon shot from a Federal battery on the right struck my horse immediately behind the saddle, killing him and throwing his body over the General's body and me upon the ground. I dragged the body from between my horse's fore and hind feet."[182]

Irvine, in later years, met a former Union soldier named Smith, who claimed to have shot Garnett. At the conclusion of the assault, he ripped the insignia from Garnett's collar and took his sword. Thus, Garnett was never identified and was buried in a mass grave near where he fell.[183] According to the accounts of Private James W. Clay and Captain Archer Campbell of the 18th Virginia Infantry Regiment, *"General Garnett's*

---

182 R.H. Irvine, "Brigadier General Richard B. Garnett." *Confederate Veteran Magazine.* Volume XXIII, 1915. 391.

183 Ibid., 391.

black warhorse came galloping toward us with a huge gash in his right shoulder, evidently struck by a piece of shell. The horse in its mad flight jumped over Captain Cambell and me."[184]

As Pickett's Virginians attempted to carry the Union position, their numbers continued to dwindle. Brigadier General Lewis A. Armistead made the charge on foot. He, along with a few hundred men, managed to break through the stone wall and breach the Federal line. Armistead and the remnants of his command soon found themselves engaged with Union reinforcements who rushed into the melee. During this action, Armistead was wounded and captured (he subsequently died from his injuries on July 5). Not far from his position Winfield Scott Hancock, a close friend of Armistead, was still mounted. He was wounded and unhorsed by a shot that entered his right upper thigh. The round struck his saddle and sent a nail into him as well. He refused to be taken from the field until the conflict had ended.

As the charge neared its end, the divisions of Major General Issac Trimble and Brigadier Johnston Pettigrew experienced similar results. Both he and Pettigrew were mounted at the time. Trimble, in his diary, recalled:

> *"We had marched at right to ¼ mile of the works it is certain we could have carried them. As it was the enemy admit they 'shook in their shoes.' I was shot through the left leg on horseback near the close of the fight and my fine mare after taking me off the field died of the same shot-Poor Jinny, noble horse. I grieve to part thus with you."*[185]

The Hancock wounding marker, with the Codori barn in the backdrop. The tree line of Seminary Ridge lies in the distance. Photograph by the author.

184 Southern Historical Society *and* R.A. Brock, Southern Historical Society *Papers Vol. 33*, (Richmond, Virginia, 1903) 29.

185 Isaac R. Trimble, "The Civil War Diary of Isaac Ridgeway Trimble." *Maryland Historical Magazine. Volume XVII. No. 1.* March 1922. Page 12.

The wounding of Hancock. Tipton and Blocher. LOC.

Prior to the charge, Pettigrew, according to Captain William H. Bond, asked of his officers, *"Gentlemen, I will lead this charge, I presume, of course, you will want to ride with me."* Pettigrew was true to his word, and as his division closed on the Union position, he had his mount shot from under him. Pettigrew was later wounded in the hand. Every member of his staff endured the same fate.[186] Both man and beast became casualties in this assault. On horseback, soldiers sat approximately three to four feet above the men who marched and made an ideal target of opportunity. It was a death sentence to their equines, as the animal became collateral damage. Perhaps one North Carolinian described the concern he had for his own mount. Captain Louis G. Young wrote following the battle:

> *"My gallant mare, and that she was gallant, her groom, James R. Norwood, a colored man, now present, who was with me all during the war, and has been my friend and servant for forty years, can testify, had succumbed to three wounds; and do not think me heartless, when I tell you, that when I placed a wounded soldier on her and sent them out, the thoughts of my heart were more with the spirited animal which borne me bravely through many perils, than with my hurt comrade."[187]*

186 James I. Metts, *Longstreet's Charge at Gettysburg, PA. Pickett's, Pettigrew's and Trimble's Divisions,* (Wilmington, N.C.: Morning Star Print, 1899) 10.

187 Louis G. Young, *The Battle of Gettysburg. An Address by Captain Louis G Young.* 1866. (https://archive.org/details/unclibraries)

The Confederate viewpoint of Cemetery Ridge. The small marker in front of the stone wall marked the approximate location and furthest point made by the 26th North Carolina. Photograph by the author.

In less than one hour, it was over. The survivors fell back across the bloodstained field to the relative safety of Seminary Ridge. Robert E. Lee had witnessed the attack from a vantage point along Seminary Ridge today known as the "Point of Woods." Mounted on Traveller, Lee rode out among his shattered troops and accepted the blame for the loss. *"This has been all my fault."* He found George Pickett and issued orders to *"look to your Division."* Lee needed to prepare for a possible Union counterattack, but Pickett overcome with grief, only managed to state succinctly, *"General Lee, I have no division."*

The Confederates suffered heavy losses as a result of this assault. Approximately 12,500 soldiers participated in the charge. The casualty count: 50% killed, wounded, missing or captured. Between 1,100 and 1,200 Confederates were killed in action in less than one hour. Pickett, his staff and animals, managed to escape the torrent unscathed. Garnett was killed in action and Pettigrew, Kemper, and Trimble were all wounded. Trimble lost his leg and fell into Union hands as a prisoner along with Kemper, who was severely wounded. Pettigrew survived his injury only to be mortally wounded on July 14, 1863 during the Confederate retreat.

Their mounts were among the dead and wounded. Despite the defeat and dreadful cost which his men paid, Lee noticed the trivial, even when it came to horses. Arthur Fremantle, a British Colonel, who was present at Gettysburg as an observer with the Confederates mused in his writings: *"When a mounted officer began licking his horse for shying at the bursting of a shell, he called out, "Don't whip him, Captain; don't whip him. I've got just such another foolish horse myself, and whipping does no good."*[188]

---

188 Arthur J. Fremantle, *Three Months in the Southern States: April-June 1863*, (New York: J. Bradburn, successor to M. Doolady, 1864) 268.

Today, the Confederate State Memorials sit along Seminary Ridge. These works of art not only pay tribute to the bravery of the soldiers of each state, but also, they mark the Confederate battle lines. The first of these monuments to be dedicated was the *State of Virginia* on June 8, 1917. Perhaps the most striking monument on the field, it portrays seven soldiers from the state of Virginia, each from a different walk of life and each from a specific branch of service. Atop this monument sits the Equestrian Statue of General Robert E. Lee, mounted on Traveller.

The Virginia State Memorial. Located on Seminary Ridge along West Confederate Avenue.
Photograph by the author.

The seven figures located at the base of Virginia State Memorial. They represent soldiers who came from various walks of life and occupations. From left to right, they represent a professional, a mechanic, an artist, a boy, a businessman, a farmer, and a youth. The soldier on horseback represents the Cavalry; The soldier firing the pistol and the bugler depict Artillery;[189] The remaining three are from the Infantry. Photograph by the author.

This monument was designed by Frederick William Sievers. Sievers, who ensured an accurate depiction of Lee, studied photographs and life masks of Lee. He also studied the skeleton of Traveller as well as a live horse of the same breed, the saddlebred, that served as a model.[190] The statue portrays Lee surveying the field as he sits erect in his saddle with the reins relaxed. Traveller looks forward with his keen eyes focused toward the front and ears turned ahead and upright, both horse and its rider alert and awaiting the outcome of the battle.

Union officer, Lieutenant Frank A. Haskell, aide de camp of Brigadier General John Gibbon, was unwittingly in the direct path at the start of the Rebel artillery barrage. Haskell was lying on the ground dozing when the guns started to fire. His horse was nearby tied to a tree eating oats. Haskell went to fetch the animal and despite the carnage that took place, the horse continued to eat. He recounted the event:

189 David G Martin, *Confederate Monuments at Gettysburg. Volume I*, (New Jersey: Longstreet House Publishing, 1986) 57.

190 Frederick W. Hawthorne, *Gettysburg: Stories of Men and Monuments as Told by Battlefield Guides*, (Gettysburg, PA.: The Association of Licensed Battlefield Guides, 1988) 38.

Atop the Virginia State Memorial, sits General Robert Edward Lee mounted on Traveller. Photograph by the author.

"I called for my horse; nobody responded. I found him tied to a tree near-by, eating oats, with an air of the greatest composure, which under the circumstances, even then struck me as exceedingly ridiculous. He alone, of all beasts or men near, was cool. I am not sure but that I learned a lesson then from a horse. Anxious alone for his oats, while I put on the bridle and adjusted the halter, he delayed me by keeping his head down, so I had time to see one of the horses of our mess wagon struck and torn by a shell."[191]

191 Frank A. Haskell, *The Battle of Gettysburg*, (Wisconsin History Commission: Democrat Printing Co., 1910) 95-96.

From his vantage point, Haskell viewed both the eastern and western slopes of Cemetery Ridge and observed the damage inflicted upon man and horse. He described the carnage sustained by Battery I, 1st U.S. Artillery, under the command of Lieutenant George Woodruff, that sat in a small patch of trees called Ziegler's Grove:

> *"The great oaks there by Woodruff's guns heave down their massy branches with a crash, as if the lightning smote them. The shells swoop down among the battery horses standing there apart. A half a dozen horses start, they tumble, their legs stiffen, their vitals and blood smear the ground."[192]*

Then Haskell looked eastward toward the Taneytown Road where Meade's HQ sat, as well as farms, such as the William Patterson Farm and Peter Frey Farm. Both were utilized as field hospitals and did not escape the fury of the Confederate bombardment. Haskell remembered:

> *"All in rear of the crest for a thousand yards, as well as among the batteries, was the field of their blind fury. Ambulances, passing down the Taneytown Road with wounded men, were struck. The hospitals near this road were riddled. The house which was General Meade's headquarters was shot through several times, and a great many horses of officers and orderlies were lying dead around it. Riderless horses, galloping madly through the fields, were brought up or down by these invisible horse-tamers, and they would not run anymore."[193]*

Meade temporarily moved his HQ to nearby Powers Hill, and soon after the cannonade concluded, Meade was able to return to Cemetery Ridge for the climax of the assault. The Confederate attack had been repulsed with heavy losses to Lee's army. Union casualties amounted to approximately 1500 men. The loss in horseflesh was keenly felt by those defending the ridge.

In the short span of three hours, the First New York Battery under the command of Captain Andrew Cowan lost 14 horses. Battery A of the 4th U. S. Artillery under the command of Lieutenant Alonzo Cushing, (who was killed in action) lost eighty-three horses out of ninety. Chief of Artillery Brigadier General Henry Hunt estimated the overall loss in artillery animals at a staggering 881.[194] One animal that did not survive was Hunt's personal mount, "Bill." During the assault, Hunt was mounted astride "Bill," firing his revolver at Confederates as they approached. Captain Andrew Cowan relayed the scenario in a letter to John Bachelder in 1866:

> *"It may be an interesting fact that Gen. Hunt, Chief of Artillery of the Army, was in my battery when the enemy was closest, and while mounted on*

192 Ibid., 100.
193 Ibid., 103.
194 OR., Series I. Vol 27. Part 1. 241.

Alexander Gardner's photograph of the Leister house following the battle. Note the dead horses in the yard and along the Taneytown Road. LOC.

Dead artillery horses near the scene of Pickett's Charge. Edwin Forbes. LOC.

the back of his black horse was shooting Rebels with his revolver, till his horse was shot under him. And I then remounted him on one of my Sergeant's horses."[195]

Haskell's mount, "Dick" had also been hit several times and he described him after the repulse: *"He was literally covered with blood. Struck repeatedly, his right thigh had been ripped open in a ghastly manner by a piece of shell, and three bullets were lodged deep in his body, and from his wounds the blood oozed and ran down his sides and legs and with the sweat formed a bloody foam."*[196]

At right: Major General George Gordon Meade. Cemetery Ridge. Photograph by the author.

The Equestrian Statue of General George Gordon Meade, which sits atop Cemetery Ridge, close to the Leister Farm. Meade is mounted on Baldy, his trusted steed and friend. This monument was sculpted by Henry Kirke Bush-Brown and dedicated June 5th, 1896. Visitors today can see these timeless works of art (Lee and Meade) forever peering at each other over the hallowed grounds.[197]

Photograph by the author.

195 John B. Bachelder. David L. Ladd, Audrey J. Ladd, and Richard Allen Sauers, *The Bachelder papers: Gettysburg in Their Own Words Volume 1*, (Dayton, Ohio: Morningside House, Inc. 1994) 367-368. Letter of Captain Andrew Cowan 1st NY Independent Battery.

196 Frank A. Haskell, *The Battle of Gettysburg*, (Wisconsin History Commission: Democrat Printing Co., 1910) 161.

197 Frederick W. Hawthorne, *Gettysburg: Stories of Men and Monuments as Told by Battlefield Guides*, (Gettysburg, PA.: The Association of Licensed Battlefield Guides, 1988) 125.

EAST CAVALRY FIELD, SOUTH CAVALRY FIELD, AND FARNSWORTH'S CHARGE

The story of man and beast did not conclude with the repulse of Longstreet's assault on July 3, as a clash of cavalry took place three miles to the east and another on the southern end of the field. The carnage was far from over. In the afternoon of July 2, Lee's wayward Lieutenant J.E.B. Stuart finally arrived. Stuart received a frosty greeting from his commanding officer and then ordered to the left flank of Lt. General Richard Ewell's Second Corps. Stuart's men and horses were in want of rest and forage, but as these orders were carried out, and at approximately 11:00 am on July 3, Stuart's division of cavalry moved along Cress Ridge situated in the vicinity of the Hanover and Low Dutch Roads, three miles east of Gettysburg.

Stuart had four brigades of cavalry and artillery numbering approximately 4800 men. There they encountered the Union cavalry division of Brigadier General David Gregg. His command had been augmented by the presence of Brigadier General George A. Custer's Brigade of Michigan troopers. This gave Gregg about 3900 men, including artillery. The Union cavalry had been sent to the right flank of the Army of the Potomac and received word around noon that a large body of Confederate cavalry was seen moving to their right. The Federal cavalry dismounted and sent skirmishers forward toward Cress Ridge to probe for Rebel troops. The opposing sides soon exchanged fire, and an artillery duel ensued. As the melee escalated, Stuart ordered a full cavalry charge. Gregg and his command responded in kind and led countercharges towards troopers of Brigadier Generals Fitzhugh Lee and Wade Hampton's brigades. Brigadier General George A. Custer with his troopers, led his mounted "Wolverines" into the fray.

Left to right: Brigadier General George A. Custer, Major General J.E.B. Stuart, Brigadier General Wade Hampton. LOC.

East Cavalry Field. Map by Hal Jespersen.

Perhaps one of the most unnerving occurrences that a rider can experience is riding at full a gallop, which on a flat level surface may approach twenty-five to thirty miles per hour. Most people don't give this a second thought. After all, driving in a car at that speed is hardly noteworthy, but on horseback, it feels as though you are traveling much faster. To sit on a horse as it moves at this speed requires skill, dexterity, proper posture, and courage, coupled with a healthy dose of respect. The animal may need to leap over obstacles in its path, only further endangering the rider. A sudden stop or turn can send the rider hurling from the saddle, resulting in severe injury or even death. This was a real danger to the soldiers and officers during the battle—as well as it is for those on horseback in the modern age.

The cavalry, in this instance, galloped toward their foe, and if one adds the noise and confusion of battle, the risk of injury grew exponentially. The horse, if adequately desensitized, can learn to act as it is cued by the rider. One must consider the trooper may inadvertently injure his own mount from an improper swing of a saber or a careless mishandling of a firearm. A saber swung abruptly into the horse's field of view can startle the animal, too.

During training, the equine was gradually exposed to the saber; it is slowly brought into view, and like other startling objects, the horse will eventually learn not to react to its presence or motion. The same approach is used with small arms fire and cannon, as well as the sound of bugles and the fluttering of flags. The sense of touch enables the horse to feel every muscle in the trooper's body tense as other animals encroach into their personal space. While chaos surrounded them in battle, they learned to act based on the cue given to them, whether by boot, spur, or rein. Eventually, cavalry in both armies grew to appreciate the importance of training exercises, which in the beginning seemed pointless.

Now in the early afternoon, it was put to the test. Captain William E. Miller of the 3rd PA Cavalry described the scene:

> "Shell and shrapnel met the advancing Confederates and tore through their ranks. Closing the gaps though nothing happened, on they came. As they drew nearer, canister was substituted by our artillerymen for shell, and horse after horse staggered and fell. Still they came on. Our mounted skirmishers rallied and fell into line; the dismounted men fell back, and a few of them reached their horses. The First Michigan, drawn up in close column of squadrons near Pennington's Battery, was ordered by Gregg to charge. Custer, who was near, placed himself at its head, and off they dashed. As the two columns approached each other the pace of each increased, when suddenly a crash, like the falling of timber, betokened the crisis. So sudden and violent was the collision that many of the horses were turned end over end and crushed their riders beneath them."[198]

198 William Brooke, Rawle, *History of the Third Pennsylvania Cavalry, Sixtieth Regiment Pennsylvania Volunteers, in the American Civil War*, (Philadelphia: Franklin Printing Company, 1905) 300.

From the Confederate perspective, a similar picture was painted:

> *"Hampton, cool, with his noble eye flashing fire, rings out 'Charge them, my brave boys, charge them.' On his fiery trooper's dash, with gleaming sabres uplifted, with a wild deafening yell. The two hostile columns tilt together, with furious clashing of sabres, intermingled with the popping of pistols; horses and riders lock together in the dread melee, friend and foe fall and are crushed beneath the angry tread."*[199]

The clash of the cavalry on July 3 held each side in check. Stuart's mounted troopers were prevented from moving any further. By the time the engagement had ended, the artillery duel along Seminary and Cemetery Ridges had not yet concluded. Some speculate that had Longstreet's assault succeeded, Stuart's cavalry was positioned in a manner to threaten the rear of the Union Army. That was not the case. Longstreet's assault failed; no further exploits took place to the right of Meade's army. Toward the south of Gettysburg, however, another clash of cavalry and infantry soon began.

The Federal cavalry, under the command of Brigadier General Judson Kilpatrick, received orders at 5:30 pm to *"attack the enemy's right and rear with my whole command."*[200] Kilpatrick's Division consisted of the brigades of Brigadier General Elon Farnsworth, and Brigadier General George A. Custer.[201] Merritt's reserve brigade of Brigadier John Buford's Division, arrived approximately 3:00 pm on July 3 and engaged Confed-

Monument to the 3rd Pennsylvania Cavalry, East Cavalry Field. Photograph by the author.

199 Ulysses R. Brooks, *Stories of the Confederacy*, Columbia, South Carolina: The State Company, 1912) 176.

200 OR., Volume 27. Series I. Part I. 993.

201 Custer did not take part in this attack; His command remained to the east of Gettysburg.

erate infantry from Georgia in a series of cavalry charges. He had initial success, but ultimately the gains were short-lived. Elon Farnsworth's task took place over far worse terrain, such as wooded fields strewn with large rocks and stone fences. The area, defended by Texas and Alabama infantry, prevented the success of this cavalry attack and forced the retreat of the Federal troopers. Elon Farnsworth lost his life as he led his men. Major William Wells of the 1st Vermont Cavalry was awarded the Medal of Honor for his leadership and bravery that day.

Michigan Cavalry Brigade monument looking toward Cress Ridge (the Confederate position) and the fields over which the charge took place. Photograph by the author.

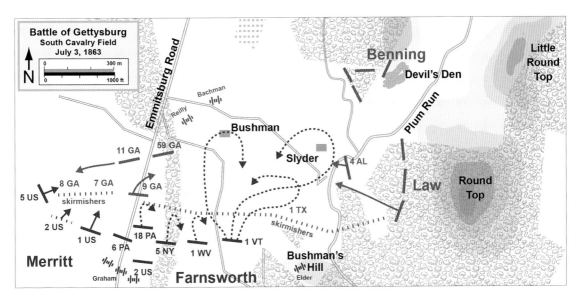

South Cavalry Field. Map by Hal Jespersen.

Portrait Statue of Major William Wells of the 1st Vermont Cavalry. Sculpted by J. Otto Schweitzer. Dedicated in 1913. Photograph by the author.

Below: Bas-relief below the Wells Statue. Wells is depicted to the left leading the charge with saber drawn. Farnsworth is to his right, falling mortally wounded from his mount. Photograph by the author.

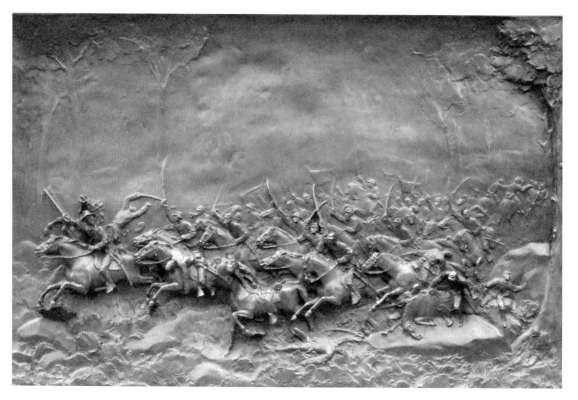

Monument to the 1st Vermont Cavalry. According to the monument's inscription, "Gen. Elon J. Farnsworth fell near this spot." Photograph by the author.

Left to right Brigadier Generals Wesley Merritt, Judson Kilpatrick, and Elon Farnsworth. LOC

CHAPTER 8

RETREAT AND AFTERMATH

The Battle of Gettysburg had ended. On the evening of July 3, heavy rains began to fall that continued through the following day. Lee began to plan his retreat to Virginia, and by the morning of July 5, he was underway. Lee had suffered approximately thirty percent casualties over the course of the battle. Now, his defeated and exhausted men must move as quickly as possible, taking with them supplies and thousands of Union prisoners, and a wagon train of wounded stretching for seventeen miles.

Lee depended upon his cavalry and mounted horseman more than ever to ensure the protection of his army. The mounted infantry of Brigadier General John Imboden's brigade spent the battle guarding the wagon trains of the Confederate army and were now utilized to help protect the supplies and wounded. J.E.B. Stuart's cavalry also played a role in protecting and screening the remaining supply wagons, infantry, and artillery. The weather did not aid Lee's retreat as torrential rains muddied the roads and resulted in wagons, soldiers, equines and mules sinking into the mire. Despite the rain and poor road conditions attacks were made by Union cavalry at Monterey Pass, which furthered the loss of life and depleted the number of horses and mules. Once the Confederates arrived at Williamsport, Lee found the Potomac River swollen and unable to be forded. Time and good fortune were needed to allow the river to subside enough to permit passage. The Confederates now prepared a defensive position from Williamsport to Falling Waters. The Confederate retreat, despite the attacks by Union cavalry, was made in an efficient manner.

Union General George Meade had won a victory. If Meade pursued Lee with vigor, perhaps he could further cripple the Army of Northern Virginia and force its surrender. This did not come without cost. The Army of the Potomac had suffered approximately 25 percent casualties. Meade's army had constantly marched and fought for three days of near-continuous combat. This undertaking had taken its toll, yet over the years, many have faulted Meade for not pursuing Lee with more effort, even though he did indeed pursue Lee. Major General John Sedgwick's Sixth Corps clashed with the rear guard of Lee's Army near the Fairfield Pass soon after the battle, and by July 6, the pursuit began in earnest. Brigadier General Henry Hunt wrote a letter in which he gave an account of the cautious nature of Meade's chase:

> "Our killed, wounded and missing 22,000, more than one fourth- very large portion of our artillery horses killed with batteries broken up by the loss of men and raw material. Ammunition running low-encumbered with the duty of burying the dead of both armies and caring for the wounded-embarrassed by the great number of prisoners we had captured and the necessity of bringing up the impediments from the far rear. All of these made our movements difficult. Then we couldn't move 'Straight' and movements depended more or less on those of the enemy. Our cavalry and artillery horses shod with contract nails, which would not hold a shoe on rocky ground for two days. Hence, after torturing the poor wretched horses, we had to submit to detention, what did the savings on a pound of horseshoe nails, say 3 or 4 cents to the contractor did deprive us of a team."[202]

As Ben Franklin had stated in Poor Richard's Almanac: "all for the want of a horseshoe nail." Meade eventually trapped Lee; however, the Army of Northern Virginia was finally able to ford the receded waters of the Potomac River, and on July 14, 1863, the last remnants of Lee's invasion force crossed the river at Williamsport and Falling Waters into relative safety. The sorry condition of his horses became apparent. In a correspondence to Lt. General James Longstreet, Lee impressed upon him the attention these animals needed:

> "I need not suggest to you the importance of causing every attention to be paid to your artillery and wagon horses, for, as little or no grain can be procured, it will be impossible for them to stand hard work without the utmost care and relief from all superfluous weight."[203]

Lee's post-battle concerns were not unfounded. In a correspondence to James A. Seddon, the Confederate Secretary of War, dated August 7, 1863, Lee wrote that due to transportation issues with freight trains and passenger trains, he received only one thousand bushels of grain per diem (day) for all of the animals of the army.[204] As the

---

202 Henry J. Hunt, Letter written to Eunice. July 28th, 1863. US Army Military History Institute Carlisle, PA. (Ford Papers) Gettysburg Military Park Library. (Henry Hunt Papers).

203 OR., Series I. Volume 27. Part 3. 1025.

204 OR., Series I. Volume 29. Part 2. 628.

Army of the Potomac continued into Virginia, Lee's scouts kept him appraised of their movements. Lee wrote to Confederate President Jefferson Davis on August 24, 1863:

"Nothing prevents my advancing now but the fear of killing our artillery horses. They are much reduced, and the hot weather and scarce forage keeps them so. The cavalry also suffer, and I fear to set them at work. Some days we get a pound of corn per horse and some days more; some none. Our limit is 5 pounds per day per horse." He later continued that "Everything is being done by me to that can be done to recruit the horses. I have been obliged to diminish the number of guns in the artillery and fear I shall have more to lose."[205]

The armies were now far from the town of Gettysburg, but the aftermath resulted in some 51,000 casualties.[206] This number is further divided into approximately 7,800 dead, 27,000 wounded, with 11,000 missing and captured. Many wounded were taken by Lee during the retreat, but a majority were left at Gettysburg with a small cadre of Union and Confederate medical staff, along with the local citizenry for care. The burial of the dead began in earnest. Many of the corpses had laid in the sun and heat since July 1, which resulted in an overwhelming stench. Burial details set out as soon as possible, and mass shallow graves were dug for the deceased soldiers. But what about the bodies of the deceased horses?

It is estimated that, at the very minimum, 3,000 horses perished. This does not include mules or the number of animals that either succumbed to their wounds, exposure or were euthanized.[207] If these numbers are added to the total numbers that perished throughout the campaign, that amount can easily exceed 5,000. Another example that illustrates the toll exacted upon these animals comes from the 16th Pennsylvania cavalry. During the period of October of 1862 through October of 1863, the 16th marched 1763 miles. They had receipts for a total of 1673 animals. This number further breaks down as follows:

Condemned and turned in: 679
Abandoned on Marches: 256
Killed in action: 47
Died of disease: 254
Captured by the enemy: 12
The number left at the end of October 1863: 425 [208]

205 Ibid., 665.
206 Casualties were killed, missing, wounded, and captured. Sources vary in the total numbers and subsequent breakdown.
207 Gregory, A. Cocco, *A Strange and Blighted Land. Gettysburg the Aftermath of a Battle,* (Gettysburg, PA: Thomas Publications, 1995) 82.
208 John Irvin Gregg, *The 16th Regiment of Pennsylvania Cavalry, For the Year Ending October 31st* (Philadelphia, PA: King and Baird Printers, 1864).

The above numbers are inclusive of the Battle of Gettysburg, although it is difficult to ascertain an exact count of the animals that were lost by this regiment during this battle. However, many of the townspeople and the remaining soldiers do give us a reasonable estimate. Soon after the battle had ended, local citizens and soldiers described the carnage that laid before them. Daniel Skelly, a teenager and local resident of Gettysburg, recalled the scene at General Meade's Headquarters (the home of Lydia Leister):

"Around the house and yard and below it lay at least 12 or 15 dead horses, shot down no doubt while aides and orderlies were delivering orders and messages to headquarters. A short distance below the house there was a stone fence dividing a field. Across this was hanging a horse which had been killed evidently just as he was jumping the fence, for its front legs were on one side and the hind legs on the other. In the road a short distance away was another horse which had been shot down while drawing an ambulance."[209]

Lydia Leister, whose house served as Meade's HQ, recounted to a visitor in 1865 the scene and subsequent aftermath:

"There was seventeen dead horses on my land. They burn five of 'em around my best peach tree and killed it; So I hadn't no peaches this year. The dead horses sp'iled(sic) my spring, so I had to have my well dug."
    She received, like property owners little if any governmental reimbursement for the damages; When asked, she simply replied, "Not much. I jest(sic) sold the bones of the dead horses. I couldn't do it till this year, for the meat hadn't off till yit(sic). I got fifty cents a hundred. There were seven hundred and fifty pounds. You can reckon up what they come to. That's all I got."[210]

Sarah Broadhead, a Gettysburg resident while en route to the Lutheran Seminary to offer aid to the wounded, remembered:

"what horrible sites present themselves on every side, the roads strewn with dead horses and the bodies of some men though the dead have nearly all been buried, and every step of the way giving evidence of the dreadful contest."[211]

209 Daniel Alexander Skelly, *A Boy's Experience During the Battles of Gettysburg* (Gettysburg, PA: Adams County Historical Society, 1932) 20-22.

210 J. T. Trobridge, "The Field of Gettysburg." *Atlantic Monthly*. Number 16. November 1865. Gettysburg National Military Park Library Files.

211 Sarah, M. Broadhead, *The Diary of a Lady of Gettysburg Pennsylvania From June 15 to July 15, 1863*. Adams County Historical Society. Page 16.

Mary Ziegler, the dorm matron of the Lutheran Theological Seminary, along with her children Lydia and Hugh were taken by wagon to the vicinity of the Round Tops while returning to Gettysburg following the battle. From the Round Tops, she decided to walk the remaining three miles. The sights and odors she experienced overwhelmed her as she related:

> *"Pen cannot describe the awful sights that met our gaze on that day. The dying and dead were all around us—men and beasts. We could count as high as twenty dead horses lying side by side. Imagine, if you can, the stench of one dead animal lying in the hot July sun for days. Here they were by the hundreds."[212]*

Along Cemetery Ridge, Captain Martin Stone of the of the 2nd Pennsylvania Cavalry noted, *"I found the ground all along the lines strewn with dead horses and in many places dead bodies. From one elevation I counted one hundred dead horses."[213]*

William T. Livermore of the 20th Maine Infantry Regiment moved with the remnants his unit toward the Emmitsburg Road. They moved toward the former position of the Rebel lines and then returned. He stated that, *"to speak safely there was one thousand dead horses that were all swollen and the smell of the horses and men was dreadful."* He soon found himself near the Trostle Farm. He remembered the sights:

> *"The ground every foot of it was covered with men, horses clothing cartridge boxes canteen guns bayonets scattered cartridges cannon balls everywhere. Caissons stood where the horses were instantly killed by a cannon ball and they piled up on the pole just as they were killed in some places on the bigness of your house there would be 8 or 10 horses & from 3 to 8 men where there guns stood one place in particular where the 5th "9th" Mass. Battery stood within three rods of a house. 19 horses lay in the bigness of your barn yard. Some of their head others their legs & some there thighs torn way."[214]*

Some of these animals indeed were buried, but others were set ablaze. The burial of the soldiers and care of the wounded took precedent. Benson Lossing visited the battlefield and wrote that:

---

212 Ziegler, Lydia Clare Ziegler and Hugh Zeigler, *The Dead and Dying Were All Around Us. Stories from the Lutheran Theological Seminary During the Battle of Gettysburg and its Aftermath.* Adams County Historical Society.

213 Diary of Captain Martin Stone, Co. I, 2nd Pennsylvania Cavalry. Gettysburg National Military Park Library Files.

214 William T. Livermore, Letter to Charles Livermore, July 6, 1863. Gettysburg National Military Park Library. See also Gregory, A. Cocco, *A Strange and Blighted Land. Gettysburg the Aftermath of the Battle.* Gettysburg, PA: Thomas Publications, 1995) 50.

"those of the horses, some untouched and some a consuming fire, were scattered thickly over the field, especially where Hancock's Batteries were, and along the Taneytown Road, near Meade's headquarters." He estimated on his tour that he had encountered no less than two hundred of *"these noble brutes, many of them on fire, the smoke of which, with the effluvium of decomposition everywhere filled the whole region of Gettysburg with unpleasant odors."*[215]

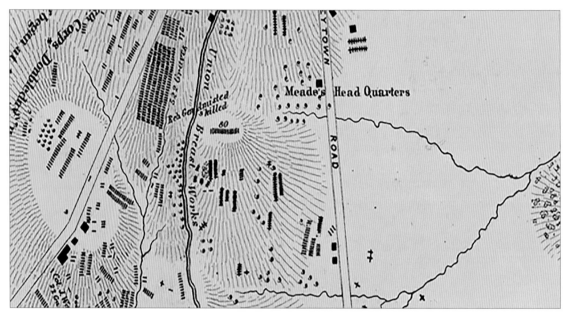

Elliot Burial Map showing a section near Meade's HQ and Cemetery Ridge. It shows both Union and Confederate burial positions. Horses were marked by the symbol that resembles a small 'g.' LOC.

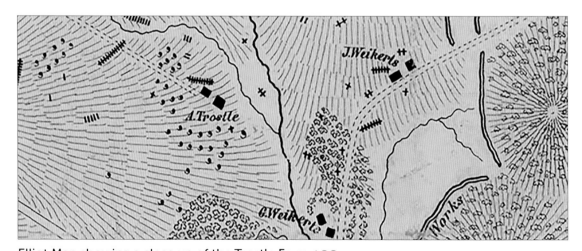

Elliot Map showing a close up of the Trostle Farm. LOC.

215 Benson Lossing, *Scenes on the Battlefield*. July 1863. Page 77. Adams County Historical Society.

CHAPTER 9

"The world will little note nor long remember what we say here but it can never forget what they did here."
— PRESIDENT ABRAHAM LINCOLN

REMEMBRANCE

The dead and debris of battle were gradually removed. The Union dead were exhumed and reburied on a parcel of land atop Cemetery Hill, which today is the Soldiers National Cemetery. 3512 reinterments, of which 979 were unable to be identified, now rest beneath the soil they defended.

On November 19, 1863, the day of dedication of the cemetery, Edward Everett gave the keynote address to a crowd estimated to approach 15,000 people. It was preceded by a parade from the town square along Baltimore Street. In that parade was one very tall person who was mounted on a horse that was too small for him, his feet nearly touching the ground. This man sat patiently while Everett delivered a two-hour-long speech. Perhaps the crowd that gathered that day were more curious to hear not Everett's speech but the man who spoke after. With little fanfare, Abraham Lincoln stood up, and in just over two minutes, delivered the most recognized speech given in American history, *The Gettysburg Address*.

Parade preceding the dedication of the Soldiers National Cemetery November 19th, 1863. Looking north along Baltimore Street. LOC.

THE GETTYSBURG ADDRESS

"Four score and seven years ago our fathers brought forth on this continent, a new nation, conceived in Liberty, and dedicated to the proposition that all men are created equal.

Now we are engaged in a great civil war, testing whether that nation, or any nation so conceived and so dedicated, can long endure. We are met on a great battlefield of that war. We have come to dedicate a portion of that field, as a final resting place for those who here gave their lives that that nation might live. It is altogether fitting and proper that we should do this.

But, in a larger sense, we can not dedicate—we can not consecrate—we can not hallow—this ground. The brave men, living and dead, who struggled here, have consecrated it, far above our poor power to add or detract. The world will little note, nor long remember what we say here, but it can never forget what they did here. It is for us the living, rather, to be dedicated here to the unfinished work which they who fought here have thus far so nobly advanced. It is rather for us to be here dedicated to the great task remaining before us—that from these honored dead we take increased devotion to that cause for which they gave the last full measure of devotion—that we here highly resolve that these dead shall not have died in vain—that this nation, under God, shall have a new birth of freedom—and that government of the people, by the people, for the people, shall not perish from the earth."

In 1864 the Gettysburg Battlefield Memorial Association was founded by David McConaughy, with its mission to preserve this historic land. Eventually, memorials, monuments, and cannons began to dot the landscape marking and memorializing this landmark battle. In 1895, the War Department took over the management of the field, after Major General Daniel Sickles pushed legislation through Congress to the desk of the President of the United States. Once signed by President Cleveland, Gettysburg National Military Park came into existence. Roads were placed and parcels of land that were significant to the history of the battle were added, which continue to this very day. The field is now managed by the National Park Service (NPS) under the auspices of the Department of the Interior, which occurred in 1933.

Today, the field has changed little. Ongoing efforts through the NPS and the Gettysburg Foundation ensure this great field will endure for years to come. Visitors to Gettysburg have numerous choices in which they can view the ground and pay tribute to the memories of Union and Confederate veterans. Guests can take advantage of the many free programs offered by Park Rangers throughout the year, especially during the Spring, Summer, and Fall.

The Gettysburg Foundation hosts not only a world-class museum but also the Cyclorama. This enormous painting (completed in 1883 by French artist Paul Philippoteaux) depicts Pickett's Charge and is brought to life through real-time narration. Battlefield tours are also available through the Gettysburg Foundation or the Association of Licensed Battlefield Guides. Battlefield Guides at Gettysburg are licensed by the NPS to conduct tours on this hallowed ground, bringing the battle to life from either bus, the privacy of your own car, bicycle, on foot, and many other modes of transportation.

The last mode of touring the field should be the least surprising, via horseback and horse-drawn carriage. There are several "horse" tour companies available, and most of these tours are given by Licensed Battlefield Guides who take the rider on the trails less

Horse drawn carriage in Devil's Den. LOC.

traveled and seen by the general public.[216] The tours also provide the riders a newfound appreciation of these incredible animals. Horse owners currently have the privilege of trailering their own animals to Gettysburg and riding them on the near seventeen miles of horse trails that traverse the battlefield.[217]

216 Tours are seasonal and book quickly. Contact each stable for rates, terms and restrictions.
217 For details, please visit https://www.nps.gov/gett/planyourvisit/horseback-riding-trails.htm for park rules and a complete map of the current trail network. Contact information is provided on this site for those wishing to contact the park directly for any additional questions or concerns.

"In the end, we don't know what horses can do. We only know that when, over the past thousands of years, we have asked something more of them, at least some of them have readily supplied it."

— JANE SMILEY

EPILOGUE

The story of the horse did not begin at Gettysburg, nor does it end there. After the conclusion of the American Civil War, the populace of the horse began its recovery, only to be followed by more wars in which they were again prepared for battle. This continued into the twentieth century, and even to the battlefields of WWII. If, but for a moment, we consider the bond between man and beast, we can begin to appreciate their sacrifice and the impact the horses had on those who rode them.

The horse depended on its master, and its master, in turn, depended on the horse. To witness one of these animals severely wounded and writhing in pain, neighing and whinnying while looking to you, its friend and companion for any aid or succor, was more than many could bear. Knowing it will not survive, you have but one recourse. You produce a pistol or rifle, and as a last act of kindness, and with one quick pull of the trigger, you end its misery by ending the life of your loyal friend and companion. This animal had a name, and now, its own quirks and personality live only in your memory.

Today, horses, like many animals, fall victim to abuse and neglect. Many may not raise a hand to the horse, but the financial inconvenience of owning the animal may cause them to be neglected or abused, nonetheless. To some, horses who are middle aged or older have outlived any usefulness to their former owners. These animals may be auctioned or sold to kill pens, where they are butchered for their meat. With growing public awareness however, many equines are saved by horse rescues every year and are given (as Lincoln expressed) a new birth of freedom.

We expected much from them, now much is expected from society. We continue to see the benefits that arise from interacting with these animals. They can serve as mounts or sometimes just as a faithful friend. In some instances, horses are utilized to rehabilitate prisoners, who learn to develop a bond of trust, accountability, and respect. Disabled Veterans and those with post-traumatic stress disorder can also benefit from their non-judgmental natures and companionship. Adults, the elderly, and children with physical, emotional and learning disabilities benefit from interacting with these animals, as they can be trained to be gentle giants. Perhaps one day, society will genuinely appreciate these animals and realize the benefits they offer. Perhaps then, they will be "Prepared for Battle" no more, forever.

"Colonel." This animal survived 18 battles of the Civil War including Gettysburg. He was the mount of Colonel Norman Hall, of the Second Corps, Army of the Potomac. LOC.

"Then I saw heaven standing open, and there before me was a white horse. And its rider is called Faithful and True. With righteousness He judges and wages war."

—REVELATION 19:11

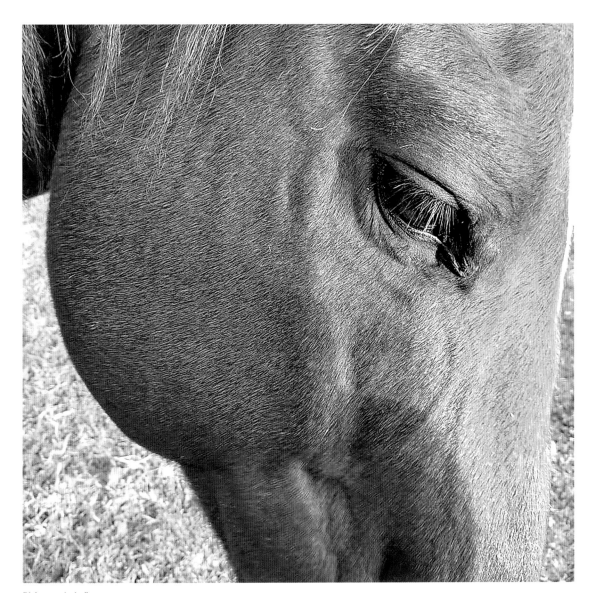

"Maverick."

APPENDIX
Order of Battle

ARMY OF THE POTOMAC

(k) Killed, (w) wounded, (mw) mortally wounded,
(c) captured, (MOH) Medal of Honor

Major General George G. Meade, **Commanding**
Maj. Gen. Daniel Butterfield, **Chief of Staff**
Brig. Gen. Gouverneur K. Warren, **Chief of Engineers**
Brig. Gen. Henry Hunt, **Chief of Artillery**
Brig. Gen. Marsena R. Patrick, **Provost Marshall General**
Brig. Gen. Seth Williams, **Asst. Adjutant General**
Brig. Gen. Rufus Ingalls, **Chief Quartermaster**
Dr. Jonathan Letterman, **Medical Director**
Capt. Lemuel B. Norton, **Chief Signal Officer**
Lieut. John R. Eadie, **Acting Chief Ordnance Officer**
93rd New York Infantry- Col. John S. Crocker
8th United States Infantry (8 cos.)- Capt. Edwin W.H. Read
2nd Pennsylvania Cavalry- Col. R. Butler Price
6th Pennsylvania Cavalry (Co's E and I)- Capt. Emlen N. Carpenter, Capt. James Starr
HQ Guard: Co. C, 32nd Massachusetts Infantry- Capt. Josiah C. Fuller
HQ Escort: Oneida (NY) Cavalry- Capt. Daniel P. Mann
Engineer Brigade- Brig. Gen. Henry W. Benham
    15th New York Engineers- Maj. Walter L. Cassin
    50th New York Engineers- Col. William H. Pettes
    US Engineer Battalion- Capt. George H. Mendell

FIRST ARMY CORPS

Maj. Gen. John F. Reynolds (k), Maj. Gen. Abner Doubleday, Maj. Gen. John Newton
Escort: Company L, 1st Maine Cavalry- Capt. Constantine Taylor

FIRST DIVISION- Brig. Gen. James S. Wadsworth
First Brigade ("Iron Brigade")- Brig. Gen. Solomon Meredith (w); Col. William W. Robinson.
   19th Indiana Infantry- Col. Samuel J. Williams
   24th Michigan Infantry- Col. Henry A. Morrow (w), Capt. Albert M. Edwards
   2nd Wisconsin Infantry- Col. Lucius Fairchild (w), Maj. John Mansfield (w), Capt. George H. Otis
   6th Wisconsin Infantry- Lt. Col. Rufus R. Dawes
   7th Wisconsin Infantry- Col. William W. Robinson, Maj. Mark Finnicum
Second Brigade -Brig. Gen. Lysander Cutler
   7th Indiana Infantry- Col. Ira G. Grover
   76th New York Infantry- Maj. Andrew J. Grover (k), Capt. John E. Cook
   84th New York Infantry (14th Militia)- Col. Edward B. Fowler
   95th New York Infantry- Col. George H. Biddle(w), Maj. Edward Pye
   147th New York Infantry- Lt. Col. Francis C. Miller (w), Maj. George Harney
   56th Pennsylvania Infantry (9 cos.)- Col. J. William Hoffman

SECOND DIVISION- Brig. Gen. John C. Robinson
First Brigade- Brig. General Gabriel R. Paul (w), Col. Samuel H. Leonard (w), Col. Adrian R. Root (w), Col. Richard Coulter (w), Col. Peter Lyle
   16th Maine Infantry- Col. Charles W. Tilden, Maj. Archibald D Leavitt
   13th Massachusetts Infantry- Col. Samuel H. Leonard, Lt. Col. N. Walter Batchelder
   94th New York Infantry- Col. Adrian R. Root, Maj. Samuel A. Moffett
   104th New York Infantry- Col. Gilbert G. Prey
   107th Pennsylvania Infantry- Lt. Col. James M. MacThomson (w), Capt. Emanuel D. Roath
Second Brigade- Brig. Gen. Henry Baxter
   12th Massachusetts Infantry- Col. James L. Bates (w), Lt. Col. David Allen, Jr.
   83rd New York Infantry (9th Militia)- Lt. Col. Joseph A. Moesch
   97th New York Infantry- Col. Charles Wheelock (w/c), Maj. Charles Northrup
   11th Pennsylvania Infantry- Col. Richard Coulter, Capt. Benjamin F. Haines (w), Capt. John B. Overmyer
   88th Pennsylvania Infantry- Maj. Benezet F. Foust (w), Capt. Edmund A. Mass (c), Capt. Henry Whiteside
   90th Pennsylvania Infantry- Col. Peter Lyle, Maj. Alfred J. Sellers (MOH)

THIRD DIVISION- Maj. Gen. Abner Doubleday, Brig. Gen. Thomas A. Rowley
First Brigade- Brig. Gen. Thomas A. Rowley, Col. Chapman Biddle
   80th New York Infantry (20th Militia)- Col. Theodore B. Gates
   121st Pennsylvania Infantry- Col. Chapman Biddle, Maj. Alexander Biddle
   142nd Pennsylvania Infantry- Col. Robert P. Cummins (mw), Lt. Col. A. B. McCalmont
   151st Pennsylvania Infantry- Lt. Col. George F. McFarland (w), Capt. Walter F. Owens, Col. Harrison Allen
Second Brigade ("Bucktail Brigade")- Col. Roy Stone (w), Col. Langhorne Wister (w), Col. Edmund L. Dana
   143rd Pennsylvania Infantry- Col. Edmund L. Dana, Lt. Col. John D. Musser

149th Pennsylvania Infantry- Lt. Col. Walton Dwight (w), Capt. James Glenn

150th Pennsylvania Infantry- Col. Langhorne Wister (w), Lt. Col. Henry S. Huidekoper (w), Capt. Cornelius C. Widdis

Third Brigade (Second Vermont Brigade)- Brig. Gen. George J. Stannard (w), Col. Francis V. Randall

12th Vermont Infantry- Col. Asa Blunt

13th Vermont Infantry- Col. Francis V. Randall, Maj. Joseph J. Boynton, Lt. Col. William D. Munson (w)

14th Vermont Infantry- Col. William T. Nichols

15th Vermont Infantry- Col. Redfield Proctor

16th Vermont Infantry- Col. Wheelock G. Veazey (MOH)

Artillery Brigade- Col. Charles S. Wainwright

Battery B, 2nd Maine Light Artillery- Capt. James A. Hall

Battery E, 5th Maine Light Artillery- Capt. Greenleaf T. Stevens (w), Lt. Edward N. Whittier

Battery L, 1st New York Light Artillery- Capt. Gilbert H. Reynolds (w), Lt. George Breck

Battery B, 1st Pennsylvania Light Artillery- Capt. James H. Cooper

Battery B, 4th United States Artillery, Battery B- Lt. James Stewart

SECOND ARMY CORPS

Maj. Gen. Winfield S. Hancock (w), Brig. Gen. John Gibbon (w)

Escort: Co's D and K, 6th New York Cavalry- Capt. Riley Johnson

FIRST DIVISION- Brig. Gen. John C. Caldwell

First Brigade- Col. Edward E. Cross (mw), Col. H. Boyd McKeen

5th New Hampshire Infantry- Lt. Col. Charles E. Hapgood

61st New York Infantry- Col. K. Oscar Broady

81st Pennsylvania Infantry- Lt. Col. Amos Stroh

148th Pennsylvania Infantry- Col. H. Boyd McKeen, Lt. Col. Robert McFarlane

Second Brigade ("Irish Brigade")- Col. Patrick Kelly

28th Massachusetts Infantry- Col. Richard Byrnes

63rd New York Infantry (2 cos.)- Lt. Col. Richard C. Bentley (w), Capt. Thomas Touhy

69th New York Infantry (2 cos.)- Capt. Richard Moroney (w), Lt. James J. Smith

88th New York Infantry (2 cos.)- Capt. Denis F. Burke

116th Pennsylvania Infantry (4 cos.)- Maj. St. Clair A. Mulholland

Third Brigade- Brig. General Samuel K. Zook (mw), Lieut. Col. John Fraser

52nd New York Infantry- Lt. Col. Charles G. Freudenberg (w), Maj. Edward Venuit (k), Capt. William Scherrer

57th New York Infantry- Lt. Col. Alford B. Chapman

66th New York Infantry- Col. Orlando H. Morris (w), Lt. Col. John S. Hammell (w), Maj. Peter Nelson

140th Pennsylvania Infantry- Col. Richard P. Roberts (k), Lt. Col. John Fraser

Fourth Brigade- Col. John R. Brooke (w)

27th Connecticut Infantry (2 cos.)- Lt. Col. Henry C. Merwin (k) , Maj. James H. Coburn

2nd Delaware Infantry- Col. William P. Bailey, Capt. Charles H. Christman

64th New York Infantry- Col. Daniel G. Bingham (w), Maj. Leman W. Bradley

53rd Pennsylvania Infantry - Lt. Col. Richard McMichael

145th Pennsylvania Infantry (7 cos.)- Col. Hiram L. Brown (w), Capt. John W. Reynolds (w), Capt. Moses W. Oliver

SECOND DIVISION- Brig. Gen. John Gibbon (w), Brig. Gen. William Harrow
First Brigade- Brig. Gen. William Harrow, Col. Francis E. Heath
    19th Maine Infantry- Col. Francis E. Heath (w), Lt. Col. Henry W. Cunningham
    15th Massachusetts Infantry- Col. George H. Ward (mw), Lt. Col. George C. Joslin
    1st Minnesota Infantry- Col. William C. Colvill, Jr., Capt. Nathan S. Messick (k), Capt. Henry C. Coates. 2nd Company Minnesota Sharpshooters attached
    82nd New York Infantry (2nd Militia)- Lt. Col. James Huston (k), Capt. John Darrow
Second Brigade ("Philadelphia Brigade")- Brig. Gen. Alexander S. Webb
    69th Pennsylvania Infantry- Col. Dennis O'Kane (mw), Capt. William Davis
    71st Pennsylvania Infantry- Col. Richard Penn Smith
    72nd Pennsylvania Infantry- Col. De Witt C. Baxter (s), Lt. Col. Theodore Hesser
    106th Pennsylvania Infantry- Lt. Col. William L. Curry
Third Brigade- Col. Norman J. Hall
    19th Massachusetts Infantry- Col. Arthur F. Devereaux
    20th Massachusetts Infantry- Col. Paul J. Revere (mw), Lt. Col. George N. Macy (w), Capt. Henry L. Abbott
    7th Michigan Infantry- Lt. Col. Amos E. Steele, Jr. (k), Maj. Sylvanus W. Curtis
    42nd New York Infantry- Col. James E. Mallon
    59th New York Infantry- Lt. Col. Max A. Thoman (mw), Capt. William McFadden
    Unattached: 1st Company, Massachusetts Sharpshooters- Capt. William Plummer, Lt. Emerson L. Bicknell

THIRD DIVISION- Brig. General Alexander Hays
First Brigade- Col. Samuel S. Carroll
    14th Indiana Infantry- Col. John Coons
    4th Ohio Infantry- Lt. Col. Leonard W. Carpenter
    8th Ohio Infantry-Lt. Col. Franklin Sawyer
    7th West Virginia Infantry- Lt. Col. Jonathan H. Lockwood
Second Brigade- Col. Thomas A. Smyth (w), Lt. Col. Francis E. Pierce
    14th Connecticut Infantry - Maj. Theodore G. Ellis
    1st Delaware Infantry- Lt. Col. Edward P. Harris, Capt. Thomas B. Hizar (w), Lieut. William Smith (k), Lt. John D. Dent
    12th New Jersey Infantry- Maj. John T. Hill
    10th New York Battalion- Maj. George F. Hopper
    108th New York Infantry- Lt. Col. Francis E. Pierce
Third Brigade- Col. George L. Willard (k), Col. Eliakim Sherrill (mw), Lieut. Col. James L. Bull
    39th New York Infantry (4 cos.)- Maj. Hugo Hildebrandt
    111th New York Infantry- Col. Clinton D. MacDougall (w), Lt. Col. Isaac M. Lusk (w), Capt. Aaron B. Seeley
    125th New York Infantry- Lt. Col. Levin Crandall
    126th New York Infantry- Col. Eliakim Sherrill, Lt. Col. James L. Bull
Artillery Brigade- Capt. John G. Hazard
    Battery B, 1st New York Light Artillery and 14th New York Battery- Capt. James K. Rorty (k), Lt. Albert S. Sheldon (w), Lt. Robert E. Rogers
    Battery A, 1st Rhode Island Artillery- Capt. William A. Arnold
    Battery B, 1st Rhode Island Artillery- Lt. T. Fred Brown
    Battery I, 1st United States Artillery- Lt. George A. Woodruff (mw), Lieut. Tully McCrea
    Battery A, 4th United States Artillery- Lt. Alonzo H. Cushing (k), Sgt. Frederick Fuger

THIRD ARMY CORPS

Maj. Gen. Daniel E. Sickles (w), Maj. Gen. David B. Birney (w)

FIRST DIVISION- Maj. Gen. David B. Birney, Brig. Gen. J. H. Hobart Ward
First Brigade- Brig. Gen. Charles K. Graham (m/c), Col. Andrew H. Tippin
    57th Pennsylvania Infantry (8 cos.)- Col. Peter Sides (w), Capt. Alanson H. Nelson
    63rd Pennsylvania Infantry- Maj. John A. Danks
    68th Pennsylvania Infantry- Col. Andrew H. Tippin, Capt. Milton S. Davis
    105th Pennsylvania Infantry- Col. Calvin A. Craig
    114th Pennsylvania Infantry- Lt. Col. Frederick F. Cavada (w), Capt. Edward R. Bowen
    141st Pennsylvania Infantry- Col. Henry J. Madill
Second Brigade-Brig. Gen. J. H. Hobart Ward, Col. Hiram Berdan
    20th Indiana Infantry- Col. John Wheeler (mw) , Lt. Col. William C. L. Taylor
    3rd Maine Infantry - Col. Moses B. Lakeman
    4th Maine (Col. Elijah Walker (), Capt. Edward Libby
    86th New York Infantry- Lt. Col. Benjamin L. Higgins
    124th New York Infantry- Col. Van Horne Ellis (k), Lt. Col. Francis L. Cummins
    99th Pennsylvania Infantry- Maj. John W. Moore
    1st United States Sharpshooters- Col. Hiram Berdan, Lt. Col. Casper Trepp
    2nd United States Sharpshooters (8 cos.)- Maj. Homer R. Stoughton
Third Brigade- Col. P. Regis De Trobriand
    17th Maine Infantry -Lt. Col. Charles B. Merrill
    3rd Michigan Infantry- Col. Byron R. Pierce(w); Lt. Col. Edward S. Pierce
    5th Michigan Infantry- Lt. Col. John Pulford (w)
    40th New York Infantry- Col. Thomas W. Egan (w)
    110th Pennsylvania (6 cos.)- Lt. Col. David M. Jones (w), Maj. Isaac Rogers

SECOND DIVISION- Brig. Gen. Andrew A. Humphreys
First Brigade- Brig. Gen. Joseph B. Carr
    1st Massachusetts Infantry- Lt. Col. Clark B. Baldwin
    11th Massachusetts Infantry- Lt. Col. Porter D. Tripp
    16th Massachusetts Infantry- Lt. Col. Waldo Merriam (w), Capt. Matthew Donovan
    12th New Hampshire Infantry- Capt. John F. Langley
    11th New Jersey Infantry- Col. Robert McAllister (w), Capt. Luther Martin (k), Capt. William H. Lloyd (w), Capt. Samuel T. Sleeper, Lt. John Schoonover (w)
    26th Pennsylvania Infantry-Maj. Robert L. Bodine
    84th Pennsylvania Infantry- Lt. Col. Milton Opp (*Train guard, not present at Gettysburg*)
Second Brigade- Col. William R. Brewster
    70th New York Infantry- Col. J. Egbert Farnum
    71st New York Infantry- Col. Henry L. Potter (w)
    72nd New York Infantry- Col. John S. Austin (w), Lt. Col. John Leonard
    73rd New York Infantry- Maj. Michael W. Burns
    74th New York Infantry- Lt. Col. Thomas Holt
    120th New York Infantry- Lt. Col. Cornelius D. Westbrook (w), Maj. John R. Tappen
Third Brigade- Col. George C. Burling
    2nd New Hampshire Infantry- Col. Edward L. Bailey (w)
    5th New Jersey Infantry- Col. William J. Sewell (w), Capt. Thomas C. Godfrey, Capt. Henry H. Woolsey (w)

6th New Jersey Infantry- Lt. Col. Stephen R. Gilkyson

7th New Jersey Infantry- Col. Louis R. Francine (mw), Maj. Fred Cooper

8th New Jersey Infantry- Col. John Ramsey (w), Capt. John G. Langston

115th Pennsylvania Infantry- Maj. John P. Dunne

Artillery Brigade- Capt. George E. Randolph (w), Capt. A. Judson Clark

2nd Battery B, 1st New Jersey Light Artillery- Capt. A. Judson Clark, Lt. Robert Sims

Battery D, 1st New York Light Artillery- Capt. George B. Winslow

4th New York Independent Battery- Capt. James E. Smith

Battery E, 1st Rhode Island Light Artillery- Lt. John K. Bucklyn (w), Lt. Benjamin Freeborn (w)

Battery K, 4th United States Artillery- Lt. Francis W. Seeley (w), Lt. Robert James

FIFTH ARMY CORPS

Maj. Gen. George Sykes

FIRST DIVISION- Brig. Gen. James Barnes, Brig. Gen. Charles Griffin

First Brigade- Col. Williams S. Tilton

18th Massachusetts Infantry -Col. Joseph Hayes

22nd Massachusetts Infantry- Lt. Col. Thomas Sherwin, Jr. 2nd Company of Massachusetts Sharpshooters Attached.

1st Michigan Infantry- Col. Ira C. Abbott (w), Lt. Col. William A. Throop

118th Pennsylvania Infantry- Lt. Col. James Gwyn

Second Brigade- Col. Jacob B. Sweitzer

9th Massachusetts Infantry- Col. Patrick R. Guiney

32nd Massachusetts Infantry- Col. George L. Prescott

4th Michigan Infantry- Col. Harrison H. Jeffords (mw), Lt. Col. George W. Lumbard

62nd Pennsylvania Infantry- Lt. Col. James C. Hull

Third Brigade- Col. Strong Vincent (mw), Col. James C. Rice

20th Maine Infantry- Col. Joshua L. Chamberlain

16th Michigan Infantry- Lt. Col. Norval E. Welch

44th New York Infantry- Col. James C. Rice, Lt. Col. Freeman Conner

83rd Pennsylvania Infantry- Capt. Orpheus S. Woodward

SECOND DIVISION- Brig. Gen. Romeyn B. Ayres

First Brigade- Col. Hannibal Day

3rd United States Infantry (6 cos.)- Capt. Henry W. Freedley (w) , Capt. Richard G. Lay

4th United States Infantry (4 cos.)- Capt. Julius W. Adams, Jr.

6th United States Infantry (5 cos.)- Capt. Levi C. Bootes

12th United States Infantry (8 cos.)- Capt. Thomas S. Dunn

14th United States Infantry (8 cos.)- Maj. Grotius R. Giddings

Second Brigade- Col. Sidney Burbank

2nd United States Infantry (6 cos.)- Maj. Arthur T. Lee (w), Capt. Samuel A. McKee

7th United States Infantry (4 cos.)- Capt. David P. Hancock

10th United States Infantry (3 cos.)- Capt. William Clinton

11th United States Infantry (6 cos.)- Maj. DeLancey Floyd-Jones

17th United States Infantry (7 cos.)- Lt. Col. J. Durell Greene

Third Brigade- Brig. Gen. Stephen H. Weed (mw), Col. Kenner Garrard

140th New York Infantry- Col. Patrick O'Rorke(k), Lt. Col. Louis Ernst

146th New York Infantry- Col. Kenner Garrard, Lt. Col. David T. Jenkins
91st Pennsylvania Infantry- Lt. Col. Joseph H. Sinex
155th Pennsylvania Infantry- Lt. Col. John H. Cain

THIRD DIVISION- Brig. Gen. Samuel W. Crawford
First Brigade- Col. William McCandless
 1st Pennsylvania Reserves (9 cos.)- Col. William C. Talley
 2nd Pennsylvania Reserves- Lt. Col. George A. Woodward
 6th Pennsylvania Reserves- Lt. Col. Wellington H. Ent
 13th Pennsylvania Reserves- Col. Charles F. Taylor (k), Maj. William R. Hartshorne
Third Brigade- Col. Joseph W. Fisher
 5th Pennsylvania Reserves- Lt. Col. George Dare
 9th Pennsylvania Reserves- Lt. James McK. Snodgrass
 10th Pennsylvania Reserves- Col. Adoniram J. Warner
 11th Pennsylvania Reserves- Col. Samuel M. Jackson
 12th Pennsylvania Reserves (9 cos.)- Col. Martin D. Hardin
Artillery Brigade- Capt. Augustus P. Martin
 Battery C, 3rd Massachusetts Light Artillery- Lt. Aaron F. Walcott
 Battery C, 1st New York Light Artillery- Capt. Almont Barnes
 Battery L, 1st Ohio Light Artillery- Capt. Frank C. Gibbs
 Battery D, 5th United States Artillery- Lt. Charles E. Hazlett (k), Lieut. Benjamin F. Rittenhouse
 Battery I, 5th United States Artillery- Lt. Malbone F. Watson (w), Lt. Charles C. MacConnell

SIXTH ARMY CORPS

Maj. Gen. John Sedgwick

FIRST DIVISION- Brig. Gen. Horatio G. Wright
First Brigade- Brig. Gen. Alfred T. A. Torbert
 1st New Jersey Infantry- Lt. Col. William Henry, Jr.
 2nd New Jersey Infantry- Lt. Col. Charles Wiebecke
 3rd New Jersey Infantry- Col. Henry W. Brown
 4th New Jersey Infantry (7 cos.)- Maj. Charles Ewing (*Train guard, not present at Gettysburg*)
 15th New Jersey Infantry- Col. William H. Penrose
Second Brigade- Brig. Gen. Joseph J. Bartlett
 5th Maine Infantry- Col. Clark S. Edwards
 121st New York Infantry- Col. Emory Upton
 95th Pennsylvania Infantry- Lt. Col. Edward Carroll
 96th Pennsylvania Infantry- Maj. William H. Lessig
Third Brigade- Brig. Gen. David A. Russell
 6th Maine Infantry- Col. Hiram Burnham
 49th Pennsylvania Infantry (4 cos.) - Lt. Col. Thomas L. Hulings
 119th Pennsylvania Infantry- Col. Peter S. Ellmaker
 5th Wisconsin Infantry- Col. Thomas S. Allen

SECOND DIVISION- Brig. Gen. Albion P. Howe
Second Brigade (First Vermont Brigade)- Col. Lewis A. Grant
 2nd Vermont Infantry- Col. James H. Walbridge
 3rd Vermont Infantry- Col. Thomas O. Seaver

4th Vermont Infantry- Col. Charles B. Stoughton
5th Vermont Infantry- Lt. Col. John R. Lewis
6th Vermont Infantry- Col. Elisha L. Barney
Third Brigade- Brig. Gen. Thomas H. Neill
    7th Maine Infantry (6 cos.)- Lt. Col. Selden Connor
    33rd New York Infantry (detach.) - Capt. Henry J. Gifford
    43rd New York Infantry- Lt. Col. John Wilson
    49th New York Infantry- Col. Daniel D. Bidwell
    77th New York Infantry- Lt. Col. Winsor B. French
    61st Pennsylvania Infantry- Lt. Col. George F. Smith

THIRD DIVISION- Maj. Gen. John Newton, Brig. Gen. Frank Wheaton
First Brigade- Brig. Gen. Alexander Shaler
    65th New York Infantry- Col. Joseph E. Hamblin
    67th New York Infantry- Col. Nelson Cross
    122nd New York Infantry- Col. Silas Titus
    23rd Pennsylvania Infantry- Lt. Col. John F. Glenn
    82nd Pennsylvania Infantry- Col. Isaac C. Bassett
Second Brigade- Col. Henry L. Eustis
    7th Massachusetts Infantry- Lt. Col. Franklin P. Harrow
    10th Massachusetts Infantry- Lt. Col. Joseph B. Parsons
    37th Massachusetts Infantry- Col. Oliver Edwards
    2nd Rhode Island Infantry- Col. Horatio Rogers, Jr.
Third Brigade- Brig. Gen. Frank Wheaton, Col. David J. Nevin
    62nd New York Infantry- Col. David J. Nevin
    93rd Pennsylvania Infantry- Maj. John I. Nevin
    98th Pennsylvania Infantry- Maj. John B. Kohler
    139th Pennsylvania Infantry- Col. Fredrick H. Collier
Artillery Brigade- Col. Charles H. Tompkins
    Battery A, 1st Massachusetts Light Artillery- Capt. William H. McCartney
    1st New York Independent Battery- Capt. Andrew Cowan
    3rd New York Independent Battery- Capt. William A. Harn
    Battery C, 1st Rhode Island Light Artillery-Capt. Richard Waterman
    Battery G, 1st Rhode Island Light Artillery- Capt. George A. Adams
    Battery D, 2nd United States Artillery-Lt. Edward B. Williston
    Battery G, 2nd United States Artillery- Lt. John H. Butler
    Battery F, 5th United States Artillery- Lt. Leonard Martin

ELEVENTH ARMY CORPS

Maj. Gen. Oliver O. Howard, Maj. Gen. Carl Schurz

FIRST DIVISION- Brig. Gen. Francis C. Barlow (w), Brig. Gen. Adelbert Ames
First Brigade- Col. Leopold von Gilsa
    41st New York Infantry (9 cos.)- Lt. Col. Detleo Von Einsiedal
    54th New York Infantry- Maj. Stephen Kovacs (c), Lt. Ernst Both
    68th New York Infantry- Col. Gotthilf Bourry
    153rd Pennsylvania Infantry- Maj. John F. Frueauff

Second Brigade- Brig. Gen. Adelbert Ames, Col. Andrew L. Harris
    17th Connecticut Infantry- Lt. Col. Douglas Fowler (k), Maj. Allen G. Brady
    25th Ohio Infantry Lt. Col. Jeremiah Williams (c), Capt. Nathaniel J. Manning (w), Lt. William Maloney, Lt. Israel White
    75th Ohio Infantry- Col. Andrew L. Harris, Capt. George B. Fox
    107th Ohio Infantry- Col. Seraphim Meyer, Capt. John M. Lutz

SECOND DIVISION- Brig. Gen. Adolph von Steinwehr
First Brigade- Col. Charles R. Coster
    134th New York Infantry- Lt. Col. Allan H. Jackson
    154th New York Infantry- Lt. Col. Daniel B. Allen
    27th Pennsylvania Infantry- Lt. Col. Lorenz Cantador
    73rd Pennsylvania Infantry- Capt. Daniel F. Kelley
Second Brigade- Col. Orlando Smith
    33rd Massachusetts Infantry- Col. Adin B. Underwood
    136th New York Infantry- Col. James Wood, Jr.
    55th Ohio Infantry- Col. Charles B. Gambee
    73rd Ohio Infantry- Lt. Col. Richard Long

THIRD DIVISION- Maj. Gen. Carl Schurz, Brig. Gen. Alexander Schimmelfennig
First Brigade- Brig. Gen. Alexander Schimmelfennig (m), Col. George Von Amsberg
    82nd Illinois Infantry- Col. Edward S. Salomon
    45th New York Infantry- Col. George Von Amsberg, Lt. Col. Adolphus Dobke
    157th New York Infantry- Col. Philip P. Brown, Jr.
    61st Ohio Infantry- Col. Stephen J. McGroarty
    74th Pennsylvania Infantry- Col. Adolph Von Hartung, Lt. Col. Alexander von Mitzel (w), Capt. Gustav Schleiter, Capt. Henry Krauseneck
Second Brigade- Col. Wladimir Krzyzanowski
    58th New York Infantry- Lt. Col. August Otto (w), Capt. Emil Koenig
    119th New York Infantry- Col. John T. Lockman (w), Lt. Col. Edward F. Lloyd
    82nd Ohio Infantry- Col. James S. Robinson (w), Lt. Col. David Thomson
    75th Pennsylvania Infantry- Col. Francis Mahler (mw), Major August Ledig
    26th Wisconsin Infantry- Lt. Col. Hans Boebel (w), Capt. John W. Fuchs
Artillery Brigade- Maj. Thomas W. Osborn
    Battery I, 1st New York Light Artillery- Capt. Michael Weidrich
    13th New York Independent Battery- Lieut. William Wheeler
    Battery I, 1st Ohio Light Artillery- Capt. Hubert Dilger
    Battery K, 1st Ohio Light Artillery- Capt. Lewis Heckman
    Battery G, 4th United States Artillery- Lt. Bayard Wilkeson (mw), Lt. Eugene A. Bancroft

TWELFTH ARMY CORPS

Maj. Gen. Henry W. Slocum, Brig. Gen. Alpheus S. Williams

FIRST DIVISION- Brig. Gen. Alpheus S. Williams, Brig. Gen. Thomas H. Ruger
First Brigade- Col. Archibald L. McDougall
    5th Connecticut Infantry- Col. Warren W. Packer
    20th Connecticut Infantry- Lt. Col. William B. Wooster
    3rd Maryland Infantry- Col. Joseph M. Sudsburg

123rd New York Infantry- Lt. Col. James C. Rogers, Capt. Adolphus H. Tanner

145th New York Infantry- Col. Edward J. Price

46th Pennsylvania Infantry- Col. James L. Selfridge

Second Brigade- Brig. Gen. Henry H. Lockwood

1st Maryland Infantry, Potomac Home Brigade- Col. William P. Maulsby

1st Maryland Infantry, Eastern Shore- Col. James Wallace

150th New York Infantry- Col. John H. Ketcham

Third Brigade- Brig. Gen. Thomas H. Ruger, Col. Silas Colgrove

27th Indiana Infantry- Col. Silas Colgrove, Lt. Col. John R. Fesler

2nd Massachusetts Infantry- Lt. Col. Charles R. Mudge (k), Maj. Charles F. Morse

13th New Jersey Infantry- Col. Ezra A. Carman

107th New York Infantry- Col. Nirom M. Crane

3rd Wisconsin Infantry- Col. William Hawley

SECOND DIVISION- Brig. Gen. John W. Geary

First Brigade- Col. Charles Candy

5th Ohio Infantry- Col. John H. Patrick

7th Ohio Infantry- Col. William R. Creighton

29th Ohio Infantry- Capt. Wilbur F. Stevens (w), Capt. Edward Hayes

66th Ohio Infantry- Lieut. Col. Eugene Powell

28th Pennsylvania Infantry- Capt. John H. Flynn

147th Pennsylvania Infantry (8 cos.)- Lt. Col. Ario Pardee, Jr.

Second Brigade- Col. George A. Cobham, Jr., Brig. Gen. Thomas L. Kane

29th Pennsylvania Infantry- Col. William Rickards, Jr.

109th Pennsylvania Infantry- Capt. Frederick L. Gimber

111th Pennsylvania Infantry- Lt. Col. Thomas L. Walker, Col. George A. Cobham, Jr.

Third Brigade- Brig. Gen. George S. Greene

60th New York Infantry- Col. Abel Godard

78th New York Infantry- Lt. Col. Herbert Von Hammerstein

102nd New York Infantry- Col. James C. Lane (w), Capt. Lewis R. Stegman

137th New York Infantry- Col. David Ireland

149th New York Infantry- Col. Henry A. Barnum, Lt. Col. Charles B. Randall (w), Capt. Nicholas Grumbach

Artillery Brigade- Lt. Edward D. Muhlenberg

Battery M, 1st New York Light Artillery- Lt. Charles E. Winegar

Battery E, Independent Pennsylvania Light Artillery- Lt. Charles A. Atwell

Battery F, 4th United States Artillery- Lt. Sylvanus T. Rugg

Battery K, 5th United States Artillery-Lt. David H. Kinzie

CAVALRY CORPS

Maj. Gen. Alfred Pleasonton

FIRST DIVISION- Brig. Gen. John Buford

First Brigade- Col. William Gamble

8th Illinois Cavalry- Maj. John L. Beveridge

12th Illinois Cavalry (6 cos.)- Col. George H. Chapman

3rd Indiana Cavalry (6 cos.)- Col. George H. Chapman
8th New York Cavalry- Lt. Col. William L. Markell
Second Brigade- Col. Thomas C. Devin
6th New York Cavalry- Maj. William E. Beardsley
9th New York Cavalry- Col. William Sackett
17th Pennsylvania Cavalry Col. Josiah H. Kellogg
3rd West Virginia Cavalry (2 cos.)- Capt. Seymour B. Conger
Reserve Brigade- Brig. Gen. Wesley Merritt
6th Pennsylvania Cavalry- Maj. James H. Haseltine
1st United States Cavalry- Capt. Richard S. C. Lord
2nd United States Cavalry- Capt. Theophilus F. Rodenbough
5th United States Cavalry- Capt. Julius W. Mason
6th United States Cavalry- Maj. Samuel H. Starr (w), Lt. Louis H. Carpenter, Lt. Nicholas Nolan,
Capt. Ira W. Claflin

SECOND DIVISION- Brig. Gen. David M. Gregg
First Brigade- Col. John B. McIntosh
1st Maryland Cavalry (11 cos.)- Lt. Col. James M. Deems
Purnell (Maryland) Legion Co. (A) (Capt. Robert E. Duvall
1st Massachusetts Cavalry- Lieut. Col. Greely S. Curtis
1st New Jersey Cavalry- Maj. Myron H. Beaumont
1st Pennsylvania Cavalry- Col. John P. Taylor
3rd Pennsylvania Cavalry- Lt. Col. Edward S. Jones
Battery H (One Section), 3rd Pennsylvania Artillery- Capt. William D. Rank
Second Brigade- Col. Pennock Huey (*Guarding trains and railroads, not present at Gettysburg*)
2nd New York Cavalry- Lt. Col. Otto Harhaus
4th New York Cavalry- Lt. Col. Augustus Pruyn
6th Ohio Cavalry (10 cos.)- Maj. William Stedman
8th Pennsylvania Cavalry- Capt. William Corrie
Third Brigade- Col. J. Irvin Gregg
1st Maine Cavalry (10 cos.)- Lt. Col. Charles H. Smith
10th New York Cavalry- Maj. M. Henry Avery
4th Pennsylvania Cavalry- Lt. Col. William E. Doster
16th Pennsylvania Cavalry- Lt. Col. John K. Robinson

THIRD DIVISION- Brig. Gen. Judson Kilpatrick, Col. Nathaniel P. Richmond
First Brigade- Brig. Gen. Elon J. Farnsworth
5th New York Cavalry- Maj. John Hammond
18th Pennsylvania Cavalry- Lt. Col. William P. Brinton
1st Vermont Cavalry- Lt. Col. Addison W. Preston
1st West Virginia Cavalry (10 cos.)- Col. Nathaniel P. Richmond, Maj. Charles E. Capehart
Second Brigade- Brig. Gen. George A. Custer
1st Michigan Cavalry- Col. Charles H. Town
5th Michigan Cavalry- Col. Russell A. Alger
6th Michigan Cavalry- Col. George Gray
7th Michigan Cavalry (10 cos.)- Col. William D. Mann

HORSE ARTILLERY

First Brigade- Capt. James M. Robertson
    9th Michigan Battery- Capt. Jabez J. Daniels
    6th New York Independent Battery- Capt. Joseph W. Martin
    Batteries B & L, 2nd United States Artillery- Lt. Edward Heaton
    Battery M, 2nd United States Artillery- Lt. A. C. M. Pennington, Jr.
    Battery E, 4th United States Artillery- Lt. Samuel S. Elder
Second Brigade- Capt. John C. Tidball
    Batteries E & G, 1st United States Artillery- Capt. Alanson M. Randol
    Battery K, 1st United States Artillery- Capt. William M. Graham
    Battery A, 2nd United States Artillery- Lt. John H. Calef
    Battery C, 3rd United States Artillery- Lt. William D. Fuller (With Huey's Cavalry Brigade arrives July 4)

ARTILLERY RESERVE

Brig. Gen. Robert O. Tyler, Capt. James M. Robertson

First Regular Brigade- Capt. Dunbar R. Ransom
    Battery H, 1st United States Artillery- Lt. Chandler P. Eakin
    Batteries F & K, 3rd United States Artillery- Lt. John G. Turnbull
    Battery C, 4th United States Artillery- Lt. Evan Thomas
    Battery C, 5th United States Artillery- Lt. Gulian V. Weir (w)
First Volunteer Brigade- Lt. Col. Freeman McGilvery
    5th Battery, Massachusetts Light Artillery- Capt. Charles A. Phillips
    9th Battery, Massachusetts Light Artillery- Capt. John Bigelow
    15th New York Independent Battery- Capt. Patrick Hart
    Batteries C & F, Pennsylvania Independent Light Artillery- Capt. James Thompson
Second Volunteer Brigade- Capt. Elijah D. Taft
    Battery B 1st Connecticut Heavy Artillery- Capt. Albert Brooker (Not engaged. Remained in Westminster, Md).
    Battery M 1st Connecticut Heavy Artillery-Captain Franklin A. Pratt (Not engaged. Remained in Westminster Md).
    2nd Connecticut Battery- Capt. John W. Sterling
    5th New York Independent Battery- Capt. Elijah D. Taft
Third Volunteer Brigade- Capt. James F. Huntington
    1st Battery, New Hampshire Light Artillery- Capt. Frederick M. Edgell
    Battery H, 1st Ohio Light Artillery- Lt. George W. Norton
    Batteries F & G, 1st Pennsylvania Light Artillery- Capt. R. Bruce Ricketts
    Battery C, 1st West Virginia Light Artillery- Capt. Wallace Hill
Fourth Volunteer Brigade- Capt. Robert H. Fitzhugh
    6th Battery (F), Maine Light Artillery- -Lt. Edwin B. Dow
    Battery A, 1st Maryland Light Artillery- Capt. James H. Rigby
    Battery A, 1st New Jersey Light Artillery- Lt. Agustin N. Parsons
    Battery G, 1st New York Light Artillery- Capt. Nelson Ames
    Battcry K, 1st New York Light Artillery and 11th New York Independent Battery - Capt. Robert H. Fitzhugh

192   *The Horse at Gettysburg*

ARMY OF THE NORTHERN VIRGINIA

(k) Killed, (w) wounded, (mw) mortally wounded, (c) captured

ARMY HEADQUARTERS

Gen. Robert E. Lee
Escort: 39th Virginia Cavalry Battalion (2 cos)
Chief of Staff, Inspector General: Col. Robert H. Chilton
Chief of Artillery: Brig. Gen. William N. Pendleton
Medical Director: Dr. Lafayette Guild
Chief of Ordnance: Lt. Col. Briscoe G. Baldwin
Chief of Commissary: Lt. Col. Robert G. Cole
Chief Quartermaster: Lt. Col. James L. Corley
Judge Advocate General: Maj. Henry E. Young
Military Secretary, Acting Asst. Chief of Artillery: Col. Armistead L. Long
Aide de Camp, Asst. Adjutant General: Lt. Col. Walter H. Taylor
Aide de Camp, Asst. Military Secretary: Maj. Charles Marshall
Aide de camp, Asst. Inspector General: Maj. Charles S. Venable
Engineer Officer: Capt. Samuel R. Johnston

FIRST CORPS

Lt. Gen. James Longstreet

McLAWS' DIVISION- Maj. Gen. Lafayette McLaws
Kershaw's Brigade- Brig. Gen. Joseph B. Kershaw
    2nd South Carolina Infantry- Col. John D. Kennedy (w), Lt. Col. F. Gaillard
    3rd South Carolina Infantry- Col. J. D. Nance, Maj. Robert C. Maffett
    7th South Carolina Infantry- Col. D. Wyatt Aiken
    8th South Carolina Infantry- Col. John W. Henagan
    15th South Carolina Infantry- Col. William DeSaussure (k), Maj. William M. Gist
    3rd South Carolina Infantry Battalion- Lt. Col. William G. Rice
Semmes' Brigade- Brig. Gen. Paul J. Semmes (mw), Col. Goode Bryan
    10th Georgia Infantry- Col. John B. Weems
    50th Georgia Infantry- Lt. Col. Francis Kearse (mw), Maj. Peter A.S. McClashan
    51st Georgia Infantry- Col. Edward Ball
    53rd Georgia Infantry- Col. James P. Simms
Barksdale's Brigade- Brig. Gen. William Barksdale (mw/c), Col. Benjamin G. Humphreys
    13th Mississippi Infantry- Col. John W. Carter (k)
    17th Mississippi Infantry- Col. William D. Holder (w), Lt. Col. John C. Fiser (w)
    18th Mississippi Infantry- Col. Thomas M. Griffin(w), Lt. Col. William H. Luse (c)
    21st Mississippi Infantry- Col. Benjamin G. Humphreys
Wofford's Brigade- Brig. Gen. William T. Wofford
    16th Georgia Infantry- Col. Goode Bryan
    18th Georgia Infantry- Lieut. Col. Solon Z. Ruff
    24th Georgia Infantry- Col. Robert McMillin
    Cobb's (Georgia) Legion Infantry- Lt. Col. Luther J. Glenn

Phillips' (Georgia) Legion Infantry- Lt. Col. Elihu S. Barclay
3rd Georgia Battalion Sharpshooters- Lt. Col. Nathan Hutchins
Cabell's Artillery Battalion- Col. Henry C. Cabell
Battery A, 1st North Carolina Artillery- Capt. Basil C. Manly
Pulaski (Georgia) Artillery- Capt. John C. Fraser (mw), Lt. William J. Furlong
1st Richmond (Virginia) Howitzers- Capt. Edward S. McCarthy
Troup (Georgia) Artillery - Capt. Henry H. Carlton (w), Lt. Columbus W. Motes

PICKETT'S DIVISION- Maj. Gen. George E. Pickett
Garnett's Brigade- Brig. Gen. Richard B. Garnett (k), Maj. C. S. Peyton
8th Virginia Infantry- Col. Eppa Hunton (w)
18th Virginia Infantry- Lt. Col. Henry A. Carrington
19th Virginia Infantry- Col. Henry Gantt (w), Lt. Col. John T. Ellis (mw)
28th Virginia Infantry- Col. Robert C. Allen (k), Lt. Col. William Watts
56th Virginia Infantry- Col. William D. Stuart (mw), Lt. Col. Philip P. Slaughter
Kemper's Brigade- Brig. Gen. James L. Kemper, Col. Joseph Mayo, Jr.
1st Virginia Infantry- Col. Lewis B. Williams (k), Lt. Col. Frederick G. Skinner
3rd Virginia Infantry- Col. Joseph Mayo, Jr., Lt. Col. Alexander D. Callcote (k)
7th Virginia Infantry- Col. Waller T. Patton (mw), Lt. Col. Charles C. Flowerree
11th Virginia Infantry- Maj. Kirkwood Otey (w)
24th Virginia Infantry- Col. William R. Terry
Armistead's Brigade- Brig. Gen. Lewis A. Armistead (mw/c), Col. William R. Aylett (w)
9th Virginia Infantry- Maj. John C. Owens (mw)
14th Virginia Infantry- Col. James G. Hodges (k), Lt. Col. William White
38th Virginia Infantry- Col. Edward C. Edmonds (k), Lt. Col. Powhatan B. Whittle (w)
53rd Virginia Infantry- Col. William R. Aylett (w), Lt. Col. Rawley W. Martin (w/c)
57th Virginia Infantry- Col. John Bowie Magruder (mw/c)
Dearing's Artillery Battalion- Maj. James Dearing
Fauquier (Virginia) Artillery- Capt. Robert M. Stribling
Richmond "Hampden" (Virginia) Artillery- Capt. William H. Caskie
Richmond "Fayette" Artillery- Capt. Miles C. Macon
Lynchburg (Virginia) Artillery- Capt. Joseph G. Blount

HOOD'S DIVISION- Maj. Gen. John B. Hood (w), Brig. Gen. Evander M. Law
Law's Brigade- Brig. Gen. Evander M. Law, Col. James L. Sheffield
4th Alabama Infantry- Col. Lawrence H. Scruggs
15th Alabama Infantry- Col. William C. Oates, Capt. Blanton A. Hill
44th Alabama Infantry- Col. William F. Perry
47th Alabama Infantry- Col. James W. Jackson, Lt. Col. J. M. Bulger (w/c), Maj. James M. Campbell
48th Alabama Infantry- Col. James L. Sheffield, Capt. T. J. Eubanks
Robertson's Brigade ("Hood's Texas Brigade")- Brig. Gen. Jerome B. Robertson
3rd Arkansas Infantry- Col. Van H. Manning (w), Lt. Col. Robert S. Taylor
1st Texas Infantry- Col. Phillip A. Work
4th Texas Infantry- Col. John C. G. Key (w), Maj. John P. Bane
5th Texas Infantry- Col. Robert M. Powell (w/c), Lt. Col. King Bryan (w), Maj. Jefferson C. Rogers

Anderson's Brigade-Brig. Gen. George T. Anderson (w), Lt. Col. William Luffman
  7th Georgia Infantry- Col. William W. White
  8th Georgia Infantry- Col. John R. Towers
  9th Georgia Infantry- Lt. Col. John C. Mounger (k), Maj. William M. Jones, Capt. George Hillyer
  11th Georgia Infantry- Col. Francis H. Little (w), Lt. Col. William Luffman (w), Maj. Henry D. McDaniel (w), Capt. William H. Mitchell
  59th Georgia Infantry- Col. William "Jack" Brown (w/c), Capt. M. G. Bass
Benning's Brigade- Brig. Gen. Henry L. Benning
  2nd Georgia Infantry- Lt. Col. William T. Harris (k), Maj. William S. Shepherd
  15th Georgia Infantry- Col. M. Dudley DuBose
  17th Georgia Infantry- Col. Wesley C. Hodges
  20th Georgia Infantry- Col. John A. Jones (k), Lt. Col. James D. Waddell
Henry's Artillery Battalion-Maj. Mathis W. Henry
  3rd North Carolina "Branch" Artillery- Capt. Alexander C. Latham
  Charleston "German" (South Carolina) Artillery- Capt. William K. Bachman
  Palmetto (South Carolina) Light Artillery- Capt. Hugh R. Garden
  1st North Carolina "Rowan" Artillery- Capt. James Reilly
First Corps Artillery Reserve- Col. James B. Walton
Alexander's Artillery Battalion- Col. Edward P. Alexander
  Ashland (Virginia) Artillery- Capt. Pichegru Woolfolk, Jr. (w), Lt. James Woolfolk
  Bedford (Virginia) Artillery- Capt. Tyler C. Jordan
  Brooks (South Carolina) Artillery- Lt. S. C. Gilbert
  Madison (Louisiana) Artillery- Capt. George V. Moody
  Richmond "Parkers" (Virginia) Battery- Capt. William W. Parke
  Bath (Virginia) Battery- Capt. Osmond B. Taylor
Washington (Louisiana) Artillery Battalion- Maj. Benjamin F. Eshleman
  1st Company- Capt. Charles W. Squires
  2nd Company- Capt. John B. Richardson
  3rd Company- Capt. Merritt B. Miller
  4th Company- Capt. Joe Norcom (w), Lt. Henry A. Battles

SECOND ARMY CORPS

Lt. Gen. Richard S. Ewell

EARLY'S DIVISION- Maj. Gen. Jubal A. Early
Hays' Brigade- Brig. Gen. Harry T. Hays
  5th Louisiana Infantry- Maj. Alexander Hart (w), Capt. Thomas H. Biscoe
  6th Louisiana Infantry- Lt. Col. Joseph Hanlon
  7th Louisiana Infantry- Col. Davidson B. Penn
  8th Louisiana Infantry- Col. Trevanion D. Lewis, Lt. Col. Alcibiades DeBlanc (w), Maj. German A. Lester
  9th Louisiana Infantry- Col. Leroy A. Stafford
Smith's Brigade- Brig. Gen. William "Extra Billy" Smith
  31st Virginia Infantry- Col. John S. Hoffman
  49th Virginia Infantry- Lt. Col. J. Catlett Gibson
  52nd Virginia Infantry- Lt. Col. James H. Skinner

Hoke's Brigade- Col. Isaac E. Avery (mw), Col. Archibald C. Godwin
 6th North Carolina Infantry- Maj. Samuel D. Tate
 21st North Carolina Infantry- Col. William W. Kirkland
 57th North Carolina Infantry- Col. Archibald C. Godwin
Gordon's Brigade- Brig. Gen. John B. Gordon
 13th Georgia Infantry- Col. James L. Smith
 26th Georgia Infantry- Col. Edmund N. Atkinson
 31st Georgia Infantry- Col. Clement A. Evans
 38th Georgia Infantry- Capt. William L. McLeod
 60th Georgia Infantry- Capt. Waters B. Jones
 61st Georgia Infantry- Col. John H. Lamar
Jones' Artillery Battalion- Lt. Col. Hilary P. Jones
 Charlottesville (Virginia) Artillery- Capt. James McD. Carrington
 Richmond "Courtney" (Virginia) Artillery- Capt. William A. Tanner
 Louisiana Guard Artillery- Capt. Charles A. Green
 Staunton (Virginia) Artillery- Capt. Asher W. Garber

RODES' DIVISION- Maj. Gen. Robert E. Rodes
Daniel's Brigade- Brig. Gen. Junius Daniel
 32nd North Carolina Infantry- Col. Edmund C. Brabble
 43rd North Carolina Infantry- Col. Thomas S. Kenan (w/c), Lt. Col. William G. Lewis
 45th North Carolina Infantry- Lt. Col. Samuel H. Boyd (c), Maj. John R. Winston (w/c), Capt. A. H. Gallaway (w), Capt. James A. Hopkins
 53rd North Carolina Infantry- Col. William A. Owens
 2nd North Carolina Infantry Battalion- Lt. Col. Hezekiah L. Andrews (w), Capt. Van Brown
Iverson's Brigade- Brig. Gen. Alfred Iverson
 5th North Carolina Infantry- Capt. Speight B. West, Capt. Benjamin Robinson
 12th North Carolina Infantry- Lt. Col. William S. Davis
 20th North Carolina Infantry- Lt. Col. Nelson Slough (w), Capt. Lewis T. Hicks
 23rd North Carolina Infantry- Col. Daniel H. Christie (mw), Capt. William H. Johnston
Doles' Brigade- Brig. Gen. George Doles
 4th Georgia Infantry- Lt. Col. David R. E. Winn (k), Maj. William H. Willis
 12th Georgia Infantry- Col. Edward Willis
 21st Georgia Infantry- Col. John T. Mercer
 44th Georgia Infantry- Col. Samuel P. Lumpkin (mw/c), Maj. William H. Peebles
Ramseur's Brigade- Brig. Gen. Stephen D. Ramseur
 2nd North Carolina Infantry- Maj. Daniel W. Hurt (W), Capt. James T. Scales
 4th North Carolina Infantry- Col. Bryan Grimes
 14th North Carolina Infantry- Col. R. Tyler Bennett (w), Maj. Joseph H. Lambeth
 30th North Carolina Infantry- Col. Francis M. Parker (w), Maj. W. W. Sillers
O'Neal's Brigade- Col. Edward A. O'Neal
 3rd Alabama Infantry- Col. Cullen A. Battle
 5th Alabama Infantry- Col. Josephus M. Hall
 6th Alabama Infantry- Col. James N. Lightfoot (w), Capt. M. L. Bowie
 12th Alabama Infantry- Col. Samuel B. Pickens
 26th Alabama Infantry- Lt. Col. John C. Goodgame
Carter's Artillery Battalion- Lt. Col. Thomas H. Carter
 Jeff Davis (Alabama) Artillery- Capt. William J. Reese

King William (Virginia) Artillery- Capt. William P. Carter
Louisa "Morris" (Virginia) Artillery- Capt. Richard C. M. Page
Richmond "Orange" (Virginia) Artillery- Capt. Charles W. Fry

JOHNSON'S DIVISION- Maj. Gen. Edward Johnson
Steuart's Brigade- Brig. Gen. George H. Steuart
1st Maryland Infantry Battalion (2nd MD Infantry, CSA)- Lt. Col. James R. Herbert (w), Maj. William W. Goldsborough (w), Capt. James P. Crane
1st North Carolina Infantry- Lt. Col. Hamilton Allen Brown
3rd North Carolina Infantry- Maj. William M. Parsley
10th Virginia Infantry- Col. Edward T. H. Warren
23rd Virginia Infantry- Lt. Col. Simeon T. Walton
37th Virginia Infantry- Maj. Henry C. Wood
Nicholls' Brigade- Col. Jesse M. Williams
1st Louisiana Infantry- Col. Michael Nolan
2nd Louisiana Infantry- Lt. Col. Ross E. Burke
10th Louisiana Infantry- Maj. Thomas N. Powell
14th Louisiana Infantry- Lt. Col. David Zable
15th Louisiana Infantry- Maj. Andrew Brady
Walker's Brigade ("Stonewall Brigade")- Brig. Gen. James Walker
2nd Virginia Infantry- Col. John Q.A. Nadenbousch
4th Virginia Infantry- Maj. William Terry
5th Virginia Infantry- Col. John H. S. Funk
27th Virginia Infantry- Lt. Col. Daniel M. Shriver
33rd Virginia Infantry- Capt. James B. Golladay
Jones' Brigade- Brig. Gen. John. M. Jones (w), Lt. Col. Robert H. Dungan
21st Virginia Infantry- Capt. William P. Moseley
25th Virginia Infantry- Col. John C. Higginbotham (w), Lt. Col. J. A. Robinson (absent)
42nd Virginia Infantry- Col. Robert Withers, Capt. Samuel H. Saunders
44th Virginia Infantry- Maj. Norval Cobb (w), Capt. Thomas R. Buckner
48th Virginia Infantry- Lt. Col. Robert H. Dungan, Maj. Oscar White
50th Virginia Infantry- Lt. Col. Logan H. N. Salyer
Latimer's Artillery Battalion- Maj. James W. Latimer (mw)
1st Maryland Battery- Capt. William F. Dement
Alleghany Rough (Virginia) Artillery- Capt. John C. Carpenter
4th Maryland "Chesapeake" Artillery- Capt. William D. Brown
Lynchburg "Lee" (Virginia) Battery- Capt. Charles I. Raine (mw), Lt. William M. Hardwicke
Second Corps Artillery Reserve- Col. J. Thompson Brown
Dance's Artillery Battalion- Capt. Willis J. Dance
2nd Richmond (Virginia) Howitzers- Capt. David Watson
3rd Richmond (Virginia) Howitzers- Capt. Benjamin H. Smith, Jr.
1st Rockbridge (Virginia) Artillery- Capt. Archibald Graham
Powhatan (Virginia) Artillery- Lt. John M. Cunningham
Salem (Virginia) Flying Artillery- Lt. Charles B. Griffin
Nelson's Artillery Battalion- Lt. Col. William Nelson
Amherst (Virginia) Artillery- Capt. Thomas J. Kirkpatrick
Fluvanna (Virginia) Artillery- Capt. John L. Massie
Georgia Battery- Capt. John Milledge, Jr.

THIRD ARMY CORPS

Lt. Gen. Ambrose P. Hill

ANDERSON'S DIVISION- Maj. Gen. Richard H. Anderson
Wilcox's Brigade- Brig. Gen. Cadmus M. Wilcox
    8th Alabama Infantry- Lt. Col. Hilary A. Herbert
    9th Alabama Infantry- Capt. J. Horace King (w)
    10th Alabama Infantry- Col. William H. Forney (w/c), Lt. Col. James E. Shelley
    11th Alabama Infantry- Col. John C. C. Sanders (w), Lt. Col. George E. Tayloe
    14th Alabama Infantry- Col. Lucius Pinckard (w/c), Lt. Col. James A. Broome
Wright's Brigade- Brig. Gen. Ambrose R. Wright, Col. William Gibson
    3rd Georgia Infantry- Col. Edward J. Walker
    22nd Georgia Infantry- Col. Joseph A. Wasden (k), Capt. Benjamin C. McCurry
    48th Georgia Infantry- Col. William Gibson (w/c), Capt. Matthew R. Hall
    2nd Georgia Infantry Battalion- Maj. George W. Ross (mw), Capt. Charles J. Moffett
Mahone's Brigade- Brig. Gen. William Mahone
    6th Virginia Infantry- Col. George T. Rogers
    12th Virginia Infantry- Col. David A. Weisiger
    16th Virginia Infantry- Col. Joseph H. Ham
    41st Virginia Infantry- Col. William A. Parham
    61st Virginia Infantry- Col. Virginius D. Groner
Perry's Brigade- Col. David Lang
    2nd Florida Infantry- Maj. Walter R. Moore
    5th Florida Infantry- Capt. Richmond N. Gardner
    8th Florida Infantry- Lt. Col. William Baya
Posey's Brigade- Brig. Gen. Carnot Posey
    12th Mississippi Infantry- Col. Walter H. Taylor
    16th Mississippi Infantry- Col. Samuel E. Baker
    19th Mississippi Infantry- Col. Nathaniel H. Harris
    48th Mississippi Infantry- Col. Joseph M. Jayne
Lane's Artillery Battalion ("Sumter Battalion", Georgia)- Maj. John Lane
    Company A - Capt. Hugh M. Ross
    Company B - Capt. George M. Patterson
    Company C - Capt. John T. Wingfield

HETH'S DIVISION- Maj. Gen. Henry Heth (w), Brig. Gen. James J. Pettigrew (w)
Pettigrew's Brigade- Brig. Gen. James J. Pettigrew, Col. James K. Marshall (k)
    11th North Carolina Infantry- Col. Collett Leventhorpe (w/c), Maj. Egbert Ross (k)
    26th North Carolina Infantry- Col. Henry K. Burgwyn (k), Lt. Col. John Lane (w), Maj. John J. Jones (w), Capt. Henry C. Albright
    47th North Carolina Infantry- Col. George H. Faribault (w), Lt. Col. John A. Graves (w/c). Maj. Archibald Crudup (w/c)
    52nd North Carolina Infantry- Col. James K. Marshall (k), Lt. Col. Marcus A. Parks
Brockenbrough's Brigade- Col. John M. Brokenbrough
    40th Virginia Infantry- Capt. T. Edwin Betts (w), Capt. R. B. Davis
    47th Virginia Infantry- Col. Robert M. Mayo
    55th Virginia Infantry- Col. William S. Christian
    22nd Virginia Infantry Battalion- Maj. John S. Bowles

Archer's Brigade- Brig. Gen. James J. Archer (c), Col. Birkett D. Fry (w), Lt. Col. Samuel G. Shepherd
    5th Alabama Infantry Battalion- Maj. Albert S. Van De Graaf
    13th Alabama Infantry- Col. Birkett D. Fry
    1st Tennessee (Provisional Army) Infantry- Maj. Felix G. Buchanan
    7th Tennessee Infantry- Lt. Col. Samuel G. Shepherd
    14th Tennessee Infantry- Capt. Bruce L. Phillips
Davis' Brigade- Brig. Gen. Joseph R. Davis
    2nd Mississippi Infantry- Col. John M. Stone
    11th Mississippi Infantry- Col. Francis M. Green
    42nd Mississippi Infantry- Col. Hugh R. Miller (mw/c)
    55th North Carolina Infantry- Col. John Kerr Connally
Garnett's Artillery Battalion- Lt. Col. John Garnett
    Donaldsville (Louisiana) Artillery- Capt. Victor Maurin)
    Norfolk "Huger's" (Virginia) Artillery- Capt. Joseph D. Moore)
    Pittsylvania "Lewis" (Virginia) Artillery- Capt. John W. Lewis)
    Norfolk (Virginia) Light Artillery Blues- Capt. Charles R. Grandy

PENDER'S DIVISION- Maj. Gen. William D. Pender (mw), Maj. Gen. Isaac Trimble (w/c), Brig. Gen. James H. Lane
Perrin's Brigade- Col. Abner Perrin
    1st South Carolina Infantry (Provisional Army)- Maj. Charles W. McCreary
    1st South Carolina Rifles- Capt. William M. Hadden
    12th South Carolina Infantry- Col. John L. Miller
    13th South Carolina Infantry- Lt. Col. Benjamin T. Brockman
    14th South Carolina Infantry- Lt. Col. Joseph N. Brown
Lane's Brigade- Brig. Gen. James H. Lane, Col. Clark M. Avery
    7th North Carolina Infantry- Maj. J. McCleod Turner (w/c), Capt. James G. Harris
    18th North Carolina Infantry- Col. John D. Barry
    28th North Carolina Infantry- Col. Samuel D. Lowe (w), Lt. Col. W. H. A. Speer (w)
    33rd North Carolina Infantry- Col. Clark M. Avery
    37th North Carolina Infantry- Col. William M. Barbour
Thomas' Brigade- Brig. Gen. Edward L. Thomas
    14th Georgia Infantry- Col. Robert W. Folsom
    35th Georgia Infantry- Col. Bolling H. Holt
    45th Georgia Infantry- Col. Thomas J. Simmons
    49th Georgia Infantry- Col. Samuel T. Player
Scales' Brigade- Brig. Gen. Alfred M. Scales, Lt. Col. George T. Gordon, Col. W. Lee. J. Lowrance
    13th North Carolina Infantry- Col. Joseph H. Hyman (w), Lt. Col. Henry A. Rogers
    16th North Carolina Infantry- Capt. Leroy W. Stowe
    22nd North Carolina Infantry- Col. James Conner
    34th North Carolina Infantry- Col. W. Lee. J. Lowrance, Lt. Col. George T. Gordon (w)
    38th North Carolina Infantry- Col. William J. Hoke (w), Lt. Col. John Ashford
Poague's Artillery Battalion- Maj. William T. Poague
    Albemarle "Everett" (Virginia) Artillery- Capt. James W. Wyatt
    1st North Carolina "Charlotte" Artillery- Capt. Joseph Graham
    Madison (Mississippi) Light Artillery- Capt. George Ward
    Warrenton (Virginia) Battery- Capt. James V. Brooke

Third Corps Artillery Reserve- Col. R. Lindsay Walker
McIntosh's Artillery Battalion- Maj. David G. McIntosh
    Danville (Virginia) Artillery- Capt. R. Sidney Rice
    Hardaway (Alabama) Artillery- Capt. William B. Hurt
    2ⁿᵈ Rockbridge (Virginia) Artillery- Lt. Samuel Wallace
    Richmond "Johnson's" (Virginia) Battery- Capt. Marmaduke Johnson
Pegram's Artillery Battalion- Maj. William J. Pegram, Capt. E. B. Brunson
    Richmond "Crenshaw's" (Virginia) Battery- Capt. William G. Crenshaw
    Fredericksburg (Virginia) Artillery- Capt. Edward A. Marye
    Richmond "Letcher" (Virginia) Artillery- Capt. Thomas A. Brander
    Pee Dee (South Carolina) Artillery- Lt. William E. Zimmerman
    Richmond "Purcell" (Virginia) Artillery- Capt. Joseph McGraw

STUART'S CAVALRY DIVISION

Maj. Gen. James E. B. Stuart
Hampton's Brigade- Brig. Gen. Wade Hampton (w), Col. Laurence S. Baker
    1ˢᵗ North Carolina Cavalry- Col. Laurence S. Baker
    1ˢᵗ South Carolina Cavalry- Col. John L. Black
    2ⁿᵈ South Carolina Cavalry- Col. Matthew C. Butler
    Cobb's Legion (Georgia)- Col. Pierce B. M. Young
    Jeff Davis Legion (Mississippi)- Col. Joseph F. Waring
    Phillips' Legion (Georgia)- Lt. Col. Jefferson C. Phillips
Fitz Lee's Brigade- Brig. Gen. Fitzhugh Lee
    1ˢᵗ Maryland Battalion Cavalry- Maj. Harry Gilmore, Maj. Ridgely Brown
    1ˢᵗ Virginia Cavalry- Col. James H. Drake
    2ⁿᵈ Virginia Cavalry- Col. Thomas T. Munford
    3ʳᵈ Virginia Cavalry- Col. Thomas H. Owen
    4ᵗʰ Virginia Cavalry- Col. William Carter Wickham
    5ᵗʰ Virginia Cavalry- Col. Thomas L. Rosser
Robertson's Brigade- Brig. Gen. Beverly H. Robertson
    4ᵗʰ North Carolina Cavalry- Col. Dennis D. Ferebee
    5ᵗʰ North Carolina Cavalry- Col. Peter G. Evans
Jenkins' Brigade- Brig. Gen. Albert G. Jenkins (w), Col. Milton J. Ferguson
    14ᵗʰ Virginia Cavalry- Maj. Benjamin F. Eakle
    16ᵗʰ Virginia Cavalry- Col. Milton J. Ferguson
    17ᵗʰ Virginia Cavalry- Col. William H. French
    34ᵗʰ Virginia Battalion- Lt. Col. Vincent A. Witcher
    36ᵗʰ Virginia Battalion- Capt. Cornelius T. Smith
    Jackson's (Virginia) Battery- Capt. Thomas E. Jackson
Jones's Brigade- Brig. Gen. William E. Jones
    6ᵗʰ Virginia Cavalry- Maj. Cabel E. Flournoy
    7ᵗʰ Virginia Cavalry- Lt. Col. Thomas Marshall
    11ᵗʰ Virginia Cavalry- Col. Lunsford L. Lomax
W. H. F. Lee's Brigade- Col. John R. Chambliss, Jr.
    2ⁿᵈ North Carolina Cavalry- Lt. Col. William Payne (c), Capt. William A. Graham (w), Lt. Joseph Baker
    9ᵗʰ Virginia Cavalry- Col. Richard L. T. Beale

10th Virginia Cavalry- Col. J. Lucius Davis
13th Virginia Cavalry- Capt. Benjamin F. Winfield
Stuart Horse Artillery- Maj. Robert F. Beckham
1st Stuart (Virginia) Horse Artillery - Capt. James Breathed
Ashby (Virginia) Horse Artillery - Capt. R. Preston Chew
2nd Baltimore (Maryland) Horse Artillery- Capt. William H. Griffin
Washington (South Carolina) Horse Artillery- Capt. James F. Hart
2nd Stuart (Virginia) Horse Artillery- Capt. William M. McGregor
Lynchburg (Virginia)Horse Artillery- Capt. Marcellus M. Moorman
Imboden's Cavalry Command- Brig. Gen. John D. Imboden
18th Virginia Cavalry- Col. George W. Imboden)
62nd Virginia Infantry, Mounted- Col. George H. Smith
Virginia Partisan Rangers- Capt. John H. McNeill
Virginia (Staunton) Battery- Capt. John H. McClanahan

Source: National Park Service. Official Records.

BIBLIOGRAPHY

INTERNET SOURCES:

American Battlefield Trust (https://www.battlefields.org)

Downunder Horsemanship (https://downunderhorsemanship.com)

Equus Magazine (https://www.equusmagazine.com)

Internet Archives (https://www.archive.org)

Hathi Trust (https://www.hathitrust.org)

Gettysburg Discussion Group (https://gdg.org/research)

Library of Congress (https://www.loc.gov)

UNC University Libraries (https://library.unc.edu)

National Archives (https://www.archives.gov)

Newspapers.com (https://www.newspapers.com)

National Museum of Civil War Medicine (http://www.civilwarmed.org/animal)

National Park Service (http://www.npshistory.com/series/symposia/gettysburg_seminars)

The Horse: Your Guide to Equine Health Care (https://thehorse.com)

Warick Schiller Performance Horsemanship (https://www.videos.warwickschiller.com)

LIBRARIES AND ORGANIZATIONS:

Adams County Historical Society. Gettysburg, Pennsylvania.

Association of Licensed Battlefield Guides Library. Gettysburg, Pennsylvania.

Gettysburg National Military Park Library. Gettysburg, Pennsylvania.

U.S. Army Heritage and Education Center. Carlisle Barracks. Carlisle, Pennsylvania.

CITED WORKS

Adelman, Garry E., Smith, Timothy A., *Devil's Den: A History and Guide,* Gettysburg, PA: Thomas Publications, 1997.

Anderson, Clinton. *Lessons Well Learned. Why My Method Works for Any Horse,* Vermont: Trafalgar Square Books, 2009.

Anderson, Clinton. *Clinton Anderson's Training on the Trail. Practical Solutions for Trail Riding,* Colorado: Equine Network, 2005.

Arlington, B.T. *The Medal of Honor at Gettysburg,* Gettysburg, PA: Thomas Publications, 1996.

Armistead, Gene C. *Horses, and Mules in the Civil War,* Jefferson, NC: McFarland Publishers, 2013.

Avery Family of North Carolina Papers #33, Southern Historical Collection, Wilson Library, The University of North Carolina at Chapel Hill (https://web.lib.unc.edu/civilwar/index.php/2013/09/03/3-september-1863).

Bachelder, John, Ladd, David L., and Ladd, Audrey J. *The Bachelder Papers: Gettysburg in Their Own Words,* Volumes I-III, Dayton, Ohio: Morningside House, 1997.

Barakat, Christine. "Your Horse's Night Vision. With the Horse's Superior Night Vision, Negotiating a Trail in the Dark is No Sweat." *Equus Magazine,* September 10th, 2003.

Barry, William F., French, William H., Hunt, Henry J. *Instruction for Field Artillery, Prepared by the Board of Artillery,* Philadelphia: J.B. Lippincott, 1860.

Baumgartner, Richard A. *Buckeye Blood, Ohio at Gettysburg,* Huntington, West Virginia: Blue Acorn Press, 2003.

Bennett, Gerald R. *Days of Uncertainty and Dread,* Camp Hill, PA: Plank's Suburban Press, 1994.

Beyer, W.F., and Keydel, O.F. *Medal of Honor. A History of Our Country's Recent Wars,* Detroit, Michigan: The Perrien-Keydel Company, 1905.

Bigelow, John, *The Peach Orchard Gettysburg July 2nd, 1863 Explained by Official Reports and Maps,* Minneapolis, Minnesota: Kimball-Storer Co., 1910.

Billings, John. *Hardtack and Coffee. The Unwritten Story of Army Life,* Boston: George M. Smith and Company, 1887.

Broadhead, Sarah M. *The Diary of a Lady of Gettysburg, Pennsylvania from June 15th to July 15th, 1863.*

Clutz, Jacob A./Hollinger, Liberty. *Some Personal Recollections of the Battle of Gettysburg,* Adams County Historical Society.

Coco, Gregory A. *A Strange and Blighted Land Gettysburg The Aftermath of a Battle,* Gettysburg, PA: Thomas Publications, 1995.

Cole Phillip M. *Civil War Artillery at Gettysburg,* Ortanna, PA: Colecraft Industries, 2002.

Conover, David A. "Killing of Geo. W. Sandoe. A Battle Story Told by David A. Conover." *Gettysburg Compiler,* September 27, 1905.

Curtis, Orson B. *History of the Twenty-Fourth Michigan of the Iron Brigade, Known as the Detroit and Wayne County Regiment,* Detroit: Winer and Hammond, 1891.

Delory, Mary. "Dentistry: A Look Inside." *The Horse Your Guide to Equine Health Care,* April 1, 2009.

Ford, Worthington C. *A Cycle of Adams Letters 1861-1865. Volume 1. 1969.* New York: Kraus Reprint Company. Courtesy of US Army Education and Heritage Center Carlisle, PA.

Freemantle, Arthur J. *Three Months in the Southern States: April-June 1863,* New York: J. Bradburn (successor to M. Doolady), 1864.

Garrand, Kenner. *Nolan's System for Training Cavalry Horses. Captain 5th Cavalry, USA*, New York: D. Van Nostrand, 1862.

Gerleman, David James. *Unchronicled Heroes: A Study of Union Cavalry Horses in the Eastern Theater Care, Treatment and Use. 1861-1865*, Ann Arbor, Michigan: UMI Dissertation Services, 1999. USAHEC

Gibbon, John. *Artillerist's Manual Compiled from Various Sources and Adapted to the Service of the United States*, New York: D. VanNostrand, 1860.

Gilbreath, Erasmus, C., Company I 20th Indiana. ALBG Library Files. U.S. Army History Institute, Carlisle Barracks, PA.

Glazier, Willard. *Three Years in the Federal Cavalry*, New York: R. H. Ferguson and Company, 1860.

Grabowski, Amelia., Reichard, Katie. "Every Man His Own Horse Doctor," *National Museum of Civil War Medicine*, August 30th, 2017.

Hall, Hillman, H., Besley, W. B., Wood, Gilbert, G. *History of the Sixth New York Cavalry (Second Ira Harris Guard) Second Brigade — First Division —Cavalry Corps, Army of the Potomac, 1861-1865*, Worcester, MA: The Blanchard Press, 1908.

Hanifen, Michael. *History of Battery B, First New Jersey Artillery*, Ottawa, Illinois: Republican-Times Printers, 1905.

Hanna, Charles. *Gettysburg Medal of Honor Recipients*, Springville, Utah: Bonneville Books, 2010.

Haskell, Frank, A. *The Battle of Gettysburg*, Wisconsin History Commission: Democrat Printing Co, 1910.

Hawthorne, Frederick W. *Gettysburg Stories of Men and Monuments as told by Battlefield Guides*, Gettysburg, PA: The Association of Licensed Battlefield Guides, 1988.

Hazelton, W.C. "The People of Gettysburg. An Address made at the Regimental Reunion." *Gettysburg Star and Sentinel*, September 1, 1891. Adams County Historical Society.

Hessler, James., Motts, Wayne E., Stanley, Steven A. *Pickett's Charge at Gettysburg. A Guide to the Most Famous Attack in American History*, El Dorado Hills, CA: Savas Beatie, 2015.

Hood, J.B., *Advance and Retreat. Personal Experiences in the United States and Confederate States Armies*. Edited by Richard N. Current, Bloomington, Indiana: Indiana University Press, 1959.

Horner, John, B. Sgt *Hugh Paxton Bigham Lincoln's Guard at Gettysburg*, Gettysburg, PA: Horner Enterprises, 1994.

Jones, Janet, L. "How Your Horse's Vision Differs From Yours." *Equus Magazine*. January 29, 2016.

Jones, Marcellus, E., *The Marcellus E. Jones Journal*, Chicago: Peregrine, Stime, Newman, Ritzman, and Bruckner, 1897.

Jordan, Brian Matthew. "The Unfortunate Colonel." *Civil War Monitor*. Volume 6:4. Winter 2016.

Kershaw, Joseph B., *Kershaw's Brigade at Gettysburg*. Gettysburg National Military Park Library.

Lee, Robert Edward Jr. *Recollections and Letters of General Robert E Lee*, New York: Doubleday Page and Company, 1905.

Longacre, Edward G. *Lee's Cavalrymen*, Mechanicsburg, PA: Stackpole Books, 2002.

Lundberg, Kathleen. "Horses' Sensitive Hearing Makes Them More Reactive to Loud Sounds—Like Fireworks." *The Ann Arbor News*, June 22, 2011.

Lynghaug, Fran, L. *The Official Horse Breeds Standards Book*, Minneapolis, Minnesota: Voyager Press, 2009.

McBane, Susan. *The Illustrated Encyclopedia of Horse Breeds*, Edison, New Jersey: Wellfleet Press, 1997.

McClellan, George B., *Regulations and Instructions for the Field Service of the United States Cavalry in Time of War*, Philadelphia: J.B. Lippincott, 1861.

McClellan, H.B. *The Life and Campaigns of Major General J.E.B. Stuart*, Boston and New York: Houghton Mifflin, 1885.

Manger, Blake. *Traveller and Co. The Horses of Gettysburg*, Gettysburg, PA: Farnsworth House Military Impressions, 1995.

Meade, George. Letter to the Commander of George G. Meade Post No.1 Dept of Penna. G.A.R. Dated March 12th, 1883.

Meade, George. *Life and Letters of George Gordon Meade. Vol. 1.* New York: Charles Scribner's Sons, 1913.

Meade, George Gordon. *With Meade at Gettysburg*, Philadelphia: John C. Winston Company, 1930.

Military Order of the Loyal Legion of the United States. *War Papers. Volume 1. District of Columbia*, Wilmington, North Carolina: Broadfoot Publishing, 1993.

Mulholland, St. Clair A. *The Story of the 116th Regiment Pennsylvania Volunteers in the War of the Rebellion. Record of a Gallant Command*, Philadelphia: F. McManus Jr., 1903.

Norton, Oliver, W., *The Attack and Defense of Little Round Top. Gettysburg, July 2, 1863*, Gettysburg, PA: Stan Clark Military Books, 1913/1992.

Norton, Oliver Wilcox. *Strong Vincent and His Brigade at Gettysburg, July 2, 1863*, Chicago, 1908.

Patrick, Sean. *The Modern Horseman's Countdown to Broke*, Vermont: Trafalgar Square Books, 2009.

Pendelton, Robert. *Traveller. General Robert E Lee's Favorite Greenbrier Warhorse*, Lutz, Florida: Robert Pendelton, 2005.

Pickernal, Tamsin. *The Majesty of the Horse an Illustrated History*, London, UK: Quintessence Edition Ltd., 2011.

Pierce, Tillie. *At Gettysburg, Or What A Girl Saw and Heard of The Battle*, New York: W. Lake Boreland, 1889.

Polley, J.B., *Hood's Texas Brigade*, Dayton, Ohio: Morning Side Bookshop, 1988.

Powell, David, A. "A Reconnaissance Gone Awry: Captain Samuel R. Johnston's Fateful Trip to Little Round Top." *Gettysburg Magazine*, Issue 23, June 2000.

Prince, A. P., *Brooks Artillery, Rhett's Battery*, South Carolina Department of Archives and History. Columbia, SC. Gettysburg National Military Park Library Files, 1898.

Regulations for the Army of the Confederate States, 1863. [2nd and only correct ed. War Department, Richmond, January 28th, 1863], James A. Seddon, Secretary of War. Richmond: J. W. Randolph, 1863.

Riley, Franklin L., *Publications of the Mississippi Historical Society. Volume XIV*, Gettysburg National Military Park Library, 1914.

Risch, Erna. *Quartermaster Support of the Army: A History of the Corps. 1775-1939*, Washington: Quartermaster Historian's Office, Office of the Quartermaster General, 1962.

Rosengarten, Joseph George, *William Reynolds Rear Admiral, John Fulton Reynolds, Major General USV, Colonel 5th US Infantry, A Memoir*, Philadelphia: J.B. Lippencott, 1880.

Seymour, Issac, *Issac Seymour Journal (Adjutant, Hay's Brigade)*, William Clements Library, University of Michigan. Transcript by K. R. George. Gettysburg National Military Park Library, 1984.

Sellnow, Les. "The Equine Eye." *The Horse: Your Guide to Equine Health Care*, October 15, 2001.

Sharrer, G. Terry. "The Great Glanders Epizootic, 1861-1866: A Civil War Legacy." *Agricultural History*, Volume 69:1, 1995.

Skelly, Daniel Alexander. *A Boy's Experiences During the Battles of Gettysburg*, 1932.

Southern Historical Society Papers (http://www.gdg.org/Research/SHSP)

Southern Historical Society and R.A. Brock, *Southern Historical Society Papers, Volume 31 and 33*, Richmond, Virginia: Virginia Historical Society, 1903.

Storrick, W.C. to Frederick Tilbert, National Park Historian, March 28, 1939. Gettysburg National Military Park Library Files.

Teague, Charles. *Gettysburg by the Numbers: The Essential Pocket Compendium of Crucial and Curious Data about the Battle*, Gettysburg, PA: Adams County Historical Society, 2006.

Tremain, Henry Edwin, *Two Days of War, a Gettysburg Narrative, and Other Excursions*, New York: Bonnell, Silver, and Bowers, 1905.

Trudeau, Noah Andrew, "Eugene Blackford." *America's Civil War*, July 2001.

Thorn Elizabeth, "Woman Keeper of Cemetery in 1863, Describes the Battle," *Gettysburg Times*, July 2, 1938.

United State Serial Congressional Serial Set. Washington: U.S. Govt. Print Off., 1893-1896 Volume 3142 Issue 1. Volume 3. John Spicer vs. The United States. (https://babel.hathitrust.org/cgi/pt?id=uc1.$b635772&view=1up&seq=587&q1=spicer).

United States Department of War. *Revised Regulations of the Army of the United States. 1861*, Mineola, New York: Dover Publications, 2013.

United States War Department, *The War of the Rebellion: A Compilation of the Official Records of the Union and Confederate Armies*. Washington, Govt. Print. Office, 1901, 1880.

United States War Dept., Obrien, Thomas M., Dieffendorf, Oliver. *General Orders of the War Department 1861-1863, Volume 2*, New York: Derby and Miller, 1864.

Watrous, J. A., *Commandry of the State of Wisconsin, Military Order of the Loyal Legion of the United States. Volume 1*, Milwaukee: Burdick, Armitage and Allen, 1891.

Weld, Stephen, M., *War Diaries and Letters of Stephen Minot Weld 1861-1865*, Cambridge, MA: The Riverside Press, 1912.

Weygant, Charles, H. *History of the One Hundred and Twenty-fourth Regiment, N.Y.S.V.* Newburgh, New York: Journal Printing House, 1877.

Whitford, Frederick., Martin, Andrew., Mattheis, Phyllis. *The Queen of American Agriculture a Biography of Virginia Claypool Meredith*, West Lafayette, Indiana: Purdue University Press, 2008.

Wilkeson, John. A Letter to His Daughter. Buffalo. July 6th, Monday, 1863. ALBG Library Files.

Ziegler, Lydia, and Ziegler, Hugh. *The Dead and Dying Were All Around Us. Stories from the Lutheran Theological Seminary during the Battle of Gettysburg and its Aftermath*, Adams County Historical Society.

ADDITIONAL SELECT BIBLIOGRAPHY:

Adkin, Mark. *The Gettysburg Companion*, Mechanicsburg, Pennsylvania: Stackpole Books, 2008.

Bonner, Laurie. "Twelve Ways to Protect your Horse from Laminitis." *Equus Magazine*, April 4th, 2014.

Busey, John W, and Martin, David W. *Regimental Strengths and Losses at Gettysburg. Fourth Edition*. Hightstown, NJ: Longstreet House, 2005.

Christ, Elwood. *Over a Wide, Hot...Crimson Plain : The Struggle for the Bliss Farm at Gettysburg, July 2nd and 3rd, 1863*, Gettysburg, PA: Stan Clark Military Books, 1998.

Coddington, Edwin. *The Gettysburg Campaign A Study in Command*, New York: Charles Scribner's Sons Macmillan, 1968.

Coggins, Jack. *Horseman's Bible*, Garden City, New York: Doubleday, 1966.

Frassanito, William A. *Early Photography at Gettysburg*, Gettysburg, PA: Thomas Publications, 1995.

Hessler, James. *Sickles at Gettysburg. The Controversial Civil War General Who Committed Murder, Abandoned Little Round Top, and Declared Himself the Hero of Gettysburg*, New York: Savas Beatie, 2009-2010.

Hessler, James A., Isenberg, Britt C. *Gettysburg's Peach Orchard. Longstreet, Sickles, and the Bloody Fight for the Commanding Ground Along the Emmitsburg Road*, El Dorado Hills, CA: Savas Beatie, 2019.

Laino, Phillip, *Gettysburg Campaign Atlas 3rd Edition*, United States of America: Gettysburg Publishing, 2014.

Petruzzi J. David and Stanley, Steven A. The Gettysburg Campaign in Numbers and Losses, El Dorado Hills, CA: Savas Beatie, 2012.

Pfanz, Harry W. *Gettysburg The First Day*, Chapel Hill & London: The University of North Carolina Press, 2002.

Pfanz, Harry W. *Gettysburg Culp's Hill and Cemetery Hill*, Chapel Hill & London: University of North Carolina Press, 1993.

Pfanz, Harry W. *Gettysburg The Second Day*, Chapel Hill & London: University of North Carolina Press, 1987.

Stollberg, Ashley. *The Ultimate Guide to Horse Colors*, La Crosse, Wisconsin: Dark Horse Publications, 2017.

Smith, Timothy A. *Farms at Gettysburg: The Fields of Battle*, Gettysburg, PA: Thomas Publications, 2007.

Wittenberg, Eric J. *Gettysburg's Forgotten Cavalry Actions: Farnsworth's Charge, South Cavalry Field and the Battle of Fairfield*, El Dorado Hills, CA: Savas Beatie, 2011.

Wittenberg, Eric J. *Protecting the Flanks at Gettysburg. The Battles for Brinkerhoff's Ridge and East Cavalry Field, July 2-3, 1863*, El Dorado Hills, CA: Savas Beatie, 2013.

Wittenberg, Eric J. *The Devil's to Pay. John Buford at Gettysburg. A History and Walking Tour*, El Dorado Hills, CA: Savas Beatie, 2014.

INDEX

ABOUT THE AUTHOR

Chris hails from Canton, Ohio, where he resides with his wife Becky. Chris has been a Registered Nurse for 31 years and currently works as a surgical nurse. He became a Licensed Battlefield Guide at Gettysburg National Military Park in 2016. He always had a love and fascination of horses from childhood which continues to this day.